Political Passions and Psychology

Social and Political Activism in Analysis

Edited by Stefano Carta
and Emilija Kiehl

Routledge
Taylor & Francis Group

LONDON AND NEW YORK

First published 2021
by Routledge
2 Park Square, Milton Park, Abingdon, Oxon OX14 4RN

and by Routledge
52 Vanderbilt Avenue, New York, NY 10017

Routledge is an imprint of the Taylor & Francis Group, an informa business

British Library Cataloguing-in-Publication Data
A catalogue record for this book is available from the British Library

Library of Congress Cataloging-in-Publication Data
Names: Carta, Stefano, editor. | Kiehl, Emilija, editor.
Title: Political passions and Jungian psychology: social and political activism in analysis / edited by Stefano Carta and Emilija Kiehl.
Description: Abingdon, Oxon; New York, NY: Routledge, 2021. | Includes bibliographical references and index.
Identifiers: LCCN 2020037729 | ISBN 9780367261726 (hardback) | ISBN 9780367261740 (paperback) | ISBN 9780429291845 (ebook)
Subjects: LCSH: Jungian psychology. | Political psychology.
Classification: LCC BF173.J85 P656 2021 |
DDC 150.19/54—dc23
LC record available at https://lccn.loc.gov/2020037729

ISBN: 978-0-367-26172-6 (hbk)
ISBN: 978-0-367-26174-0 (pbk)
ISBN: 978-0-429-29184-5 (ebk)

Typeset in Times New Roman
by codeMantra

"This book is a record of various significant and stimulating contributions of Analytical Psychology to possible solutions for the social, political and cultural problems that have been affecting our world for centuries, such as immigration and suffering caused by war, poverty, racial, social and gender prejudices, environmental catastrophes, etc. Each chapter presents the psychotherapeutic point of view applied in areas of work outside the consulting room, thus overcoming the split between the inner and outer, personal and social aspects of life. It is a highly recommendable book not only for psychologists, who will see new ways of applying their work, but also those involved in other fields of knowledge, as well as general readers. All will find that psychology can bring new light to the understanding of social problems."

Toshio Kawai
President, International Association for
Analytical Psychology

"This compilation of a selection of presentations from the third Analysis and Activism Conference held in Prague in December 2017, builds on and furthers the exploration of the vibrant, yet also very difficult and at times imperceptible, link between the psychological, the cultural, the social, the political and the ecological. Framed within a post-modern and archetypal perspective, the authors explore the often murky and less-than-obvious, yet crucial, link between the psychological and such diverse areas as migration and refugees, the environment, our perspective on history, and the political. Each presenter, in their own unique manner, seeks to break down walls of resistance and to build bridges to a wider and more inclusive perspective. What at first may seem like disparate and unrelated perspectives on this topic, in the end contribute to providing the reader with a kaleidoscopic perspective on the intricate, yet not so obvious, intimate relationship between these diverse topics and how the psychological is irrefutably embedded within and part of a wider matrix that necessarily includes the social and the political. The last article offers an example of how this can then be incorporated into the training of young analysts. As Jung succinctly stated, individuation does not take place in a bubble or in isolation, it is a process very much connected to the collective.

The publication of this book could not be more timely as the world finds itself in the midst of the current Covid-19 pandemic, a dramatic example of the interconnectedness these authors aim to bring to light and of the impact of social policy on the collective and on the psychological state of its citizens.

I highly recommend this book and am confident that readers will be nourished by the multiple perspectives provided and inspired to consider analysis and activism as allies and not as mutually exclusive fields of interest."

Tom Kelly
Co-Editor-in-Chief, *Journal of Analytical Psychology*

Political Passions and Jungian Psychology

In this book, a multidisciplinary and international selection of Jungian clinicians and academics discuss some of the most compelling issues in contemporary politics.

Presented in five parts, each chapter offers an in-depth and timely discussion on themes including migration, climate change, walls and boundaries, future developments, and the psyche. Taken together, the book presents an account of current thinking in the psychotherapeutic community as well as the role of practitioners in working with the results of racism, forced relocation, colonialism, and ecological damage.

Ultimately, this book encourages analysts, scholars, psychotherapists, sociologists, and students to actively engage in shaping current and future political, socio-economic, and cultural developments in this increasingly complex and challenging time.

Stefano Carta is a Jungian analyst practising in Rome, Italy. He is professor of Dynamic and Clinical Psychology at the University of Cagliari, Italy, and a member of the International Association for Analytical Psychology (IAAP) and of the Associazione Italiana di Psicologia Analitica (AIPA), of which he was President for the 2002–2006 term.

Emilija Kiehl, MSc, is a Jungian analyst practising in London. She is Vice President of the International Association for Analytical Psychology (IAAP), former Chair of the British Jungian Analytic Association (BJAA), and a senior member of the British Psychotherapy Foundation (BPF).

Contents

About the authors

John Beebe is a psychiatrist and Jungian analyst, practises psychotherapy in San Francisco. The author of *Integrity in Depth* **and** *Energies and Patterns in Psychological Type: The Reservoir of Consciousness*, he co-authored *Psychiatric Treatment: Crisis, Clinic and Consultation* and *The Presence of the Feminine in Film* and edited *Terror, Violence and the Impulse to Destroy* and C. G. Jung's *Aspects of the Masculine*. He founded *The San Francisco Jung Institute Library Journal* (now *Jung Journal: Culture and Psyche*) and was the first American editor of the *Journal of Analytical Psychology*. He regards himself as a citizen of the world.

Stefano Carta is a psychologist and a Jungian analyst graduated at the C.G. Jung Institute in Zurich, Switzerland. He is Professor of Dynamic and Clinical Psychology at the University of Cagliari, Italy. He is *Honorary Professor* at the Department of Psychoanalytic Studies of the University of Essex, UK, and has been visiting professor at Kyoto University, Japan. He is a member of the International Association of Analytical Psychology, and of the Associazione Italiana di Psicologia Analitica (AIPA), the oldest Jungian Psycho-analytical society in Italy, of which he has been the President for the 2002–2006 term. He has been the representative for Italy at the United Nations' International Union of Psychological Sciences and consultant for UNESCO, for which he has edited a three-volume entry – Psychology – for the *Encyclopedia of Life Support Systems*.

As a consultant, he worked in the field of ethno-psychology in the refugee camp of Daadab, Kenya, and in Rwanda. He supervises and carries out counsellings and psychotherapy to migrants in Italy, and supervises several centres that belong to the national "Sistema di protezione per richiedenti asilo e rifugiati".

He is the co-director of the oldest Jungian journal in Italy: the *Rivista di Psicologia Analitica* and has been *Deputy Editor for Europe* of the *Journal of Analytical Psychology* for six years (2013–19). He has been guest lecturer in Germany, Switzerland, the UK, the USA, Japan, Slovenia, Greece, and Denmark and has published over 90 articles and books.

He has participated in and organized several international conferences in Italy and abroad, among which the second, third, and fourth conferences were on ANALYSIS AND ACTIVISM: SOCIAL AND POLITICAL CONTRIBUTIONS OF JUNGIAN PSYCHOLOGY. He lives between Rome and Cagliari, Italy.

Heather Formaini, PhD, is Australian by birth though European by choice. She spent exhilarating years as a broadcaster and documentary-maker before becoming a Jungian analyst. She has worked in the refugee courts in London, in some refugee detention centres (prison camps) in Australia, and now divides her time between the hills of Lucca doing permaculture and the juvenile court in Florence, with lawyers advocating the rights of the people we know as Roma. It is because of this work she wants to work alongside activists of other professions. Her abiding interests lie in the sociology of the lack of knowledge, masculinities, and fathering.

Lynn Alicia Franco, LCSW, works bilingually (Spanish/English) from a multicultural relational perspective as a Jungian Psychoanalyst in private practice in Berkeley, California. She is an active member of the Extended Education Committee of the C. G. Jung Institute of San Francisco and is on the Ad Hoc Committee on Diversity. At the Psychotherapy Institute in Berkeley, she is a faculty member and founder of the Supervision Study Program and the Psychological Study of Cultural Identities. She has consulted to the University of California S.F. community mental health services and to the Woman's Therapy Center addressing group dynamics as related to cultural and racial diversity.

Gražina Gudaitė, PhD, is Professor of Psychology at Vilnius University and a Jungian psychoanalyst as well as President of the Lithuanian Association for Analytical Psychology. She is the author of several books and articles on analytical psychology and co-editor with Murray Stein of *Confronting Cultural Trauma: Jungian Approaches to Understanding and Healing.* She has a private practice in Vilnius and teaches in the Analyst Training programme in Lithuania.

Scott Hyder is a Jungian psychoanalyst, member of AGAP. Since 2012 he is in private practice in Zürich, Switzerland. From 1989 to 1994 in Vancouver, BC, Canada, he facilitated and expanded efforts to provide community programmes through the existing CG Jung Society of Vancouver. Later, returning to his home state of Idaho, USA, he also provided public forums for depth psychology in book stores and coffee shops in Twin Falls and Sun Valley (Java*Jung). From 2002 to 2012, in Boise, he hosted a panelled presentation on environmental crises at the public library, as well as films, guest speakers and workshops through the Idaho Friends of

Jung, a non-profit organization he co-founded and led, and which continues to serve community awareness and growth.

Emilija Kiehl, MSc, is Vice President of the International Association for Analytical Psychology (IAAP). She is a training analyst and former chair of the British Jungian Analytic Association (BJAA) and a senior member of the British Psychotherapy Foundation (bpf). She works in private practice in London and lectures and teaches in the UK and abroad.

Gao Lan, PhD, is Professor of Psychology (South China Normal University and the City University of Macao), Jungian analyst/IAAP, Sandplay Therapist/ISST/STA, president of the Chinese Society of Sandplay Therapy, and main organizer of the "Garden of the Heart and Soul" project.

Antonio Karim Lanfranchi, MD, PA, is a cardiologist and an analyst (trained at the Carl Gustav Jung Institute (CGJI)), currently based in Milan. Author of *The Asclepius Complex: Current Myths and Medical Consumerism* (2015, in Italian) and "Cairo: The Mother of the World" *in Psyche and the City: A Soul's Guide to the Modern Metropolis* edited by Thomas Singer (2010).

Monica Luci, PhD, is an analytical psychologist, a member of AIPA – Rome, and a relational psychoanalyst. She has extensive experience in psycho-social and psychotherapeutic work with asylum seekers and refugees who have survived torture. Her work in this field developed in a Post-Traumatic Stress Service of the Italian National Health System, within NGOs defending human rights, in reception centres for asylum seekers and refugees, in academia at the Centre for Psychoanalytic Studies of University of Essex, and in private practice. She has contributed to a number of international conferences on the topics of the consequences of torture, identification of survivors, and post-traumatic states in psychological assessment, psychotherapy, and research. She is author of a psycho-social study entitled *Torture, Psychoanalysis and Human Rights* (2017).

Begum Maitra is a psychotherapist, trainer, and supervisor in London (UK). Her long career as a psychiatrist, and personal experience in India, alerted her to how the problem of difference is managed through biological constructions, located within ephemeral national boundaries, and re-workings of history. These subjects continue to influence her reading, clinical work, and writing. Apart from writing papers and book chapters she has co-edited *Critical Voices in Child and Adolescent Mental Health* (2006) with Sami Timimi, made the film *How Culture Matters* (2014) with Morag Livingstone, and co-authored *Culture and Madness* (2014) with Inga-Britt Krause.

Dennis Merritt has a PhD in insect pathology (microbial control of insect pests) from UC-Berkeley and is a graduate of the C. G. Jung Institute, Zurich. He practises as a Jungian analyst and ecopsychologist in Madison and Milwaukee, Wisconsin, and authored four volumes of *The Dairy Farmer's Guide to the Universe – Jung, Hermes, and Ecopsychology.* He wrote the chapter on ecopsychology in a forthcoming Routledge textbook entitled *Rethinking Nature, Challenging Disciplinary Boundaries* that explores the new alignments in academia to address environmental issues. (EcoJung.com)

Jörg Rasche is Jungian Analyst trained in Berlin and Zurich (Sandplay Therapy with Dora Kalff) and psychiatrist for children, private practice in Berlin. Former president of the German Jungian Association and former vice president of IAAP. Currently president of the German Association for Sandplay Therapy. Also a trained musician, he has published many papers and some books about mythology, music, Sandplay Therapy, and analytical psychology. He is co-editor (with Tom Singer) of *Europe's Many Souls. Exploring Cultural Complexes and Identities* (2016). He teaches in Central European countries and was honoured for his engagement for people's reconciliation by the Polish president with the Golden Cross of Merit. He gives concert-lectures all over the world.

Heyong Shen, PhD, is professor of psychology at CityU (the City University of Macao), and SCNU (South China Normal University), Jungian analyst/IAAP, Sandplay Therapist/ISST/STA, founding president of the Chinese Federation for Analytical Psychology and Sandplay Therapy, the main organizer of the International Conference of Analytical Psychology and Chinese Culture (since 1998), speaker of Eranos Conferences (1997/2007), chief editor for the Chinese translation of the Collected Works of C.G. Jung, and chief editor of the *Chinese Journal of Analytical Psychology.*

Thomas Singer, MD, is a psychiatrist and Jungian analyst, practising in San Francisco. His interests have included studying the relationship between myth, politics, and psyche in *The Vision Thing.* He has conducted researches in several countries on the cultural complex theory. He serves as President of The Archive for Research in Archetypal Symbolism (ARAS), an online archive, which explores symbolic imagery from all cultures and eras. He is the author and editor of many articles and books, the most recent of which are *Europe's Many Souls* with Joerg Rasche and "Trump and the American Selfie: Archetypal Defenses of the Group Spirit" in *A Clear and Present Danger: Narcissism in the Era of Donald Trump.*

Yasuhiro Tanaka, PhD, is a Professor of Clinical Psychology at the Graduate School of Education, Kyoto University. He is also a Senior Analyst and Honorary Secretary of the Association of Jungian Analysts, Japan (AJAJ).

Tristan Troudart, MD, is a psychiatrist, psychotherapist, and Jungian analyst, born in Chile, lives in Israel, member of the Israel Institute of Jungian Psychology (IIJP). Formerly director of the Day Hospitalization Department at the Jerusalem Mental Health Center, Kfar – Shaul Hospital. He is active in human rights work, has participated in projects of training and cooperation between Israeli and Palestinian mental health professionals, supported by Physicians for Human Rights-Israel, and of interviewing and diagnosing victims of torture with the Public Committee Against Torture in Israel. He is currently in private practice in Jerusalem.

Heba Zaphiriou-Zarifi is an Analytical Psychologist and a Dance-Movement Therapist. She is a teacher and practitioner of Authentic Movement, and the founder of the Central London Authentic Movement Group. She is a Leadership-trained BodySoul Rhythms® therapist from The Marion Woodman Foundation. Heba is a Chartres Labyrinth facilitator and founder of The Silence Retreats. Her practice is based in London and Greece, and she consults on Psycho-Social projects in the Middle East. Heba has devised a method of working with Collective Trauma and building Resilience in tune with cultural differences. Her doctorate thesis in Philosophy was on "The Metaphysics of Time".

Ali Zarbafi (UK), D An Psych, is Jungian Analyst, Psychotherapist, and Clinical Supervisor. He is a Member of the Society of Analytical Psychology where he teaches and supervises trainees. He is a founder member of the Multi-lingual Psychotherapy Centre and has been involved in Social Dreaming since 1996. He is co-author of *Social Dreaming in the 21st Century: The World We Are Losing* with John Clare. Ali has an academic background in Middle Eastern politics and international relations and has run workshops over a number of years on the Refugee Experience. He has been involved in work with refugees since 1982. He currently works in private practice and the National Health Service. Email: zarbafiali@gmail.com

Introduction

Why is social and political activism necessary for psychological understanding?

Stefano Carta and Emilija Kiehl

A while has passed since the Analysis & Activism group of Jungian analysts and academics gathered together in Prague for the III international conference in December 2017. Between then and now, as we are currently working on the preparations for the Analysis & Activism IV to be held in Berkeley in October of 2020, many new members across the planet have joined the movement while the urgency of the timeless themes that were explored in Prague has accelerated and the critical issues such as environmental disasters, rising socio-economic inequality and the corresponding class, race and gender-related unrests continue to escalate around the world. Jungian thinking has more and more to contribute to humanity's attempts to address the urgency of the seemingly unstoppable events we witness.

This book presents the proceedings from the Prague conference which was the continuation of the initiative that began with the first Analysis and Activism conference held in London in December 2014, closely followed by the second conference in Rome in 2015. The Proceedings from the London and Rome conferences were published in 2016 (eds. Kiehl, Saban, Samuels) and 2017 (eds. Carta, Adorisio, Mercurio). Therefore, this publication is part of an ongoing process of re-evaluation and analysis of the complex relationship between the conceptual and practical domains, which have within modernity been kept separate as the "inner" – psychological – dimension on one side, and the "outer" – social/political on the other.

The international endeavour to re-think the Jungian analytical model (and this may be extended to other models of analytical / psychodynamic thinking) in the context of the socio-political aspect of the life of the psyche contained in this and the previous two publications represents an attempt to overcome this untenable division between the supposedly "inner" and "outer" dimensions of human experience.

We are fully aware that, as analysts, we do not yet possess the necessary tools for a new conceptualization, which might heal this ontological split that belongs to modernity. We are also aware that many of our colleagues around the world may still hold the view that the social, economic, cultural and political spheres of existence in both the analysts' and their patients' lives must be kept separate from what is thought of as the "personal" sphere, imagined as a separate ontological entity, or a specific place which would cause – or would be caused by – the social, economic, political as well as cultural by-products.

In our view, this corresponds to a form of psychological reductionism, to a large extent because all schools of psychoanalysis – although in quite different degrees and with different characteristics – still reflect the imprint of the age in which they were conceptualized and practised – the age of modernity, where the very notions of *subject* and *object* were thought of as separate *substances*, in some way related to each other and where, depending on the point of view, one would be the cause of the other. Moreover, in the age of modernity, the subject was implicitly tailored and conceptualized by the Eurocentric and anthropocentric standards.

However, if we look at the cultural context beyond the analytic circles, the preoccupations, the efforts and the themes that are at the core of the Analysis and Activism conferences and the subsequent publications (including the present one) have already been deeply challenged and de-construed within the post-modern debate to such a degree that, at this point, some aspects of these supposed divisions and oppositions between the psycho and the socio dimensions may even be considered already resolved and outdated.

In fact, the post-modern paradigm has already transcended the polarities that these conferences mainly deal with. Some much more radical conceptual transformations have been taking place, where the complexity of human life entirely transcends such anthropocentric bias (not to mention the Eurocentric bias, which has ignored other cultural and scientific ways of conceptualizing life, such as the Chinese Taoist tradition or the Japanese Shinto). This bias fences off the domains of psychology, sociology and politics within the supposedly autonomous "human" domains, leaving out everything that involves non-human domains, those of animals, plants, and the inorganic environment in which humans are embedded.

From the post-modern perspective, it is not just the split between the imagined substantial "inner" human psychological spaces vs. a substantial "outer" human object-world organized within the social, political or economic relationships, which makes no sense, but even the very division between *anthropos* and animals/nature, which also no longer makes sense. Moreover, such a clear-cut ontological division would, at this point, make it actually *impossible* to adequately interpret and understand the human (and not only human) predicament (see: Derrida, 2008).

As one of us has attempted to point out (Carta, 2017), in our analytical conceptualizations, and therefore in our daily clinical practice, it is imperative that we develop that part of the Jungian legacy where the "Self" can no longer be conceptualized solely as one substantial entity in relationship with other substantial entities (i.e., "Other" than the "Self"). This "inter-personal" paradigm, in the post-modern thinking, must be reframed as a "trans-personal" structure whereby the "Self" is an emergent, ongoing, dynamic identity process, not in addition to, but embedded *in* the Other, and emerging from a multi-layered, embodied complex relational flow which ecologically includes the "chain of all beings" – Unus Mundus.

The notion of a "chaosmos" (Guattari, 1995) may be of help here as an image of this highly dynamic ongoing complex relational flow out of which all forms (and identities) emerge and transform themselves.

As Braidotti (2019) points out, this interconnectedness is not so much chaotic as *dynamic and self-organizing*, and, we may add, based on the revolutionary step – for the Western ontology – where the Aristotelian category of Substance, the first and foremost classical category – is substituted by that of Relationship (Carta, 2017). This radical shift of focus entails a new view of all oppositional conceptualizations, such as "inner" vs. "outer", or, at different levels of analysis: psychology vs. sociology-politics, or, again at other levels of conceptualization, of sameness-identity vs. otherness, or, also importantly for our discussion, between the concepts of the Persona vs. Anima/Animus.

Put another way, what is perceived as being outside, i.e., our "objects" must actually be found *inside*, in an *inside-out* relational process which shapes the very nature of the analytical field. Parallelly, what is "inside" – one's feeling of sameness, self-ness and identity – must be found *outside-in,* via the Other.

On an epistemological ground, this means that the individual is conceptualized as living in a society without, while containing a society within – an individual, therefore, who is made by and at the same time, in a circular way, makes the society. Thus, the society – in all its manifestations, may they be political, economic, religious, linguistic, etc. – is conceptualized as existing without the subject only insofar as it is shared and nourished by the individuals' inner space.

Yet, such a description is still faulty, as it cannot really adhere to the necessary de-construction of those two polarities (psychology/sociology), which still seem to be thought of as substances in a reciprocal relationship. Within the post-modern horizon, this view is intrinsically reductive and, after all, dissociative.

The recognition that psychology and social politics are actually polarized actualizations of an *implicit unitary something* (here the quasi Buddhist idea of Winnicott's False Self – a pure, innate, "empty" sphere of potential-being, always concealed like God's face *from which existence flows* – may be of help) within space-time, applies also to personal selfhood and identity.

For the American anthropologist Clifford Geertz, for instance:

> The western concept of identity, meaning a contained, interiorized, unique personality, more or less integrated within a cognitive and motivational universe – a dynamic center of awareness, emotion and (individually) organized action – seems a quite peculiar idea, if we look

at it in the context of other cultures [...] To try to understand the "others" means to put such a view aside and to try to read their experiences within the context of their ideas about what identity means.

(Geertz, 1983, p. 126)

In fact, as Waldenfels (2010) notices, all features that we normally ascribe to our identity actually belong to the Other:

- Our origin, which we cannot own and which pre-existed to our birth: we "arrive late" by being born into conditions already there.
- Our name, which is given to us by others and others call us by that name.
- Or our language that we are contained by and which has been spoken by others before we could speak to others.
- Our body, which, at the same time, we own as an object – the body that we see "out there", in the mirror, and the body that we perceive and with which we tend to identify.
- Our face, which was never meant to be seen by us, the subject and the object of the disturbing surprise of the *unheimlich* (Freud) when the subject sees herself/himself as an *Other*.

Some of the chapters in this volume, as well as in the publications from the previous two conferences (Kiehl et al., 2016; Carta et al., 2017), show that under the social/anthropological and political levels of human reality, a constitutive role that the Other plays in the Self's feeling of sameness is largely given to minorities, migrants or those "Other others" (Papadopoulos, 2002) whose difference is *used* to maintain the reductive, defensive, paranoid fear and the need for sameness and shared identity.

To these considerations, which dislocate our subjectivity and move it into our objects, and therefore, at a different level, de-localize psychology into "sociology" and vice versa, refer fundamental and scientifically sound empirical observations about human ontogenesis and the ontogenesis of our subjectivity and selfhood (i.e., of our own psychology). We are referring, for example, to the funding role of the mirroring function of the (m)other's face (Ogden), the sight of her and her facial expressions, which, thanks to their variable degree of difference and tuning with the baby's inner emotional state, make it possible for the infant to *find herself* in the very moment in which she discovers – feels – and identifies her own feelings.

From the brilliant clinical observations by Winnicott to the recent experiments by Tronick (Adamson & Frick, 2003; Tronick, 2007), we know that the mirror in which we lose ourselves is the physical mirror that *exactly* replicates our image, or the collusive contiguous archaic relational situations, which return our image too faithfully, whereas the one through which we see *that we are* is the living mirror made by the subjectivity of the Other.

This paradoxical, scaffolded, multi-layered relatedness, that the Self is, and within which the Self emerges (like a stable melody that emerges from a musical temporal flow) is grounded in the vast, concordant body of contemporary infant research. This research is based on sophisticated, sound empirical evidence and proves the fundamental inter-subjective and *socio-cultural* nature of the human baby (for a comprehensive discussion see: Tomasello, 2019). Far from being the product of a castration complex, human pro-sociality – from the first experiences of perspective shared-attention, intentions and emotional states (around the first year of life), to the development of pro-sociality, sense of fairness, collaboration, co-ordination of decision-making, rule formation, enforcement, normativity, ethical and moral values, etc. (from three years of age on) – prove the fundamental social nature of healthy psychology, and therefore, the profound psychological nature of human's healthy sociality.[1]

This point of view clearly carries the potentially catastrophic risk of the loss of feeling of our inner space – our sense of selfhood, identity, continuity and agency – into the "outer", "collective" realm, hence reducing psychology, both our own, and psychology as a form of knowledge, to sociology. We, as analysts, do not have to, nor need to become sociologists, or anthropologists (just as we do not need to become biologists either), as our task is to reach the levels of psychological reality and human experience *from within*, i.e., "inside out".

How then to conceptualize Self and identity? How to preserve the central protagonist of psychology itself – the space within the subject – if this is actually made possible by the object, and if we must abandon the illusion of a stable, substantial Self?

Fortunately, some of Jung's, and Bergson's ideas may help us here, as they may have been the forerunners of today's post-modern paradigm. In our view, the description of such a complex, dynamic, multi-layered, embedded and embodied flow not only between humans (as this would be a limitative, partial, reductive anthropocentric view) but also between every animate and "inanimate", organic and inorganic component is similar to the cosmogonic image of the libidinal flow as described by Jung in his seminal work *Symbols of Transformation*, (which encompasses the central 40 years of Jung's intellectual career) or by Bergson's *Elan vital*.

In fact, the true subject in Jungian psychology is not the Self as such, but libido – libido, which, in its ever-becoming, multifocal, multi-layered Proteus-like flow, takes on specific *symbolic* forms.

We believe that Jung has essentially indicated a possible way to reconceptualize our psychological experience – hence the experience *of* and *with* our patients – precisely as embedded into such a flow. Or, to put it another way, Jung has indicated a way to imagine and reconceptualize our nature as that of *being, ourselves, symbolic forms of a constant transformative relational dynamics.*

Therefore, this dynamic, relational flow embodies itself in a multiplicity of symbolic forms. It is precisely such embodiments that we may call "Selves", and such selves are psychologically meaningful – i.e., symbolic – only if and when they wholly express this constant transformative movement. Otherwise, they split into positional polarities and lose themselves either in a normotic Persona (Bollas, 1987) or in a psychotic Anima/Animus (however, these concepts may be understood).

We briefly referred to the extensive body of infant research, which was not available to Jung, and even less to Freud. Nevertheless, its findings may support an aspect of Jung's theory where what we call "individuation" may actually refer to a constant, embedded, multi-layered, dynamic relational process in which the opposites of subject and object, or psychology and sociology, inner and outer, or individual and "collective" reveal their common symbolic (meaningful) co-implication within each other.

Within such a view, a healthy Self – i.e., a process of constant formation of identity through change – is, and cannot but also be a *social, political self*. And, conversely, a society cannot be a healthy society if it does not enable the "emotional minds" (as from the theory of minds) of its members, to express and relate.

All this, of course, involves a definition of the *Persona* as the real means, not the obstacle, for the Anima or the Animus to embody within the subject's personal and historical biography. This embodiment does not stop at the inter-subjective level, but – as contemporary research makes soundly evident – actually continues and reaches its zenith at the social- and group-level through the development of the infant's and child's potential social embeddedness, normativity and morality. In this sense, no depth psychology can claim to be teleological, as Jungian psychology rightly does, without including not just the inter-subjective and interpersonal relational fields, but also the social and cultural multi-layered relational flow between all other human (as well as animals, living and non-living, organic and inorganic) beings. A flow that substantiates itself in its economic and above all "political" forms.

Within this flow, the idea of the Self, not as a metaphysical substance, but as a true affective potential emerging organizer, is perhaps similar to the "true Self" as envisioned not only by Jung but also by Winnicott. This would be a Self rooted in the ontological reality of the fact that each and every Self while being a part of a universal (ecological) relational flow, is at the same time also embedded into, and occupies a very *specific* – i.e., *unique* – position in space-time and history. A position which has, from the beginning been made unique both by the primal relationship of the foetus with the mother through the placenta and by the endowment of a genome common to all, and also (like the brain) embodied as a specific, unique individual-in-the-making.[2]

With these few thoughts, we hope to explain the background of the Analysis and Activism endeavour and the conferences from which this book and those that preceded it originate. The necessity for developing a new language, a new vision, for any depth psychology that wishes to encompass the (wonderful) complexity of the human (and not only human) being as an embodied hyper-complex relational flow, and embedded in Jung's "natural" and historical unfolding of the libido (see especially: Jung, *Aion*, 1959) has informed it from inception.

Within such a

> [...] post-human convergence [... the] capacity to produce knowledge is not the exclusive prerogative of humans alone but is distributed across all living matter and throughout self-organizing technological networks.
>
> (Braidotti, 2019, p. 51)

In this extensive post-modern broadening of the co-protagonists of the *chaosmos*, the self-organizing, interconnected, multi-layered, dynamic relational flow transcends anthropocentrism, Euro-centrism and even the dominant preoccupations of the human *Bios*, *vs.* a shift towards the transformations and organization of the natural *Zoe*. This perfectly matches one of the fundamental features of the archetype: its *transgressive nature*. As a matter of fact, strange as it may seem at first, the political and the social dimensions may be integrated in the psychological realm together with *all* its co-protagonists (human, non- human, organic and inorganic, living and non-living, material and imaginal) if we look at them through the archetypal lens.

Here we are clearly not limiting our reference to the archetypes to their relationship with the "instinct" but are looking at their powerful epistemic and heuristic character. From this perspective, it is not at all surprising that the "deepest" layer of human psychology – the archetype – would *not* be a personal construct, but a social one[3] and that, as Jung wrote, an image, a dream, a vision, when imbued with an archetypal character would be shared with the whole social community. At the bottom of psychology, we find sociology (and vice versa).

Hence, the question as to what may or may not be "Jungian" or indeed "analytical" needs to be considered from a non-reductive position where the socio-political level of reality is part and parcel of human life.

Such a reality is a supremely pragmatic one. It is the world we live in and the world we make, and make sense of at the same time. And, as the theoretical comprehension of its fluid and transgressive character is difficult to conceptualize because of its paradoxical nature, in this case, an *active* approach may prove to be the most suitable one.

From this point of view, the understanding of a patient's predicament may develop from the analyst's *active* – dialectical – participation in her world – a participation which should range from the patient's world of "inner" images and dreams, all the way to their social, economic and, therefore, cultural and political belonging.

Therefore, we will find some facets of the post-modern *chaosmos* referred to in each chapter of this book under the form of theoretical, but most of all *empirical and practical* preoccupations that, within the analytical setting, fully involve the analyst and the patient at all levels – from the imaginal to the inter-subjective, and the political.

The compass for such a multi-layered, transgressive (analytical) relationship is its intrinsic symbolic nature. After all, the analyst's aim will be the same old one: to look – together with the real expert within the shared therapeutic field (the patient) – for what *context* might reveal the lost meaning of the patient's symptomatic *text*. A symptom, embedded into its adequate context, will bloom into a potential symbolic sense, and therefore will make it possible for the Self to embody itself into its proper symbolic process-form.

Jung's fundamental clinical advice: "Go *where* the patient is" remains as valid as ever, if not even more valid than before as such a "where" will in the post-modern thinking be interpreted as transgressive, fluid, empirical, embodied reality that spans from the body to dreams, to the intimate inter-subjective transpersonal field, all the way to the cultural, economic, linguistic, ecological, political and historical levels of existence.

Notes

1 Seen under this view, the castration complex would seem "unnatural" and symptomatic. Yet, this leaves open the question of the paradoxical possibility – always maintained by Jung – that human psychopathology is a psychological necessity *contra naturam* (against nature), intrinsic to creativity and symbol-formation (Hillman, 1976).
2 At a deeper level, the uniqueness of each Self is rooted in the constant quantum collapse of each perception and mental activity from its wave form into a localized particle-like experience.
3 Jung, of course, referred to its "collective" character, yet often conflating the negative traits of the behaviour of the "masses" (in Le Bon's sociology), with the complexity of society, seen as one of the contexts in which we humans are "archetypically" embedded.

References

Adamson, L.B., & Frick, J.E. (2013). "The Still Face: A History of a Shared Experimental Paradigm." *Infancy*. 4(4): pp. 451–473.
Bollas, C. (1987). *The Shadow of the Object: Psychoanalysis of the Unthought Known*. New York: Columbia University Press.
Braidotti, R. (2019). *Posthuman, All Too Human*. Cambridge: Polity Press.
Carta, S., Adorisio A., & Mercurio R. (2017). *The Analyst in the Polis*. 2 vol. Streetlib.
Derrida, J. (2008). *The Animal That Therefore I Am*. New York: Fordham University Press.
Geertz, C. (1983). *Local Knowledge. Further Essays in Interpretive Anthropology*. New York: Basic Books.

Guattari, Felix. 1995. *Chaosmosis: An Ethico-aesthetic Paradigm.* Sydney: Power Publications.

Hillman, J. (1976). *Re-Visioning Psychology.* New York: Harper and Row.

Jung, C.G. (1959). *Aion.* Collected Works, Vol 9ii. Bollingen Series XX (translated by R.F.C. Hull). Princeton, NJ: Princeton University Press.

Kiehl, E., Saban, M., & Samuels, A. (Eds.) (2016). *Analysis and Activism: Social and Political Contributions of Jungian Psychology.* New York: Routledge.

Papadopoulos, R. (2002). "The Other Other: When the Exotic Other Subjugates the Familiar Other." *Journal of Analytical Psychology.* 47(2): pp. 163–188.

Tomasello, M. (2019). *Becoming Human. A Theory of Ontogeny.* Cambridge, MA: The Bellknap Press.

Tronick, E. (2007). *The Neurobehavioral and Social-Emotional Development of Infants and Children (Norton Series on Interpersonal Neurobiology).* New York: W.W. Norton.

Waldenfelds, B. (2008). *Fenomenologia dell'Estraneo.* Milano: Cortina.

Section 1

Leaders, led, migration

Chapter 1

Extinction anxiety

Where the spirit of the depths meets the spirit of the times

Thomas Singer

The purpose of this chapter is to introduce the term "extinction anxiety" as an apt clinical descriptor for a symptom that affects all of us.

Apocalyptic fantasies are as old as time but the term "extinction anxiety" which originates in such fears has not been used to describe the psychic state of individuals and groups that are either consciously or unconsciously gripped by the dread of extinction.

As we have learned from Freud, anxiety is a warning signal that danger is present and that overwhelming emotions may be felt, giving rise to unmanageable helplessness. The danger may be perceived as arising from internal or external sources and be the response to a variety of powerful fantasies in the unconscious mind.

It is my hypothesis that extinction anxiety is flooding the planet, although it frequently expresses itself in a displaced form of group or cultural anxiety rather than in the direct experience of the fear of extinction. It is timely to give a clinical name to "extinction anxiety" as a type of warning signal that danger is present whether it is originating in irrational fear and/or irrefutable objective evidence. In the recently published book *The Dangerous Case of Donald Trump*, Noam Chomsky writes quite simply:

> There are two huge dangers that the human species face. We are in a situation where we need to decide whether the species survives in any decent form. One is the rising danger of nuclear war, which is quite serious, and the other is environmental catastrophe.
>
> (Lee, 2017, p. 357)[1]

We know of the dangers, but we have not named "extinction anxiety" as a source of worldwide psychic distress.

It may seem surprising that this term has not been introduced to describe this profound disturbance in the individual and collective psyche. When I first began to consider the term, I did a search and discovered that the only use of "extinction anxiety" is to denote the extinction of a symptom in a behaviorist model. In that model, the term is used to describe the attempt to "extinguish conditioned fear." When I use the term "extinction anxiety" I am not talking about the extinction of fear; I am talking about the fear of extinction.

Perhaps the closest we have come in the history of our profession to naming such anxiety is "existential anxiety." Existential anxiety, born out of the dis-illusioning and dismembering experiences of World War I, the Great Depression, and World War II, convinced many that the universe was absurd and without meaning. "Existence precedes essence" was a way of saying that life did not come into being with a preexisting meaning but that meaning or "essence" had to be created out of one's own being. Finding oneself in a mean-ingless universe is not the same as facing the extinction of life as we know it. In other words, existential anxiety and extinction anxiety emerge out of different fears, although both are profoundly disorienting in the sense that we have lost our "place" in a world that had given us meaning with a feeling of relative safety. "Extinction anxiety" as part of the "spirit of our times" is different from the "spirit of the times" that gave rise to existential anxiety.

I am not writing this chapter to prophesize the end of times. Rather, my purpose in writing this chapter is to say that the intense, contemporary anx-iety about the approaching end of time is real and needs to be taken with the utmost seriousness. Although "extinction anxiety" finds direct expression in environmental groups and those concerned about nuclear war (Christensen, 2017),[2] it finds less direct expression in other groups and individuals that are in fear of their own annihilation but who do not consciously link their deeply felt precarious status to the fear of the extinction of the world.

Appropriately enough, the term "extinction anxiety" literally popped into mind when I was working on a paper about Donald Trump. I was thinking about all the diverse groups around the world who fear that their unique identi-ties and very existence are threatened. Whites, Blacks, Women, Men, Latinos, Palestinians, Jews, Muslims, Gays, 60 million refugees around the globe, are just a few of the groups in the grips of fear for their own survival. Could it be that they are all tapping into a deeper, underlying "extinction anxiety" which is the collective psyche's equivalent of the anxiety about death in the individual?

I believe that extinction anxiety acts as a psychic radioactive background in our global society and that it fuels many of our concerns. For instance, climate change deniers on the right in the US may be seen as denying the very real possibility of the planet's destruction as a way of defending them-selves against the fear of extinction. Aligning himself with this attitude, Trump offers to staunch "extinction anxiety" by denying it is real and ap-pointing a well-known climate change denier as his energy adviser. As we know, denial—whether at the individual or group level—is the most primi-tive defense in the psyche's arsenal of defenses to protect itself.

I believe that C.G. Jung was right in suggesting that the psyche has multi-ple layers that go down or up or around the individual to the family, to the clan, to the nation, to larger groups such as European or Asian, and even to primate and animal ancestors, finally finding its source in what Jung called the "central fire." We also know that there are fault lines at every level of our global society. The fault lines that demarcate divisions between groups of people and nations run deep along gender, tribal, national, religious, racial and ethnic lines. It is my hypothesis that extinction anxiety emerges from the deepest levels of the psyche through these fault lines or channels that run back and forth from the depths of the very source of life and psyche on the planet, Jung's "central fire," all the way up to the individual. We can imagine that extinction anxiety courses up and down along these channels as the carrier of the signal of alarm and great danger, not unlike the flow of lava that comes from deep beneath the surface of the earth until it breaks through the surface in a volcanic eruption.

We can also imagine that along these fault lines, extinction anxiety is where the spirit of the times and the spirit of the depths meet. To tease out the notion that the spirit of the depths and the spirit of the times merge with one another in the phenomenon of extinction anxiety, I want to circle around these two spirits in relation to extinction anxiety.

The spirit of the depths and extinction anxiety

"The spirit of the depths" refers to ancient and recurring themes of deepest concern to human beings: themes of death and rebirth, of meaning and meaninglessness, of suffering and joy, of loss and repair, of what is fleeting and what is eternal. From the "spirit of the depths" humankind has been experiencing apocalyptic fantasies since the dawn of human history. Zarathustra, The Book of Daniel, The Book of Revelations—all are steeped in the apocalyptic vision of the end of time.[3] Perhaps the most moving modern expression of this vision from the spirit of the depths is Yeats' "The Second Coming" written in 1919 at the end of World War I:[4]

The second coming

> Turning and turning in the widening gyre
> The falcon cannot hear the falconer;
> Things fall apart; the centre cannot hold;
> Mere anarchy is loosed upon the world,
> The blood-dimmed tide is loosed, and everywhere
> The ceremony of innocence is drowned;
> The best lack all conviction, while the worst
> Are full of passionate intensity.
> Surely some revelation is at hand;
> Surely the Second Coming is at hand.
> The Second Coming! Hardly are those words out
> When a vast image out of *Spiritus Mundi*

Troubles my sight: somewhere in sands of the desert
A shape with lion body and the head of a man,
A gaze blank and pitiless as the sun,
Is moving its slow thighs, while all about it
Reel shadows of the indignant desert birds.
The darkness drops again; but now I know
That twenty centuries of stony sleep
Were vexed to nightmare by a rocking cradle,
And what rough beast, its hour come round at last,
Slouches towards Bethlehem to be born?

(Yeats, 1989, p. 187)

Apocalyptic fantasy from the spirit of the depths is alive and well today in the longing of Christian fundamentalists for the end of times in the rapture at Armageddon. And it has been alive and well in Isis and its Islamic apocalyptic vision of the end of times in the yearning to create the Caliphate. These fantasies can be thought of as emerging from the depths of the "human psyche" that is grounded in the origins of life itself—not just human life but all plant and animal life on the planet. We can also imagine, along with the Hindus, that whatever forces give birth to life on the planet can do just the opposite and take back into itself all of life and psyche as in Vishnu's reabsorption into himself of the whole of the created cosmos.

The Doomsday Clock
pictured at its most recent
setting of "two and a half
minutes to midnight."

Figure 1.1 "The spirit of the times" and extinction anxiety: The Doomsday Clock.

Our "spirit of the times" remains anchored mostly in the scientific mind which has become wedded to technology and materialist consumerism. It is no accident that the Bulletin of Atomic Scientists has created and maintained a Doomsday Clock since the dawn of the nuclear age in 1947 when the clock was set at seven minutes before midnight. Midnight marks the extinction of the human race (see Figure 1.1). Since its inception, the clock has fluctuated in predicting how much time we have left. In 1953, it was moved up to two minutes before midnight when both the US and the Soviet Union exploded hydrogen bombs. It drifted back to three minutes before midnight until the election of Donald Trump and it is currently set at two minutes before midnight.[5]

In "the spirit of the times," our extinction anxiety is fueled by undeniable objective evidence that life on the planet is seriously endangered. We know, for instance, that we have already entered the "sixth mass extinction event" in which it is predicted that one half of the world's land and marine species could disappear by 2100 unless there is some other annihilating or transforming event that precedes the "natural unfolding" of the sixth mass extinction event. As human beings, we are instinctually and archetypally connected with all life. The threat of the loss of all these non-human species contributes to extinction anxiety.[6]

What if the human psyche carries within it the deep memory of biological and geological evolution, that our evolutionary heritage is mapped in the brain? In what scientists call "deep time" the Earth has experienced five mass extinctions. Four of these were triggered by climate change and were followed by large-scale reorganizations in the biosphere opening gateways that ultimately led to the evolution of the human species. Does the "deep psyche" have a memory of "deep time" and these previous extinctions as reflected in the Hindu religious imagination? It is interesting to contemplate how this might be manifesting in our current spirit of the times.

More immediately, on a day-to-day basis, we are flooded with news of devastating fires, massive storms, terrorist attacks and random mass killings. All of this heightens the horrifying fear that something is terribly amiss in the world. As Yeats wrote:

> And what rough beast, its hour come round at last,
> Slouches towards Bethlehem to be born?[7]
> (Yeats, "The Second Coming.")

Not only are we being flooded with way too much information and the staggering explosion of the global population, but also perhaps with too much interconnectivity. Imagine for a moment that everyone you see walking down the street or sitting in a coffee house communicating on their cellphones or computers is actually sending out billions of the same daily latent message: "It hasn't happened yet." What if our frantic interconnectivity is a global SOS expression of extinction anxiety and that we are desperately clinging to one another in an effort to reassure ourselves we are not on a sinking or exploding ship?

Again, we might imagine extinction anxiety to be flowing like lava up and down the layers of the ancient and contemporary global psyche that includes evolutionary time, circulating in an accelerating negative feedback loop, up from the spirit of the depths to the spirit of the times, and back "down" again, in which guns, storms, droughts, and nuclear threats merge with old and new apocalyptic visions.

The obvious next question is—so what? What can we do about this? Does it help to make conscious the unconscious extinction anxiety which is fortified today by the very real scarcity that stalks much of the world's population and that pits all sorts of groups against one another in the most intractable conflicts? I wonder if increased consciousness and political activism based on the awareness of global extinction anxiety offers some slim hope of humankind being able to make informed choices?

Conclusion

If extinction anxiety is sounding an alarm on behalf of the whole of creation where the spirit of the depths and the spirit of the times meet at every level of human experience, then our response needs to come from the whole of the psyche in harnessing all of our scientific, political, psychological and spiritual efforts to forge a unity of deep action on behalf of the creation and against those forces which would destroy it. This effort may well require the extinction of our current world view, which is focused almost exclusively on materialist reductionisms of all kinds.

No one has more vividly conveyed what is at stake than Cormack McCarthy in his strangely intimate post-apocalyptic novel, *The Road*, which has created for me a parallel universe along whose devastated and dangerous road I often find myself walking in reverie. I find myself in a world without electricity, cars, hot water, enough food and the constant threat of murderous human beings that have lost all their humanity. In the mood of that reverie, I debate whether or not to buy a gun to protect my family—but we Americans already have more guns than people, some 350 million of them, and they don't seem to be protecting us from anything. Surely the wish to own a gun is an instinctive response to defend oneself in the face of heightened extinction anxiety. This is what "extinction anxiety" does to us!

Listen to the voice of extinction anxiety in the last lines of McCormack's book:

Once there were brook trout in the streams in the mountains. You could see them standing in the amber current where the white edges of their fins wimpled softly in the flow. They smelled of moss in your hand. Polished and muscular and torsional. On their backs were vermiculate patterns that were maps of the world in its becoming. Maps and mazes. Of a thing which could not be put back. Not be made right again. In the deep glens where they lived all things were older than man and they hummed of mystery (McCarthy, 2006, pp. 306–307).[8]

Notes

1 Brandy Lee, *The Dangerous Case of Donald Trump* (New York: Thomas Dunne Books, St. Martin's Press, 2017), 357.
2 Jen Christensen, "16,000 Scientists Sign Dire Warning to Humanity over Health of Planet," *CNN,* November 15, 2017, http://www.cnn.com/2017/11/14/health/scientists-warn-humanity/index.html.
3 For this section, I am indebted to Richard Stein, M.D., whose "Living on the Edge of the Apocalypse: What Isis, The Christian Right, and Climate Change Deniers Have in Common" appears in The San Francisco Jung Institute Presidential Papers of 2016: https://aras.org/newsletters/aras-connections-special-edition-2016-presidency-papers.
4 William Butler Yeats, "The Second Coming," Poetry Foundation, https://www.poetryfoundation.org/poems/43290/the-second-coming. From *The Collected Poems of W. B. Yeats* (New York: Macmillan, 1989), 187.
5 Bulletin of the Atomic Scientists, Doomsday Clock, https://thebulletin.org/timeline.
6 I am indebted to Jeffrey Kiehl for personal communications about the section on "mass extinction events."
7 Yeats, "The Second Coming."
8 Cormac McCarthy, *The Road* (New York: Alfred A. Knopf, 2006), 306–307.

Chapter 2

Relationship with authority

Moving from helplessness towards experience of authorship

Gražina Gudaitė

The relationship with authority is an important psychosocial phenomenon that affects both individuals and groups, as well as the whole of society. The quality of the relationship with authority depends on the development of a particular human being, together with specific systems of relationship within society. The experience of authority is a controversial phenomenon. In fact, the relationship with authority is important for the formation of psychic structures and for the possibility to confront and withstand chaos; for spiritual development and even for getting a sense of inspiration. However, the experience of authority is directly connected to the power principle. Authority is defined as a power to influence another or others, which entail repression towards both the single individual and a whole group.

Repressions and the destructive influence of authority, with the consequences of an authoritarian regime may be a very significant theme in analysis.

It is interesting to note that the psychological issues of the experience of authority were raised in the countries that were recently liberated from authoritarian regimes. H. Dieckman (1977) and H. Wilke (1977) in Germany, M. Šebek from Check (Sebek, 1996), Ratković-Njegovan, Vukadinović, and Grubić Nešić from Serbia (2011), Kalinenko and Slutskaya in Russia, Gudaitė (2014, 2016), Grigutytė and Rukšaitė (2016), Petronytė- Kvedarauskienė (2018) in Lithuania published their works on different aspects of the experience of the relationship towards authority.

M. Šebek pointed out that the immaturity of the individual and of a society depends on the characteristics of figures of authority, who have great influence on the development of the individual.

Among others, the lack of respect for individuality, a tendency to own the other and to manipulate him/her and to induce dependence were common features in the relationship with authority in totalitarian regimes (Sebek, 1996).

S. Kalinenko and M. Slutskaya stated that from the weakening of the individual self and the obedience to the "Father of the people" develops the tendency to identify with large groups, in which one can find shelter and the expectation that somebody will take care of him/her. Idealization and splitting of the Father complex is the central part of the negative cultural complex in the Russian cultural space.

> Having a split attitude towards authoritarian figures is typical: one simultaneously hates them and loves them, blames them for cruelty, stupidity and corruption and admires their "strength" which ensured victory in the Second World War, established "order" in the country, gave a sense of stability and provided a global role for the country...the totalitarian authority benefits from maintaining that split which means infantilizing and depersonalizing people, turning them into small cogs in a huge system.
> (Kalinenko & Slutskaya, 2014, p. 108)

Research conducted in Lithuania showed that a high prevalence of self-destructive behaviour and suicides, alcohol problems and the loss of significance of the male roles within society and the family, the destruction of personal initiative and regressive behaviours were all related to past traumatic experiences and to disturbed relationships with authority (Gailienė & Kazlauskas, 2005; Gudaitė, 2014). The following characteristics were common in disturbed relationship with authority: the perception of authority as a power which exists only in the outer world; the development of one-sided, defensive attitudes towards authority; the difficulty to differentiate its qualities, together with dependence on authority even when it is destructive (Gudaitė, 2016).

The confrontation with the authority complex (be it personal or cultural) and the efforts to break free from its imprisonment are important themes in those psychotherapies that deal with the need to heal from the consequences of authoritarian regimes. Studies on the effectiveness of psychotherapy showed that analytical psychotherapy can be helpful in such a process. In fact, as H. Dieckman writes:

> Individuation, especially in the analytical situation, can bring about not only a changing, and rebirth, of the inner nature of man, but, to the same degree, a change and rebirth as regards structure and authority.
> (Dieckman, 1977, p. 236)

In this chapter I would like to discuss some ideas about the complexity of the relationship with authority, with a special focus on the attainment of a deeper understanding of the manifestations of the authority complex, and of the process that leads to its healing.

This discussion is based on a research project – "Revelation of personality's integrity: problem of relation with authority and psychotherapy" – and on doctoral studies carried out at the Vilnius University in 2014–2018.

A group of researchers from the Clinical Psychology Department (now: "Centre for research of the psychodynamics of the personality") carried out a research project on the experience of authority. Clinical psychologists, some holding a PhD, others still doing their doctoral studies at the Department of Psychology at Vilnius University, were members of the research group. A semi-structured interview and a questionnaire aimed at describing different types of relationship with authority were used. The main method of our research was the analysis of the course of a number of psychotherapies, with a special focus on the dynamics of the relationship with authority in psychotherapy and the retrospective analysis of long-term cases.

More than 700 participants took part in different stages of the research. The discussion of the results that follows does not include the full presentation of our studies, as the main idea of this chapter focusses on a deeper understanding of the process of psychotherapy, ranging from helplessness to authorship. In a further publication I will present the main themes to describe this process.

Defensive attitude towards authority versus recognition

One of the themes of our research was the need to have a constructive relationship with authority. The analysis of the interviews and of the psychotherapies showed that, in our culture, authority is usually perceived as a powerful force existing in the outer world, in regard to which the individual takes a passive or defensive position. Certain types of authority affect the individual's specific defensive position:

Diffuse authority. This position reflects the influence of an impersonal force which does not have a definite shape, or as somebody who may have many changing shapes.

It is hard to predict or to control such an influence. "You never know what to expect from it", "it is like an invisible power, which emerges from nowhere", "energy of a black demon".

Such and other expressions were used to describe the actions of such type of authority.

When a person experiences such inner representations it is very hard to maintain or to develop any relationship with this kind of authority. Paralysing insecurity, helplessness, permeability of personal boundaries can be the nuclear components of this authority complex. The individual subjected to its influence will use all possible defences to protect him/herself in the interaction with such a tricksterish power.

Destructive authority. In this case, authority has a clear shape, its functioning is felt and described as expansive, attacking and enslaving the other. Traumatic experiences and the influence of a dominating power principle are closely connected to the manifestation of this type of authority.

Our study showed that such descriptions of authority are common to the second generation of cultural trauma of survivors. We explored more than 100 cases of analytical therapy (Dreams and dream series, and memory episodes from personal and family histories) and we found that the authority complex was one of the main complexes in the majority of the cases. Approximately 60% of cases showed that authority was perceived as dangerous and destructive (Gudaitė, 2014).

Even many years later, authority figures, such as communist leaders, KGB officials or military officers (belonging to the Soviet or German armies), appeared in dreams or memories. They were felt to be dangerous because they could, or would, kill, torture or persecute.

For those individuals, this form of the authority complex, consisting of suppressed anger and or feelings of unsafety mixed with expectations of danger from the one who holds a position of power or a higher social ranking, was rather common. In their relationship with authority, these subjects used a number of defence strategies, such as denial, splitting, projection and idealization.

Weak authority. Our research showed that the experience of weak authority was also perceived as difficult, and that this was especially problematic for men.

> My father did not have any power at home. Maybe he was too old, or maybe ill. I do not know. I was the king, and I took whatever I wanted.... Even now I can get everything, but the problem is I do not have wishes anymore.

Experience of the other's power, competence or prestige may be accepted as an inspiring force and an important step towards developing a relationship with authority. "I do not need any authorities", "I am the main authority of my life". Such a position was common among young people.

Individuals need to identify with authority in some life situations: they need to have experience that they can influence the development of the events and that something depend on them. Yet, if a person remains fixated in such a position and if he or she tries to be the only authority in every possible life situation – this complicates his/her life very much. According to J. Bochenski, such an approach is false, as it distorts the very notion of the relationship with authority and blocks the idea of the interpersonal vertical axis of experience.

Distant authority. In this case, individuals accept their need and longing for someone who represents a real authority figure, although such a relationship is not possible, since the authority figure is not open for any communication.

> Everybody admired my father, but he did not notice me... I think I was rather a pitiful creature for him. I was longing for him. I tried to read books he liked, I was running marathons, but that did not help.

This and other examples show that the search and longing for authority could be part of an "authority complex". This complex may manifest itself in low self-esteem and a lack of feeling of an *inner* authority, and by the individual's efforts to fit in with the authority figures' expectations, together with the disappointment when this doesn't happen and the person doesn't get the blessing he/she was looking for.

Distant or expansive, diffuse or weak forms of authority all can create problems not only at an individual level, but also at cultural level. In one way or another they are all connected to an authoritarian style, which could be dangerous in many ways. In fact, if an authoritarian person takes a position of authority, and if he/she is not open to the opinions of others, he/she can make really wrong decisions, as he/she does not possess the necessary competences for managing all the possible situations that he/she will face in their position of power. Such distant authority blocks the initiative of others and this may cause all forms of passive and regressive behaviours, which emerge in the course of analysis as the consequences of authoritarian regime.

On the other hand, the authoritarian style is not a remainder of the past. In fact, we witness many of its manifestations also in our present time. Roots of the authority complex are archetypal. This means that relationship or identification with authority is a universal feature and, regardless of historical conditions they are part and parcel of each individual's experience. Therefore, the individual needs to be conscious of the issues that involve authority.

The manifestation of authority is a dynamic process. It may be creative or destructive, inspiring or repressing. It may bring peace or chaos. The issue of the relationship towards authority is an essential part of the individual's relational system. Therefore, the growing consciousness about complexity of its manifestation can be essential to confront authority's destructive power.

Confronting the authority complex in psychotherapy

Studies on psychotherapy effectiveness showed that long-term analytical psychotherapy can be helpful in the process of confrontation with the authority complex. The effectiveness of this approach depends on the aetiology of the complex, on the development of the individual, on the stage of psychotherapy and on the culture in which the individual lives. Confronting the authority complex (be it personal or cultural) means facing the shadow side of our personal and cultural life.

Destructive and regressive impulses, weakness and helplessness when encountering frightening aggressive forces, feelings of inferiority and socially unacceptable impulses could be interpreted as contents of the Shadow.

According to Jungian authors, not all Shadow images are horrific. Nevertheless, they remain difficult to face. Facing the Shadow requires love and compassion, and not only towards the other's weakness or inferiority but it also requires an understanding of one's own undeveloped or destroyed parts, our inner limitedness or sickness.

The shadow can be socially unacceptable and even evil, it is important that it is carried by us, which means that we do not project our unacceptable parts onto others and or act them out. This is an ethical responsibility (Marlan, 2010, p. 8).

The authority complex is part of our Shadow. Withdrawing our projections and taking responsibility for our own strength, together with confronting the dominating power principle and being open to the Eros principle to emerge, are all fundamental conditions for the healing of the disturbed relationship with authority.

The healing process may manifest itself in different ways. All of the following and other qualities are important in confronting the authority complex: the possibility to create a safe and empathetic space; fostering the ability to both take a position of authority and leave it at right time; being attentive to the signs of other's inner authority; being open to the manifestation of a transcendental authority; the encouragement and ability to tolerate frustration and to maintain a deep trust in the other.

Moving from being dependent on authority towards being able to rebel against the powerful object are significant moments within the healing process of authority-related psychological issues. Our retrospective case analysis showed that the ability to stand up to great power contained in the authoritarian object, the ability to remain open to meeting him/her – the ability to face the aggressor – are all important parts of the confrontation with the authority complex.

It is interesting to note that the theme of "rebel" came up not only in trauma survivors, but also in younger individuals. Our research towards a deeper understanding of the healing moments in psychotherapy showed that clients accepted their experience as rebels against the psychotherapist and other authority figures as one of the most important healing moments in their psychotherapy (Petronytė-Kvedarauskienė, 2018).

The courage to confront authority in the outer world is a relevant condition for the formation of an inner authority principle. Nevertheless, if an individual remains fixed in the rebellious position, this will limit his or her adaptation and expression of creativity. Some recent studies of social psychology (Passini & Morselli, 2009) suggest that in the life of a human being both the positions of obedience and disobedience to authority are meaningful experiences. Obedience to authority is an important condition for the continuity of the society and for the group's life. Disobedience is crucial in preventing the authority-based relationship from degenerating into an authoritarian mode. People who integrate both obedience and disobedience are more democratic than those who recognize only the value of obedience and consider disobedience as a threat to the *status quo* and for well-being (Passini & Morselli, 2009).

The ability to recognize one's own limitedness and helplessness is part of the individual's maturation process. Even in the Hero mythology the theme of submission is part of the hero's actions. The question when to rebel and when to submit comes up again and again. In the words of J. Campbell:

> The hero is the man of self-achieved submission. But submission to what? That precisely is the riddle that today we have to ask ourselves and that it is everywhere the primary virtue and historic deed of the hero to have solved.
>
> (Campbell, 2015, p. 24)

When the individual takes a position of authority – when he or she has great power or exceptional competence – still, he/she should be able to be submissive and to keep a relationship with somebody superior, more powerful and wiser than him/herself. This opens an opportunity for renewal and for finding new sources of vitality. Vice versa, ignoring the relationship of the vertical dimension leads to stagnation and authoritarianism.

Another theme that emerged in the results of our study was the withdrawal of projections from outer figures and the development of a sense of inner authority. Taking active position and experiencing moments of rebellion towards authority indicates that the person is finding sources of inner strength and is able to stand for his/her own position.

Disagreement with a powerful object is a challenging experience, as it may cause conflict, rejection and isolation. The confrontation with outer authority is a risk, yet it is also the way to express one's own strength and to try to carry certain Shadow aspects on one's own shoulders.

The withdrawal of projections of authority is a complex process, as the essential transformations take place in the depths of our psyche. Our study confirmed the idea that dreams can be good guides for a deeper understanding of the possibilities for transformation.

> I was in a big room. Somebody big and powerful was near me. I was afraid, and I felt my heart beating violently. I did not know whether God or something evil was standing behind me, but I decided to risk meeting him. There was a big pause... Then I felt as if a wind touched my whole body. I felt a great energy and was able to rise up. I could move and I could choose the direction.

This is an episode from the dream of a man who was facing the consequences of an authoritarian regime. The dream speaks by itself about the phenomenology of the change of relationship towards the powerful object/image. Openness and the courage to meet someone who holds great power, the ability to take risks, patience, these are some of the conditions that emerge within this process of change.

Such an experience is closely related with another important theme of psychotherapy – i.e. with discovering one's own sense of authorship.

Moving from helplessness towards a sense of authorship

Usually the aetiology of the term "authority" is linked to the Latin word "Auctoritas" (lt), which refers to the power and influence exercised to direct actions of other people. The second meaning of the word is the ability to be an author (the one who can create). Therefore, authorship is defined as the ability to produce something from oneself, or as an appropriate ability to relate with the source of Creation.

Our study showed that the ability to express one's creativity and sense of authorship are fundamental in confronting the authority complex. In fact, the ability to work and create something original is the deepest antidote to the feeling of helpless, of being used or manipulated by the powerful other. Our sense of authorship confirms the value of our subjectivity and uniqueness. Regaining our subjectivity may entail our growing openness towards what is yet unknown and our liberation from a strong system of defences.

The emergence of a creative force and a growing awareness of it were reflected as important moments in our study.

Dreams gave hints about the emergence of such a possibility.

...I was making some little drawing on paper. To my surprise, the drawing became colourful and I could see a sunflower. Then, it changed on its own and became a three- dimensional sculpture, and was a really nice piece of art.

This is a fragment from a dream of a woman who was working on authority issues. In that moment of psychotherapy her developing sense of authorship was the essential theme. Spontaneity and openness to the unknown, awareness that things may happen of their own accord, trust in the power of the subject's internal reality and the trust in the process –all these were key features in the confrontation with the authority complex, together with the defensiveness and the avoidant behaviour that it constellated.

Sometimes dreams and associations refer to the way one experiences authorship. A client had a dream of an artist ceramist. These are her associations to the dream figure:

When one is making a vessel, he or she needs to feel the centre very clearly. The shape of the pot comes up in the rotation. One should hold the clay firmly but flexibly, because it is the centrifugal force that helps to make the shape.

Relatedness to the inner centre, the ability to give direction to the energy flow and to create a vessel while holding it with firm and flexible hands could be understood as metaphoric expressions and good references not only for pot-making, but also for creating new forms in a broader, symbolic, sense. The ability to create inner forms and structures is the basis for a developed system of relationships.

The feeling of authorship is important not only for analysing the creative process of some specific product, but also for a deeper understanding of the person's participation in life.

Who am I? Am I just a role-playing figure? Or am I the performer in my life situations? These questions are common to any psychotherapeutic process and to the growing awareness of the moments that refer to one's authorship in general life situations.

The great masters of creative works draw our attention to the big difference between the impulse to create and its final product. The creative impulse may come from nowhere. It may be inspiring and attractive, but if it does not have a shape, it will remain in a primary state and will never be available to others.

A creative person needs to do a lot of work until their impulse to create acquires its right shape – a shape which will speak by itself. Finding such a right form may take days, months or even years, and this is an intrinsic part of the creative process and of the authorship that we may then experience.

We can witness the same tendency in the process of psychological maturation too. There are many situations when a person can discover his/her inner power, or reach a position of power in society. Yet, this will not solve any authority issues. In fact, one needs to work a lot in order to find the right forms for expression of authority and to communicate it to others.

So, the confrontation with the authority complex and the discovery of one's own of authorship is a complex experience: it may manifest itself as the discovery of an inner authority principle and as an ability to realize one's own creative force. At the same time, it may be reflected in an appropriate ability to communicate with the source of creativity.

Important aspects of this process are: the development of an open attitude towards the unknown, the exercise of patience and hard work in order to search for the right forms for those impulses that come to us from within, and the constant search for the right words and narratives to express the meaning of our experiences.

Conclusion

I would like to conclude my chapter with a quotation from Jung's *Red Book*.

> We miss nothing more than divine force... And thus we speak and stand and look around to see whether somewhere something might happen.

Something always happens, but we do not happen, since our God is sick…We must think of his healing. And yet again I feel it quite clearly that my life would have broken in half had I failed to heal my God.

(Jung, 2009)

This quotation occurs in *Liber Secundus*, where Jung describes his experiences in active imagination and his own dialogues with powerful inner figures such as The Red One, Ammonius, and Izdubar. Many existential questions are raised in these dialogues. Are individuals able to know that their God is "sick"? Is it realistic to think about healing the transcendent power if this doesn't depend on the will of the individual? In his inner dialogues Jung does not speak about trauma. He develops the hypothesis that God became sick because modern man does not express the need for the divine reality anymore – that he puts science in the position of the main authority, and that he has lost his capacity to believe.

In the context of Jung's reflections of his experiences as recorded in the *Red Book*, the healing of the psyche means the restoration and nurturance of the relationship with the transcendent. It means remembering that human beings have a soul; and it means nourishing the inner subjective world of the individual, and searching for bridges between the inner and the outer. Such ideas fit in a deeper understanding of the relationship with authority. It is important to search for bridges between inner and outer, between the personal and the cultural, between moments of destruction and creativity, between emptiness and fertility. The confrontation with the authority complex (personal and cultural) is full of challenges, but it may also carry moments of blessing, which may open new sources of vitality and meaning, inspiration and creativity.

References

Bochenski, J. M. (2004). *Who is Authority? Introduction to Logics of Authority.* Vilnius, Lithuania: Mintis. Printed in Lithuanian language.

Campbell, J. (2015). *The Hero with a Thousand Faces.* Vilnius, Lithuania: Tyto Alba. Printed in Lithuanian language.

Dieckmann, H. (1977). Some aspects of the development of authority. *Journal of Analytical Psychology*, 22(3), 230–242.

Gailienė, D., & Kazlauskas, E. (2005). Fifty years on: The long-term psychological effects of soviet repression in Lithuania. In D. Gailienė (Ed.), *The Psychology of Extreme Traumatization: The Aftermath of Political Repression* (pp. 67–108). Vilnius, Lithuania: Akreta.

Grigutytė, N., & Rukšaitė, G. (2016). Lithuanian historical heritage: Relationship with authority and psychological well-being. *The European Proceedings of Social and Behavioral Sciences,* 274–284.

Gudaitė, G. (2014) Restoration of Continuity: Desperation or hope in Facing the Consequences of Cultural Trauma. In G. Gudaitė and M. Stein (Eds.) *Confronting cultural trauma: Jungian approaches to understanding and healing* (pp. 227–243). New Orleans, LA: Spring Journal Books.

Gudaitė, G. (2016). *Relationship with Authority and Sense of Personal Power.* Vilnius, Lithuania: Vilnius University Press. Printed in Lithuanian language.

Jung, C. G. (2009). *The Red Book. Liber Novus.* (Ed.), S. Shamdasani. New York and London: W.W. Norton and Company.

Kalinenko, V., & Slutskaya, M. (2014). "Father of the people versus enemies of the people": A split-father complex as the foundation for collective trauma in Russia. In G. Gudaitė and M. Stein (Eds.), *Confronting Cultural Trauma: Jungian Approaches to Understanding and Healing* (pp. 95–113). New Orleans, LA: Spring Journal Books.

Marlan, S. (2010). Facing the shadow. In M. Stein (Ed.), *Jungian Psychoanalysis: Working in the Spirit of C.G. Jung* (pp. 5–14). Chicago, IL: Open Court.

Passini, S., & Morselli, D. (2009). Authority relationships between obedience and disobedience. *New Ideas in Psychology,* 27, 96–106. doi:10.1016/j.newideapsych.

Ratković-Njegovan, B., Vukadinović, M., & Grubić Nešić, L. (2011). Characteristics and types of authority: The attitudes of young people. A case study. *Sociológia,* 43(6), 657–673.

Sebek, M. (1996). The fate of the totalitarian object. *International Forum of Psychoanalysis,* 5, 289–294.

Wilke, H. J. (1977). The authority complex and the authoritarian personality. *Journal of Analytical Psychology,* 22(3), 243–249.

Chapter 3

Racial awareness in analysis
Philosophical, ethical, and political considerations[1]

Antonio Karim Lanfranchi

Introduction

The title of this article originated in a presentation at the 2017 third conference on Analysis and Activism held in Prague, supported by the International Association of Analytical Psychology. It was initially inspired by the following question posed in a Google group: is "white supremacism" the ultimate expression of an innate, archetypal trend? I answered with another question: isn't its current manifestation in a globalizing world a relatively recent cultural acquisition, linked to the modern idea of human progress as opposed to the "archaic" or the "primitive", and also a formidable economic tool which arose with the advent of transatlantic slavery? White supremacy is not biologically innate; it is a social, cultural and political construct with a clearly traceable history. De Gobineau's essay on *The Inequality of Human Races* was written in 1855 (1915), but the process had started several centuries earlier with the first plantations in 16th-century Brazil, the first step towards globalization. Slavery was a rich source of cheap labour and in several ways is still related to structural predation as a fundamental component of liberal capitalism. As Mbembe has shown [2013] (2017), colonial and orientalist literature, including that of liberal Enlightenment thinkers such as De Toqueville, as well as Voltaire, Montesquieu, Kant, Fichte, Hegel and others, is based on a split between racial exclusivism and the advocacy of supposedly "universal" human rights. The liberal concept of freedom has been elitist since its very beginnings: De Toqueville corresponded with De Gobineau; their letters are preserved at Strasbourg's Bibliothèque Nationale Universitaire (BNU) (Marsan & Shemann, 1909).

Philosophical considerations

These ideas have prompted me to reflect further on the possibility of cross-fertilization between political philosophy and psychoanalysis, with particular reference to Agamben. He has shown how the split in liberal thinkers between racial exclusivism and supposedly "universal" human rights can be traced back to Aristotle. According to Agamben, in Aristotle's *Politics* autarky (*autarkeia*, 2018, p. 1203) was the threshold of articulation between two distinct communities: on the one hand a community of the simply living (plants, animals, slaves, women, infants and the elderly) and on the other the *polis* as the domain of political living (politically active men as citizens). Through this postulation of a limited number of citizens, the threshold between these two separate communities became a biological concept which reflected the Peripatetic philosopher's distinction between *zoe* and *bios*: on the one hand, natural life, or life as such, on the other political life – virtuous life, or a life that is worth living. Taking this idea as his starting point, in his seminal project *Homo Sacer* Agamben introduced the concept of bare life. Bare life is the result of the splitting of natural life from its form, as a result of the exclusion from the polis of vegetative life, as opposed to sensitive and intellective life. This exclusion of bare life is followed by its reacceptance in the principle of power. Bare life is thus the result of an inclusive exclusion which is both the origin and the founding principle of the law (Agamben, 2018, pp. 17–26). It designates the life of *homo sacer*, "sacred man" – life which is excluded from the realm of lawfulness but included as the threshold between natural life and politically qualified life. This inclusive exclusion is a zone of indeterminacy of the law. This indeterminacy puts it at constant risk of being placed outside the law, a condition which can be proclaimed by a sovereign decision, which thus transcends the framework of the law (see Agamben, 2018; Carl Schmitt, [1922] 2005; Walter Benjamin, [1913–1926] (1996). The same conditions that make the nation state possible create a distinction between those whom the state protects – its biopolitical body – and those whom it does not protect. Bare life becomes the life of human beings who are connected with the political sphere of the state, but only as an exception to its laws.

Ancient slavery, which was thus central to the functioning of the polis, was seen as a means of eliminating work from existence – the status of a slave making it possible for others to be human, thus occupying an intermediate zone between nature and culture, *physis* and *nomos*, not belonging exclusively either to the sphere of nature or to that of justice. *Nomos* was the personification of the spirit of the laws, the father of *Dike* (justice). The slave, as the bare life which defines the threshold that both separates and interconnects natural and political life, was the repressed aspect of an anthropology which later developed on the basis of the paradigm of the free man. The re-emergence of the slave in modern labour might be seen as the return of the repressed in pathological form, further reified in terms of production and profit (Agamben, 2018, pp. 1036–1037). In modern times bare life is linked to the nation state, in the form of colonized populations, refugees, unregistered workers, inhabitants of reservations or internment camps, unemployed individuals in suburban ghettoes, tribal areas and occupied territories, people who, often because of the colour of their skin, are seen as "life not worth living".

Aristotle's distinction between *zoe* and *bios* is reflected in his doctrine of potency and act. According to this doctrine, the birth of the verbal is the principle of anthropogenesis: humanity arises out of language. These concepts of an obscure substance presupposed by language – the birth of the verbal as the principle of anthropogenesis – and the primacy of act and operativity in the definition of being are the philosophical basis of the modern concept of primitivity as an original condition of all humanity, and of civilization in its constant process of development and overcoming of the non-human, cultivating the promise and illusion of man's control of nature, of culture as superior to nature. As we shall see, Freud and Jung based their concepts on this progressive idea of humanity, which has remained the basis of subsequent developments in psychology.

The Aristotelian ontological divide is related to the coexistence in language of two polarities. On the one hand, there is a performative polarity: "Be!", the utterance of the divine, which decrees the pre-eminence of language as the agent of being, via an act of commandment and prohibition (*imperium* or sovereignty). On the other hand, there is an explicative or denotative polarity: "This is", the utterance of science. The coexistence of these two polarities, and their periodic alternation and reversal, were the dual force that drove history, in a dialectic between *auctoritas* and *potestas*, temporal and spiritual powers. In modern times, an imbalance in favour of the explicative pole, which has left the performative pole uncontrolled (outside the framework of the law) and unleashed its manifestation on a global scale, has provided the fuel for an incredibly self-fulfilling, violent European impulse not only to conquer and colonize the physical world, but also to cognitively define, categorize and possess all that is living and non-living on earth.

With the advent of capitalism the colonized become in the first place the psychically colonized, invisible other, which are systematically devalued and destroyed for profit. To reduce the other – the "negro", the woman, the different – to animal status is to render them dispensable and deny them any legitimate subjectivity. Particularly significant in this respect are Achille Mbembe's [2000] (2001) comments on Hegel's observations in *The Phenomenology of the Spirit* about the autonomy and non-autonomy of self-consciousness and the relationship between master and slave (IV, A):

[...] the historical free individual – the self-creating subject – is only thinkable if defined in opposition to another, external reality reduced to the condition of object, of thing posited as inessential because "it barely is." The relationship the constituting subject can have with this thing benumbed in natural existence can only be a relation of unilateral sovereignty. The thing to which the subject is opposed can only be an elementary and inarticulate entity [...]

(Mbembe, [2000] 2001, p. 191)

Without recognition, each of the two self-consciousnesses, exposed to one another in immediate face-to-face, naturally enjoys self-certainty, but this self-certainty as yet lacks truth. To be a subject, my singularity must posit itself as totality within the consciousness of the other. I must stake all my "appearing totality," my life, against the others. I must stake it in such a way that, in the end, I can recognize myself in the other's consciousness as that particular totality that is not content to exclude the other but "seeks the death of the other." But, in seeking actively to encompass the death of the other, I am necessarily obliged to risk my own life

(Mbembe, [2000] 2001, p. 192)

According to Hegel, when one consciousness, engaged in such a struggle for life with another consciousness, proves incapable of pursuing it to the end, of rising above the biological instinct for self-preservation, and yields to the other, it submits and recognizes the other without reciprocity: this leads to the primordial act which creates lordship and bondage. The status of master derives from this proof of the superiority of the "victorious consciousness" over biological existence and the natural world in general (*zoe*). A slave's history is something that simply cannot exist, for the defeated consciousness is subsumed by that of the master, and its life and experiences are reduced to an animal process. Not only can no history of the defeated exist, in line with the well-known truism that history is always narrated by the victorious, but the life of the excluded is pushed into the shadows. The result is universal domination by the power of language and civilization over a postulated "underlying obscure substance" projected onto the subaltern, which has become the reified living realm of indifference and animal abjection.

[...] what holds for the animal holds for the colonized, as what holds for the act of colonizing holds for the act of hunting. "When you have caught the rhythm of Africa, you find that it is the same in all her music. What I learned from the game of the country was useful to me in my dealings with the native people" – whom indeed, it is not easy to know – "[I]f you frightened them they could withdraw into a world of their own, in a second, like wild animals which at an abrupt movement from you are gone – simply are not there." Try and force intimacy on the natives, and they will behave "like ants, when you poke a stick into their ant-hill".

(Mbembe, [2000] 2001, p. 193)

Historical and political considerations

In her book *The Origins of Totalitarianism* Hannah Arendt [1951] (1958) significantly titled the last chapter of the section on imperialism "The End of the Nation-State and the Decline of the Rights of Man":

The conception of human rights, based upon the assumed existence of a human being as such, broke down at the very moment when those who professed to believe in it were for the first time confronted with people who had indeed lost all other qualities and specific relationships – except that they were still human. The world found nothing sacred in the abstract nakedness of being human

(Arendt, [1951] 1958, p. 299).

According to Agamben (2018, pp. 117–123), in our time the figure of the refugee, who should have coincided with the ideal of the man of rights, marks a radical crisis of the concept of human rights, and constitutes a limiting concept, advocating the urgent need to formulate new categories of thought, beyond the still unresolved relationships between nation and state, birth and nation, man and citizen.

After Kant, the invention of a universal progressive (post-traditional) historical subject became the source of Liberalism. But this does not mean that so-called liberals aren't still deeply embedded in this ontological split, unable to give up their share of the structural advantages of racial privilege. For centuries non-whites were not only reified, sold and subdued, but ignored, removed from existence, pushed into desolation and the violating grasp of interiorized inferiority (autophobia). Consequently, *extra muros* (beyond the walls of "Europe") the exact opposite of the ideal of secure attachment of developmental psychology was systematically applied.

Furthermore, the liberal conception itself ignores the way its failures create space for the very populisms it demonizes. *Intra muros* the split between nature and culture has produced a further split between civilization and culture. The ethical failure of international organizations in our times is a consequence of an alleged principle of universality of human rights, whose inapplicability is obvious to all; this indicates an implicit inability to resolve the split. The advent of a geographically secluded ethnocentric liberalism was, and in many ways still is, *de facto* linked to the continued, racially selective reification of human beings. To infer a "natural" sympathy for white supremacy in the souls of "raw", "uncultivated", white racial illiterates is a misrepresentation of a deliberate historical process which is deeply seated in the mercantilist Western mentality. The existence of a white supremacist "participation mystique" (a term derived from Lucien Lévy-Bruhl, 1857–1939, and adopted in French by Jung [1921] 1971, par. 781, which indicates "a peculiar kind of psychological connection with objects whereby the subject cannot clearly distinguish him- or herself from the object but is bound to it by a direct relationship amounting to partial identity") appears to be secondary to an artificial collective narrative of human origins, implying a denial of otherness. Its relation to the shadow (in this sense there is an archetypal component: as in every dynamic of projection, what is archetypal here is a psychological dynamic rather than a racial outlook) is akin to the process of war precipitation, the invention of which is collectively constituted well before it reaches the point of being acted out (Fornari, 1974). To suggest that white supremacy is archetypal, or even that the way we conceive of "white" and "black" is archetypal, is related to the problem of essentialism in gender. Claims that "nature made it so" preclude an understanding of our implication in all the processes (historical, social, narrative) that have historically and socially "made it so", as with origin myths that create a narrative which justifies the political status and superiority of the people who claim it.

A dominant factor in the richest Western countries is the Protestant ethic, which is based on the myth of material wealth as the expression of grace and predestination, achieved through work and accumulation, whereas colonized peoples are both outwardly and inwardly overwhelmed by an insatiable desire for glittering merchandise (*techne*) and bourgeois commodities – objects radiating desire, an illusion to which poverty can only too easily succumb, and which is sometimes even more powerful than hunger. The concrete merchant-object has captured non-white desire and turned it into concrete consumption, removing it from the imaginal containers previously provided by traditional cultures. The split is therefore also between the traditional subject (the closed system), conceived of as something dead, dated, outmoded, and the historic subject, imagined as being founded on a new ethnocentric paradigm (the so-called Open Society). The current dialectic has further degenerated into a titanic conflict between, on the one hand, populist authoritarianism, which is typically localist, and on the other hand, financial capitalism, for which connectivity is a founding myth – made real by the immensity of the planet's interdependent infrastructural development (Khanna, 2016). Now, after the Cold War, the face-off between financial capital and populist authoritarianism has just begun; it is a game which has already reduced most middle-class liberals to powerlessness, while the elites are secluded in private enclaves. The myth of the economy has become the only legitimizing transpersonal force that is left. To most people corporate citizenship is the only possible safeguard against poverty, and the only possible access to the consumerist chain of desire, owing to the failure of many states to fulfil the task of social development. Social mobility and freedom of movement are restricted to a few talented individuals who belong to the elites. The idea of the subject as a sovereign individual is at the heart of this modern myth, and is shared by psychoanalysis.

Humanism developed as a model of civilization, conveying a "certain idea of Europe as the universalizing power of self-reflective reason, in a regulatory and a rather self-congratulatory vision, a self-portrait way above any average possibility of human accomplishment" (Braidotti, 2017). An entire generation of scholars has identified this mode of self-representation as Eurocentrism. The unprecedented scale of wars and massacres in both colonial and post-colonial times negated the division between reason, on the one hand, and domination and genocide, on the other. As many scholars have pointed out, among them Edward Said (1993, following Michel Foucault), reason and rationality, on the one hand, and violence and delusion, on the other, are not incompatible and can perfectly coexist well n the deeds and the thoughts of humankind (Braidotti, 2017).

Resisted and attacked by all the "marginalized" groups against which it has discriminated, the dominant evolutionist model of white male subjectivity still embodies a symbol largely indexing access to power. Hence racism, sexism, ableism, xenophobia, homophobia, transphobia, etc., can be seen under the common denominator of a patriarchal bias, in the intersectionality of their resistance to the cognitive and biopolitical aspects of power. Advanced capitalism has fully re-captured this post-humanist shift by going truly global. White masculinity is undergoing a profound crisis as a result of this post-Eurocentric leap taken by cognitive (algorithmic) capitalism and because of its greater intolerance of disposability: white men are now resisting their own objectification. Trump and other populisms may seem to be an expression of this phenomenon. In this connection the opioid epidemic in the post-industrial eastern US states is revealing. Capitalistic predation by Purdue-Pharma, the producer of Oxycontin, owned by the philanthropic Sackler family, is described in a 2017 New Yorker article, "The Family who Built an Empire of Pain" (Radden Keefe, 2017).

Analytical considerations

Psychoanalysis has certainly helped to reveal the aggression inherent in civilization, but in accordance with the spirit of the times it has retained humanism and a colonial attitude in many of its premises. The new position of many scholars of the humanities is not relativism but perspectivism: the view that perception, experience and reason change in accordance with the viewer's perspective and interpretation. The current progressive paradigmatic shift in psychoanalysis is attributed to relational psychology, an embodied, intersubjective, dynamic positioning vis-à-vis the other. However, as Celia Brickman (2017) has shown in her book on race and primitivity in psychoanalysis, Freud's colonial assumptions continue to pervade all contemporary schools of psychoanalytic thought. The use of the concept of primitivity in psychoanalysis, with its elements of Lamarckism (the inheritability of acquired characters), Haeckelism (the recapitulation hypothesis) and evolutionism (Malthus, Spencer, Galton), is the hidden shadow of the claim of the universality of the psyche, which creates a covert racial subtext allowing for a continuous slippage between the (developmental) psychological and (evolutionist) anthropological registers.

Jung further developed the configuration of racial otherness implicated in the psychoanalytic construction of subjectivity. His vision of the collective unconscious takes on strong shades of social Darwinism, even if one does not attempt to see beyond his colonial persona, an effort Farhad Dalal, in his article denouncing Jung's racism in the British Journal of Psychotherapy in the eighties (1988), certainly did not attempt to make. Carrie B. Dohe's (2016) *Jung's Wandering Archetype: Race and Religion in Analytical Psychology* is a wide-ranging and incisive discussion of Jung's racism; this might be a useful reference, especially as she is able to identify a direct link between Jung's borrowing of Norse mythology and its overt (mis)use in white supremacist ideologies.

I don't think Jung can be exonerated on the grounds that he was a man of his time; however, a reappraisal of his patriarchal and colonial shadow is useful and may be productive for the practice of Analytical Psychology today. A constructive way of making such an appraisal would be to explore how his epistemology might change if it were enhanced with the latest neuroscientific and biogenetic discoveries. Neumann's new ethic partly addressed – in an early Jungian framework – the need to recognize and overcome the racial and cultural shadow of Jung's ethnocentric prejudices with respect to the dynamics of the collective unconscious and anti-Semitism. More recent studies have highlighted Jung's tendency to interiorize and "absorb" the other (Saban, 2019), as when he seems to state that a real live woman is purely an "anima", or that the "negro" or Arab are purely primitive beings, turning them into purely imaginal figures. Furthermore, Jungians tend to combine the prospective method, concerning adaptive psychological tasks in an individual person's life, with broader, more general teleological explanations. However, when transposed to the collective level, these teleological explanations tend to reproduce universalizing views which exclude Europe's raced others by retaining an outmoded social-evolutionary framework. This happens even when it is not consciously intended, like a "slip of the tongue", when the argument shifts from the individual to the collective level.

The Jungian school needs to give expression to a balanced and diversified scholarship which is critical of Jung's racial and sexist prejudices, while paying due respect to the value of his tradition of analytical thought. Only if we refuse to be either defensive or condescending can we make a critical judgement of Jung's awareness of the crisis of himself as a representative subject of his times and gain insight for the present day. After all, his complexity and genius have produced the theory of complexes, the framework of a polycentric teleological / prospective analysis (not positing that *Where "Es" was, there "Ich" must become*), active imagination, dream theory, alchemical epistemology and the acknowledgment of countertransference, making him in many respects a precursor and transcending the possible reactive or non-engaging defences concerning these issues.

Societal tensions, mirroring individual complexity, are embedded in the polarization of different conceptualizations of diversity, which always produce aporetic dynamics of exclusion / inclusion, competing in the appropriation of the ontological power of language. Thus, comparative studies on violence, law and language should in my view be taken into consideration in a new intersectional critique of the concept of the collective. If, as Agamben suggests, the past is the only really important factor in the understanding of the present as it flees, then the methodological importance of language and words is central to any attempt at archaeological research. Jung appeared to ignore this, at least in part, when he adapted the past and its images to his own archetypal evolutionary or "scientific" scheme, thus inscribing symbols in a "new" modern – and implicitly political – container (a choice very adaptive to the spirit of his time), often freely passing from the individual to the collective register, with explicit racist implications, as when he postulates identifiable psychologies or evolutionary traits associated with nations, religions or races. The recent transposition of his theory of complexes onto the collective level (Singer & Kimbles, 2004) would benefit from a deeper examination of the relation between the idea of group spirit, that of the group as nation and the central issue of the relationship between language and image. Jungians inherit the unresolved dualism between Jung's romantic / naturalistic / deterministic soul on one side and his positivistic / rationalistic / finalistic soul on the other, and should accept the risk of moving away from Jung as the *arche* – both master and origin – of his own school.

Let us now consider the case of psychoanalysis: a normative and sexist interpretation of the Oedipus complex in Freud and Lacan is an obvious limitation. Furthermore, in object relations, the term "primitive" is associated with the paranoid-schizoid position, whereas in more recent times it has also been associated with non-representational states in the clinical encounter – with a tendency to value, but also pathologize, preverbal or presymbolic instances. These approaches do not fully reveal the influence of the Aristotelian perspective, that of assuming the non-representational (and hence the potential, non-actual) as "archaic" or "primitive". The obscure notion of something that "precedes" the representational and the verbal has retained its influence, accompanied by the implications of darkness and unnameability, even as with the fading of time. These states have been explored, though with an involuntary evolutionary nuance (emphasized by the use of the terms "primitive" or "archaic"), by psychoanalysts such as Thomas H. Ogden (1989) in his concept of the autistic-contiguous position.

Jessica Benjamin's ideas (2018) about the "Moral Third" and the lawfulness of mutuality and recognition, in contrast to the Oedipean law which sacrifices the maternal and the presymbolic, may point in this direction. She posits her idea of the "Moral Third" as an alternative to the Hegelian "only one can live" ontology of self-consciousness, which is very much in accordance with analytical complementarity and a colonial attitude. Jessica Benjamin comes close to an ontological, and not merely psychological, paradigmatic shift based on the singularity of experience in the analytical encounter:

> In impasses and enactments, finding a way to negotiate surrender without submission to the other's demand to replace your reality with theirs

can be quite elusive for the analyst. It was actually towards this end – finding a position of surrender in relation to impasses and complementary oppositions involving submission and dissociation that I initially reflected upon Lacan's idea of the Third. The Third was conceived as that which differentiates us from the imaginary relationship of kill or be killed, presented by Hegel as a struggle in which the weaker party substitutes slavery for death, while the victor gains freedom and dominion. More recently, I suggested the formulation of this complementary opposition, in which each person struggles for recognition by imposing or defending their own version of reality without recognizing the other, as corresponding to the fantasy of "Only one can live". Part of the project of recognition theory is to articulate both the dynamic forces behind this breakdown as well as those that create the material, psychological conditions for the third position in which this complementarity can be overcome.

(Benjamin, 2018, p. 94)

As I near the conclusion of this chapter, I would like to add that it is crucial to deactivate the paradigms of sovereignty embedded in our language – prejudices whose polarities tend to maintain the political tension in a conservative fashion, however hard one tries to avoid this. The idea of "taking action" is also easily caught up in the same paradigms (the ubiquitous silencing presence of patriarchy, and nowadays the principle of sovereignty embedded in the economic network). The voice of the unheard may be respected (Latin *respicere*, to reflect, recognize) through the active creation of the space of mutuality, which necessarily becomes political when it deals with collective instances, as in the case of communities exposed to Continuous Traumatic Stress (CTS): ongoing traumatic experiences in contexts of structural violence, including repressive state violence or pervasive community violence (Straker & The Sanctuaries Counselling Team, 1987). Mental health professionals who operate in the threatened social fabric of post-colonial, occupied or marginalized societies (e.g. Palestine) clearly state that the current individual paradigm in psychotherapy is insufficient as a way of dealing with collective trauma. A different approach is needed, addressing the impact of ongoing traumas and overcoming the individualistic bias regarding collective identity traumas, i.e. resulting from intergroup conflict and / or structural, institutional and ecological violence (Kira et al., 2013).

As Agamben has shown (2018, pp. 1278–1279), exposing the complexity of the ubiquitous nature of power could be an important step, only *if it actively contains the space where answers are not needed but presence is.* Not inhabiting a space of impotence but contemplating one's power of activity – undoing the ontological device of sovereignty, as a means of freeing new potential within the active space of one's life. This function is not transcendent, but immanent and is related to the impersonal circulating character of affect; compare Spinoza, *Ethics* III 53:

> When, therefore, the mind is able to contemplate itself, (...) the pleasure (*laetitia,* joy) will be greater in proportion to the distinctness, wherewith it is able to conceive itself and its own power of activity.
>
> (Spinoza, [1677] 1955); (note: always as limited by a greater power of activity)

It may be in this context that a new critical and truly post-Jungian approach could add value to political activism, especially dealing with the question of affect as a trans-individual dimension of the political, developing beyond and among subjectivities. I believe Jung's polycentrism could find analogies with philosophical and political research about Spinoza's *conatus* and its relation to imagination as an impersonal conductor of affect. If affect is more than the subject and interiority is both its source and effect, then affect overflows the scene of the subject and expands the scene of agency (Williams, 2010). This Spinozian view is based on a semiotic coincidence of the natural with the cultural (*natura naturans*), traversing the subject as a field of possibilities (Williams, 2010): circulating trans-individual natural forces and symbols, imaginatively mediated by affect, determine the interaction between bodies, a conceptualization which may have much in common with archetypal psychology, without however bearing the essentializing risks connected to the latter.

Conclusions

Human rights have become *just one axiom among others.* Advanced capitalism has made a further step: it has become post-European, computational and biogenetic, without relinquishing its anthropocentric deeds, that is without adopting an embodied distributive ethos, with a propensity to a self-congratulatory search for the trans-human, through the combination of mega-data and biogenetics, aiming at potentiating the brain's computational capacity in order to bridge the gap between the human mind and computers, the expression of a somewhat fragmented *anthropos.* A metaphysical belief in the techno-sciences, and in the possibility of a technofix, is more or less unconsciously maintained, notwithstanding the destruction of the planet, while necropolitics (the ultimate expression of sovereignty, based on the ability to inflict and apportion death as the ultimate expression of the power of coercion) continues to play an essential role in the shifting algorithmic world order, especially in the face of geopolitical issues and processes of de- or re-territorialization.

The only knowledge considered valuable by today's technocrats is algorithmic; the rest is reduced to mere intellectualization, which includes cultural studies and psychoanalysis. The consumeristic realm of absolute desire has been normalized, with an active unlearning, or perhaps simply ignorance, of the historic deposits of desire's symbolism, conveyed by traditions, initiations, narratives and experiences.

There is a growing desire among the Western middle classes today for psychological disciplines to re-appropriate circular time, the animal time of the body, in order to compensate for the unidirectional, hyper-aroused, performance-oriented operativity of our time: mindfulness as meditation, Zen, massage, Yoga, Shiatsu, hypnosis, Chinese medicine, acupuncture (though often restricted to its analgesic dimension), more or less syncretistic liturgies, singing, pet therapy, music therapy, dance therapy, etc. These methods are learned from ancient traditional knowledge and stimulate the vagal-parasympathetic system by the mere fact of being communal, relational and non-competitive. Meanwhile, nihilism, the death wish of capitalism, is realized through the immensity of current destruction as a result of demography, supply chains, relational impoverishment, moral indifference and a lack of respect for other beings and the environment. This respect should extend beyond the human sphere to include the diversity of the animal and plant worlds. A renewed sense of intimacy with the animal world – but also with plants, forests, mountains, rivers and seas (the "ecosystem", the earth as a sentient being) – provides a sense of limit and of renewed presence to oneself, thus preventing or containing human one-sidedness, beyond the limits of anthropocentrism.

Reclaiming the respect of bare life on a psychological level is a demanding process, requiring us to develop, or regain, a capacity to acknowledge death, to feel the closeness of, and therefore bring into existence, the time and the space of grief and mourning for the discarded. A first, fundamental step is overcoming, at an individual level, the ubiquitous temptations of defensive dissociation; comprehending, and not only in an intellectual sense, that the life of the discarded *can* be dignified, and the lives of victims given value, by acknowledging the wrong that has been done (Benjamin, 2018, p. 227) and admitting that their lives *are worth mourning*, as Judith Butler put it (2004). It requires the creation of an inner space of recognition and an outer space of narration, which alone can lead to vital non-violent political action. However, only political agency can address the issue of collective identity trauma and structural violence and thus appears to be indispensable if we are to contrast and / or prevent further shaming. The idea of opening up a different space, of immanence and contact, unburdened by the Western stratifications of thought concerning the concept of relation, could be a step towards really acknowledging and dignifying the lives of the drowned (Levi, [1986] 2017), beyond the obligations of "the clinic".

In conclusion, the current paradigmatic shift in psychoanalysis needs to abandon its intrinsic universalizing tendencies and dissolve its Eurocentric glass of isolation, embracing its political potential, engaging its responsibilities and constantly and actively recognizing the preeminence of the unknowable.

Note

1   I would like to acknowledge three persons for their support and assistance in this work: Celia Brickman, with whom I had a significant and rich exchange on relevant matters, Francesco Baucia, who helped me with the philosophical part and advised on the structure of the text, and Jonathan Hunt, who reviewed the English style of most of the text. All of them helped me clarify several passages of a difficult text.

References

Agamben, G. [1995–2015] (2018) Italian edition (the latest and final version of the Homo Sacer project): *Homo Sacer, Edizione Integrale 1995–2015*, Macerata: Quodlibet. English version, 2017: *The Omnibus Homo Sacer*, translated by various translators, Redwood City, CA: Stanford University Press.

Analysis & Activism 3rd Conference, IAAP Symposium (2017) *More Social and Political Contributions of Jungian psychology*, Prague.

Arendt, H. [1951] (1958) *The Origins of Totalitarianism*, Meridian Books, Cleveland, OH and New York: The World Publishing Company.

Benjamin, J. (2018) *Beyond Doer and Done to: Recognition Theory, Intersubjectivity and the Third*, London and New York: Routledge.

Benjamin, W. [1913–1926] (1996) *Critique of Violence, Selected Writings*, Cambridge, MA: Harvard University Press.

Braidotti, R. (2017) *Posthuman, All Too Human*, Durham Castle Lecture, Durham University, 25 January, Durham, UK. Available at: https://www.youtube.com/watch?v=JZ7GnwelrM0 (accessed November 2019).

Brickman, C. (2017) *Race in Psychoanalysis: Aboriginal Populations in the Mind*, New York: Routledge. First Edition: Brickman, C. (2003) *Aboriginal Populations in the Mind: Race and Primitivity in Psychoanalysis*, London and New York: Columbia University Press.

Butler, J. (2004) *Precarious Life, The Powers of Mourning and Violence*, London and New York: Verso Books.

Dalal, F. (1988) Jung: A Racist, *British Journal of Psychotherapy*, 4 (3): 263–279.

De Gobineau, J.A. Arthur, [1855] (1915) *The Inequality of the Human Races*, London: William Heinemann.

Dohe, C.B. (2016) *Jung's Wandering Archetype: Race and Religion in Analytical Psychology*, London and New York: Routledge.

Fornari, F. (1974) *The Psychoanalysis of War*, Norwell, MA: Anchor Press.

Jung, C.G. [1921] (1971) *Psychologische Typen. Psychological Types*, Bollingen Series XX, Vol. 6 of the Collected Works of C.G. Jung, A revision by Richard Francis Carrington Hull of the translation by Helton Godwin Baynes, Princeton, NJ: Princeton University Press.

Khanna, P. (2016) *Connectography, Mapping the Future of Global Civilization*, New York: Random House.

Kira, I.A., Ashby, J.S., Lewandowski, L., Alawneh, A.N., Mohanesh, J., & Odenat, L. (2013) Advances in Continuous Traumatic Stress Theory: Traumatogenic Dynamics and Consequences of Intergroup Conflict: The Palestinian Adolescents Case, *Psychology*, 4 (4): 396–409.

Levi, P. [1986] (2017). trans. Raymond Rosenthal, 1988, *The Drowned and the Saved*, New York: Simon & Schuster.

Marsan, J., & Schemann, L. (1909) Correspondance entre Alexis de Tocqueville et Arthur de Gobineau (1843–1859), In: Revue d'histoire moderne et contemporaine, tome 13 N°3,1909.

Mbembe, A. [2000] (2001) *On the Postcolony, Studies on the History of Society and Culture*, Berkeley, CA, Los Angeles, CA and London: University of California Press.

Mbembe, A. [2013] (2017) *Critique of Black Reason*, translated by Laurent Dubois, Durham, NC: Duke University Press.

Ogden, T.H. (1989) On the Concept of an Autistic Contiguous Position, *International Journal of Psycho-Analysis*, 70: 127–140.

Radden Keefe, P. (2017) *The Family That Built An Empire of Pain. The Sackler dynasty's ruthless marketing of painkillers has generated billions of dollars—and millions of addicts*. Available at: https://www.newyorker.com/magazine/2017/10/30/the-family-that-built-an-empire-of-pain (accessed, November 2019).

Saban, M. (2019) *"Two Souls Alas": Jung's Two Personalities and the Making of Analytical Psychology*, The Zurich Lecture Series, Volume 2, Asheville, NC: Chiron Publications.

Said, E. (1993) *Culture and Imperialism*, New York: Vintage Books (Random House).

Schmitt, C. [1922] (2005) *Political Theology, Four Chapters on the Concept of Sovereignty*, George Schwab (trans.), Chicago, IL: University of Chicago Press.

Singer, T., & Kimbles, S. (2004) *The Cultural Complex, Contemporary Jungian Perspectives on Psyche and Society*, London and New York: Routledge.

(De) Spinoza, B. [1677] (1955) *On the Improvement of the Understanding. The Ethics. Correspondance*, Unabridged Elwes Translation, Minneola, NY: Dover Publications.

Straker, G., & The Sanctuaries Counselling Team (1987) The Continuous Traumatic Stress Syndrome: The Single Therapeutic Interview, *Psychology in Society*, 8: 46–79.

Williams, C. (2010) Affective Processes without a Subject: Rethinking the Relation between Subjectivity and Affect with Spinoza, *Subjectivity: Politics and the Unconscious*, 3, doi:10.1057/sub.2010.15.

Ecological and other crises

Chapter 4

When fathers are made absent by tortures, wars, and migrations

Clinical and symbolical perspectives

Tristan Troudart

The making of an absent father

The subject of the Absent Father is presented to us in as an increasingly frequent phenomenon in the western world. Often the attention is confined to family dynamics and to the influence of the absence of the father in the development of the son or the daughter. Some authors have written about the industrial revolution as the turning point in distancing the fathers from their children and the weakening of their role as mentors. Before that, fathers were working together with their children in agrarian, artisanal and mercantile professions, teaching them their trade and educating them in their values (Bly, 2004). The father in the film Padre Padrone of the Taviani brothers is a Terrible Father, but he is not an absent father and he is very present in transferring to his son his knowledge in sheep herding. Special attention has been given to the influence of the missing father on his son's development of masculinity (Corneau, 1991).

In a sense, speaking individually and not collectively about the absence of the father is a privilege of rich Western countries, and within them it is related to the father's place in class society. In underdeveloped, poor societies absent fathers are the norm, as a result of poverty and social inequality. As an adolescent growing up in a middle-class environment in Chile I knew that in the South of Chile there were regions where many working-class men emigrated to work in the coal mines of the Argentinian Patagonia, some of them leaving their families behind, and "naturally" became absent fathers. At the same time, many poor women from the South emigrated to Santiago, the capital, to work as house maids, whom I met when they worked in my home, and told me that they had left their children with their grandmothers,

becoming absent mothers for their children, while they took care of middle-
and upper-class children.

Therefore, there are societies where for men, being "absent fathers by
choice", for example, choosing to separate from their wives and their children, is a luxury that few can afford. At the same time, many men become
fathers that are made absent by external circumstances, like torture, wars
and migrations, when they emigrate "to make a living", an expression that
has both a symbolic and a very concrete meaning to it.

A dangerous hero's journey

As an example of my volunteer work, I will present the case of Jeff (the name
and some details have been changed). He is 27 years old, born in an African
country. He has been living in Jerusalem for six years. He was referred to
me four years ago for psychiatric treatment. His father has been in the Army
for ten years, coming home once a year. When he was 18, Jeff had to be recruited to the Army, so he escaped to a neighbouring country, where he was
detained for months and was severely beaten by policemen. Then he was
sent back to his country where he was recruited to the army and endured
prolonged torture in an Army jail. He was closed in a dark underground cell
together with more than 100 prisoners in very hot weather, without windows
and sleeping on the floor without beds and with very scarce food.

At the beginning they were severely beaten. Later the punishment eased,
and he received a basic training and became a soldier, still in a regime of
severe discipline. During his Army service, he married. After two years in
the Army he was successful in escaping to Sinai, where he was tortured and
mugged by bandits, but at the end he was successful in crossing the border
to Israel. The crossing of the Sinai desert then became the only solution and
the expression of an archetypal hero-journey for all the Asylum seekers.

In Israel he was jailed for 30 days in the Saharonim prison, in the Negev
desert. There he suffered from a reactivation of post-traumatic stress syndrome, with worsening of his sleeping disturbance, nightmares, flashbacks,
lack of appetite and lack of interest in other people. He says that in Israel he
was not tortured, and that the food was enough. At the end he got a visa that
officially forbid him to work, but he was told by the immigration authorities
that he could work while the visa is in order.

He moved to one of the big cities in Israel, where he now works in occasional jobs, most of the time cooking and helping in restaurants kitchens. Two
years ago, his wife migrated to another country. She left behind their child,
an eight-year-old girl whom Jeff has never met, and who lives with her grand-
mother – Jeff's mother – who is aged and has difficulties raising the child alone.

Since he defected from the Army, Jeff has been suffering from a
post-traumatic stress disorder (PTSD) with symptoms related to the torture
episodes. On examination his personal hygiene was good. He was sensitive,

shy and polite. At the beginning he told me that he suffered from frequent intrusive memories, difficulties in getting sleep, terrifying nightmares that woke him up every night, flashbacks in which he sees the face of the men that beat him, permanent anxiety, tension, irritability, depressive mood and emotional instability, outbursts of crying, sensitivity to noise that causes avoidance from going to crowded places and social meetings, headache, disturbances in functioning, despair and death thoughts.

Jeff gets support from the JACC, the Jerusalem African Community Center, an NGO that assists African asylum seekers, a community which lacks legal status, and which assists them in fulfilling legal, medical and occupational rights. It offers them psychological and humanitarian aid and social and cultural activities. The asylum seekers can get individual therapy, and at the Centre there is group therapy for women who suffer from psychic trauma. I volunteer with them to give psychiatric assessment and treatment.

A social worker manages his case, and a student of social work meets him for supportive therapy sessions and psychosocial interventions. Apart from his PTSD symptoms, he suffers from anxiety as a result of the constant harassment from the Ministry of Interior. He had to present himself for an interview to renew his visa every two months, and for a long time he was under threat of deportation to Holot, a detention centre in the Negev desert. In times of hardenings in the policy of the government he was under treat of being deported from the country. Moreover, his refugee status recognition was not advanced, like most cases of asylum seekers.

These procedures are part of the pressure that Israeli government applies with the purpose of expelling the asylum seekers, who are called "infiltrators" – a negative labelling that was given to them by the government.

Jeff was referred to me by the J.A.C.C. for psychiatric treatment, He gets an antidepressant and antianxiety drug and a medication for sleep problems.

Every two months I wrote for him a document certifying that the frequent interviews cause a re-activation of his post-traumatic symptoms, and deportation to Holot detention centre or, much worse, his expulsion from Israel could cause a severe worsening of his mental health and could increase the danger of suicide.

Gradually, there has been a mild improvement in his condition, and his functioning at work is better, although he still needs some medication. Yet, there was something missing – the contact with his daughter. This lack of contact was the inspiration for this chapter, stimulated by my own father complex, centred on an absent father.

In fact, for the first time, I saw Jeff as an absent father. Gradually, with the support of his therapist and a positive father transference to me, he became more interested in his daughter and started to mention her in our sessions, and later to hold telephone conversations with her. This contact has been very emotionally rewarding for him.

Our psyche is a part of the world

Jeff personifies the tragedy of the asylum seekers in Israel.

They come mostly from Eritrea and Sudan, where many of them escaped from situations of wars, political persecutions, torture and forced military conscription. Nowadays around 30,000 asylum seekers live in Israel. Thousands of them were detained in camps in the Sinai desert run by criminal bands that murdered, tortured and raped the migrants. This migration, and the concentration camps that exploited the massive movement of people, stopped when Israel completed the construction of a fence in 2013. Holot detention centre was closed in March 2018, as a result of demonstrations of asylum seekers, advocacy by Israeli human rights NGOs and petitions to the High Court of justice.

In Israel, most of the asylum seekers live in the South of Tel Aviv, a poor and neglected area of the big city. There they are supported by human rights organizations and sympathetic residents, while they are rejected by hostile residents of the area, with the support and the incitement of extreme right racist groups and prominent members of the government majority party that relate to them as scapegoats and call them "a cancer". It is not surprising that the Israeli governmental system, that has such a low consideration for the human rights of the Palestinians, could behave in a better way towards other people seeking refuge. There have been passionate demonstrations both in favour and against the asylum seekers living in the neighbourhood. Those that defend them remind the public of the plight of the Jews seeking refuge from persecutions during the Second World War.

Jeff is an absent father, both physically and emotionally. He is also the son of an absent father, a second generation of absence and non-functioning as a father. He suffered from oppressiveness that constellates the Archetype of the Terrible Father. In Jeff's case, the roughness of the negative pole of the archetype is not softened enough by the feminine, by his wife who is an absent mother, and his mother, who can hardly cope with the child. However, his daughter as an anima figure is intensifying her presence in his internal world. The weakness of the masculine is also evident, with father and grandfather being absent. As shown in research on attachment, contrary to psychoanalytic ideas, the quality of a father's relationship with his child depends on the direct relationship with the father and not from the mediation by the mother, who is not available in this case (Samuels, 1993). In collective terms, the society replaces the individual father, partly with authoritarian values that undermine those of the good-enough father with positive patriarchal values.

The secondary effects can be the weakening of the mother and the feminine that if they were stronger could insufflate the men's souls with the transformative power of the anima. But then, when we discuss the possibilities of Jeff's internal transformation, what can be done if his physical and psychological absence is compulsory and inevitable? And finally, how is an absent father born?

In the case of Jeff, we cannot separate his absence as a father and his post-traumatic symptoms from the dramatic social circumstances that are common to thousands of men who went through the same journey of crossing the desert. Many men like Jeff suffered from a destruction and fragmentation of their family network, being separated from their wives, children, parents and other family members. Hillman admitted that psychological distress cannot be cordoned off from the distresses of the world of which one is a part. Liberation psychologists have said that it is impossible to separate individual symptoms from the cultural pathology (Watkins & Shulman, 2008) In this case this formulation includes not only the reaction to oppression, but also the influence of the rejection by a rigid state bureaucracy.

As the clinical improvement in this case shows, the feelings of alienation and the symptoms of post-traumatic stress can be attenuated by curative relational factors like the maternal support and holding of the community centre, the psychosocial therapeutic intervention and the positive father transference that he has with me. The relationship he is developing with his daughter can be a new factor that could transform him into a more present father and constellate in him new anima energies.

References

Bly, R. (2004) *Iron John, a book about men*. Cambridge: Da Capo Press.
Corneau, G. (1991) *Absent fathers, lost sons*. Boston and London: Shambhala. C. G. Jung Foundation Books Series.
Samuels, A. (1993) *The political psyche*. London and New York: Routledge.
Watkins, M., & Shulman, H. (2008) *Towards psychologies of liberation*. New York: Palgrave Mac Millan.

Chapter 5

The Garden of Heart & Soul
Working with orphans in China –
symbolic and clinical reflections

Gao Lan and Heyong Shen

There are about 1 million orphans in the mainland of China, around 15% of whom live in the orphanages. Some of the orphans are born with severe diseases such as CP (cerebral palsy), DS (Down's syndrome), and CHD (congenital heart disease), and physical disabilities. They, our orphans, really need psychological help and support.

We set up the first workstation of The Garden of Heart & Soul at an orphanage in China ten years ago in 2007, using Jungian Psychology and Sandplay to help the psychological development of orphans. After the psychological relief work for the 2008 Wenchuan Earthquake, and the 2010 Yushu Earthquake (Tibet zone), our workstations, which people named the "Garden of the Heart & Soul," moved forward, spreading to 76 in number over the mainland of China. There are over 1,000 volunteers who joined us in the project.

The basic idea for this work has been to build the psychological container, The Garden of Heart & Soul, an inner home for the orphans. We later realized, that The Garden of Heart & Soul, the inner home, is not just for the orphans and trauma victims, but for ourselves too, for our own Heart and Soul. Being so close to the orphans and feeling their suffering and their needs, we started to understand the meaning of the word "orphan" in Chinese, and the meaning of its archetypal image.

The suffering, the knowledge

As volunteers of The Garden of Heart & Soul, we were involved in the psychological relief work in the area of the Three Rivers after the earthquake in 2008, where we encountered three cultural archetypes (Dayu, Shennong, Fuxi – which we will describe further on.). One year later, we went to the far-off, high-altitude area of Yushu (in Tibet) which was hit by a powerful earthquake in 2010, where we encountered the original headstreams of the three rivers, and the archetypal mountains in the local culture. This experience added to our understanding of suffering which we gained through our work in orphanages, with our orphans, in The Garden of Heart & Soul.

We take our work as "self-redemption." Going through the suffering, we are close to our psyche and nature, just as in the saying from antiquity: The Suffering, The Knowledge! This knowledge, originally from the oracle of Delphi, is also the Self-knowledge according to C.G. Jung and Analytical Psychology.

The tremendous 2018 "512 earthquake" in Wenchuan, South-West of China was a disaster. Over 100,000 people died or are missing, 360,000 were severely wounded, and 45,00,0000 were affected by the earthquake. Our volunteers from The Garden of Heart & Soul went to the earthquake zone in the first week following the earthquake and have continued their work there until today.

We have set up seven workstations at the earthquake zone, especially for the Qiang people, a special minority, whose history goes back to the origin of Chinese civilization, Shennong, under the Yan Emperor.

Luigi Zoja and Eva Pattis, with their son and daughters, came to the China earthquake zone to join our work. Betty Jackson, Thomas Kirsch and Jean Kirsch, Murray Stein, John Beebe, International Association for Analytical Psychology (IAAP), and Internationals Society for Sandplay Therapy (ISST), also gave us a lot of support.

Yushu was an old land of Qiang people, and it is now an area of Tibet, located on the Qing-Zhang plateau, with an average altitude of 4,500 meters above sea level. Yushu is the headwater for the three main rivers in China: the Yellow River, Yangtze River, and Lanchang River. After the powerful earthquake hit Yushu in 2010, we went to the earthquake zone, set up three Gardens of Heart & Soul, and have continued our work there until today.

In the midst of his great treatise "Science and Civilization in China," Joseph Needham tells the following 5th Century CE anecdote taken from "A New Account of Tails of the World": Mr. Yin, from Jinzhou, is reported to have asked a Chan Monk (Huiyuan), "What is really the fundamental idea of the I Ching?," to which the monk is said to have replied: "The fundamental idea of the I Ching can be expressed in one single word, Resonance (Gan)," Then, Mr. Yin from Jinzhou asked again: "The Tong (copper) Mountain shaking in the West, and the Ling (spiritual) bell resonating in East, is that called I (I Ching)?" The Monk kept silence. He didn't answer (Yiqing, 2007, p. 420).

The Wenchuan Earthquake was just like the Tong-Mountain shaking in the West. Similarly, the work of our Chinese Jungian society is like the Ling Bell resonating. It echoes the meaning of Hexagram 31 of the I Ching, "Heartfelt-response," with the symbolic meaning of Hexagram 61, the "Inner Truth" which states: "A crane calling in the shade. Its young answers it" (Wilhelm, 1950, p. 237). R. Wilhelm further wrote: "this is the affection of the inmost heart" (ibid, p. 237). This is precisely what the psychology of the Heart and The Garden of Heart & Soul are about and what the aim is of this work.

During our earthquake relief work in Wenchuan and Yushu, we encountered three archetypal images and had the opportunity for great learning. First from Dayu (2200 BC deity famous for ability to control floods and for naming mountains and rivers), where we explored and gained an insight into the cultural archetypal image and meaning of naming and initiating. "Naming" in Chinese has two characters, Ming (as fate, order from Heaven, to make) and Ming (as name, self-destiny, self-enlightenment). The "initiating" here carries the meaning of awakening and initiating the Heart-nature inside all things. Second, from Shennong (4300 BC deity who initiated farming, agriculture, and Chinese medicine), where we explored and gained insight into the cultural archetypal images and meaning for taming, nurturing and healing. Dayu's father's side originates from the Yellow Emperor and mother's side stems from Yan-di Shennong. Dayu is the union and bond between these two Chinese ancestors. Chinese people refer to themselves as descendants of Yan and the Yellow Emperor. Yan-di is also called Jiang (the image of the character for this contains both "female" and "sheep"). Third, from Fuxi (4700 BC, who founded the eight hexagrams and the I Ching). Here we explored and gained an insight into the cultural archetypal image and meaning for timing and transformation. According to the Chinese legend, Fuxi drew the first Yang line in order to start the Chinese civilization with the eight hexagrams, to communicate with the virtue of heaven and to express the feelings of all things. The I Ching was called The Book of Changes, which conveys the wisdom of timing and change and the meaning of transformation. In the Chinese cultural tradition, the sages used the I Ching to cleanse the heart.

The way of the work, and reflection

Here we will use some clinical material to present the work in The Garden of Heart & Soul. About seven years ago, in a town in China, a (psychotic) man killed his wife and their three children, and committed suicide by jumping from a building.

His eldest daughter was then about ten years old. She received first aid, and survived and was sent to the orphanage where we have The Garden of Heart & Soul workstation. We will call her Xiao-Xiao (Daybreak). When the work started, Xiao-Xiao had many nightmares, she was easily frightened, often crying out "don't kill me," and crying for her mother. For several months Xiao-Xiao needed a lot of medication to calm her down and help her sleep. The policewoman, who rescued her and took her to hospital, became her first therapist (this policewoman is a qualified clinical psychologist and one of our volunteers at The Garden of Heart & Soul). We supervised her work.

Sandplay was the main modality for the work with Xiao-Xiao. Through the earlier sandtrays, Xiao-Xiao expressed her suffering, and her dreadful experiences. She didn't use any miniatures but just played with the sand. She touched the sand very slowly, like a wounded cat walking around carefully.

Figure 5.1 The fifth Sandtray by Xiao-Xiao.

Then after several sessions, even though she still only played with sand, Xiao-Xiao started to try to make something. She poured some water on the sand and began to create some forms.

At the fifth Sandtray (see Figure 5.1), Xiao-Xiao created a strange face, "a horrified face", she said. Within the free and protected space, as the relationship was being built between Xiao-Xiao and her therapist, she could begin to face some difficult feelings.

Six months later, in the 12th sandtray, it seemed that Xiao-Xiao tried to deal with what happened to her family, the tragedy. She put a male figure, dressed in dark clothes at the right side of the sandtray, and said that this man killed three people (she then buried three figurines in the center of the sandtray). At the same time, Xiao-Xiao placed a boat in the left lower corner and a mermaid in the right lower corner. The therapist paid special attention to the three parts: the tragic killing, the boat (for rescue), and mermaid (which could be the growing inner resource of Xiao-Xiao).

Throughout about one year of this work, Xiao-Xiao slowly changed. One of the main things she did in the Sandplay was that she tried very hard to protect and take care of two children figures (who could be her dead sister and brother). She tried to rescue the children using some medical tools in the Sandplay. In the process, many animals appeared in her sandtrays, and Xiao-Xiao was cooking and feeding the animals. That could be related to the symbolic meaning of preparing her inner energy.

Xiao-Xiao liked the Sandplay work in The Garden of Heart & Soul. She and her therapist were able to build a very good relationship. At the 38th sandtray (see Figure 5.2), Xiao-Xiao spent 30 minutes carefully making a "mother" with a "child" in her sandtray.

Figure 5.2 The 38th Sandtray of Xiao-Xiao.

Xiao-Xiao drew in the sand the face of the mother with long braids. She used some water and worked very carefully. Then, she chose some jade and colored stones, to decorate the mother's portrait, even adding earrings. For that moment, the mother emerged and was alive. Then, Xiao-Xiao placed a doll on mother's chest. She was immersed in this Sandplay. The therapist was deeply touched.

After that, Xiao-Xiao continued to play with the two children figures, trying to take care of them, to put them to "bed," to feed them and look after them (see Figure 5.3). In the process, more animals, especially aquatic creatures emerged. Xiao-Xiao played with the mermaid in some sandtrays, and the mermaid was growing. She even made a world for the home of the mermaid.

Figure 5.3 The last Sandtray of Xiao-xiao.

The last Sandtray of Xiao-Xiao

This was the last sandtray of Xiao-Xiao. By then she was about 15 years old and was ready for boarding school. A new life was beginning for her.

Principles for our relief work within The Garden of Heart & Soul

Based on Analytical Psychology and Chinese Culture, we made the following principles for our relief work within The Garden of Heart & Soul:

First, we build an effective therapeutic relationship: a contained, free, and protected space to re-establish and increase our clients' and trauma victims' sense of reality and safety. Some expressive and embodied methods, such as music, dance, and rituals, together with some breathing and bodywork, are used to produce embodied resonance and foster the contained relationship.

Second, based on the established relationship, we work to enhance the therapeutic containment by "attending and accompanying," and actively listening with the heart (the Chinese character for "listening," combined with ear, growing, ten eyes, and the heart). We start with Sandplay or other related expressive methods, such as music and drawing, embodied dreamwork and archetypal psychodrama, to work with the clients individually and in groups.

Third, we offer sustained psychological support using the principles of the Psychology of the Heart. We apply the principles of "loving-grief" (Ci-bei, the image of the characters conveys the way to work with trauma and healing) and Gan-ying' (whole-hearted influence); and the healing and transformative function of the cultural archetypes (Dayu for Naming and Initiating; Shennong for Taming and Nurturing; and Fuxi for Timing and Transforming).

The image and the meaning, the psychology of the heart

People refer to our work at The Garden of Heart & Soul as "Healing by 'Ci-bei' "(loving-grief-compassion therapy)." The Chinese images for "Ci-Bei" reflect action from heart to heart (see Figure 5.4). The first character Ci means love, associated with the heart and the second character, Bei, is grief and means loss of the heart. When we hold and contain love and grief together, within The Garden of Heart & Soul, then we have the chance to experience the transcendent function and compassion.

Compassion, Ci-Bei in Chinese, also means great love. The archetypal image of love in the oracle bone script form is expressed in the character in Figure 5.4.

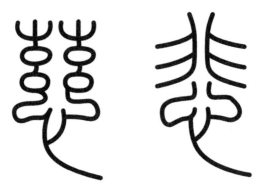

Figure 5.4 The Chinese images for 'Ci-Bei'.

Figure 5.5 The archetypal image of love in oracle bone script form.

The upper part of the character is the symbol of trust and sincerity. This symbol is precisely the image in the I Ching for hexagram 61, "The Inner Truth". The second figure in the middle is a symbol of protection, giving the image of the womb – the mother's or the Great Mother's womb. The third lower part is "hand in hand" and it means support and harmony. At its center or core is the image of the heart.

The principle of Inner Truth with heartfelt influence for transformation has formed our basic attitude and guiding principle as the way to do the work of The Garden of Heart & Soul. This means offering "psychological aid," not only "intervention" by following the image in order to reach the deeper meaning. Being guided by the image and working to extract the meaning, our work is that of "healing," not only "therapy."

Figure 5.6 Chinese character of Zhi.

Both therapy (Zhi-liao) and healing (Zhi-yu) share the first character Zhi in Chinese (see Figure 5.6):

Originally with the image and meaning of "dealing with water" (preventing flood by water control). The left part of the character is the image of water, and the right part is an image of a high plateau on earth.

This fits in with the five elements theory, according to which the earth could conquer water. In the Chinese language system, medical and psychological therapy (cure and treatment), the words to manage and the word for management, scholarship and study, and politics, all take the image and meaning of water and control and all are related to how to deal with "water."

The image of the Chinese character for "healing," in its oracle bone script form, is represented in Figure 5.7.

The upper part of the character references the image and meaning of how to make a boat or a canoe. In making a boat or a canoe, the most important thing is that it is empty and steady or in equilibrium. This equilibrium rests at the philosophical as well as physical level and also at the psychological (or psychotherapeutic) level. The lower part of the character of healing is the image of the heart. This Chinese image for healing, "the boat on the heart," offers a beautiful gift to our imagination.

With the image of the Chinese character for healing, the meaning of water in therapy acquires a new dimension, bringing in a new relationship between boat and water in comparison to the image of earth being used as a defense against water: if there is not enough water, the boat cannot move; if the water is not deep enough, a big boat cannot travel. There is something inspiring in this Chinese image for our Jungian analysis and depth

Figure 5.7 Chinese character of healing.

psychotherapy. In the Chinese image and meaning for healing, defending against water brings about a new situation, the one that is not only about defense, but also about "riding" and "sailing" across.

As the old Chinese proverb says: "Boat supporting/benefiting the world." For therapy, or therapy with healing, as Jungian analysts and depth psychotherapists, we should remember this image and this meaning: to find, or to build the "boat of the heart" with our patients. Or, as the old Chinese saying goes, (in being a therapist) The Heaven/God is using you as a boat, as an oar and a row.

C.G. Jung, in *AION: Researches into the Phenomenology of the Self,* used the image of water with Tao: "For this reason the ancients often compared the symbol to water, a case in point being Tao, where yang and yin are united. Tao is the 'valley spirit,' the winding course of a river" (Jung, 1950, *CW.* 9-ii.§281). Jung wrote that: "The undiscovered vein within us is a living part of the psyche; classical Chinese philosophy names this interior way 'Tao,' and likens it to a flow of water that moves irresistibly towards its goal. To rest in Tao means fulfillment, wholeness, one's destination reached, one's mission done; the beginning, end, and perfect realization of the meaning of existence innate in all things. Personality is Tao" (Jung, 1939, *CW.* 17.§23). Dora Kalff's last words in her ground-breaking book on the Sandplay Therapy, after she described the image of water with the 29 hexagram of I Ching were: "Remember this in Sandplay. And remember that when we do succeed with the work of bringing about the inner harmony that defines a personality, we speak of grace" (Kalff, 2003, p. 140).

Based on the Psychology of the Heart, we take together the image of "healing" in Chinese (boat on the Heart) combined with "therapy," for our

Jungian Analysis and Sandplay practice, and for the work in The Garden of Heart & Soul.

References

Jung, C.G. (1939). *Development of Personality*. CW. 17.

Jung, C.G. (1950). *AION: Researches into the Phenomenology of the Self*. CW. 9–ii.

Kalff, D. (2003). *Sandplay: A Psychotherapeutic Approach to the Psyche*. Conclusion Hot Springs:. Temenos Press.

Yiqing, L. (2007). "Kingdom of Song" in '*A New Account of Tales of the World*'. Beijing: Zhonghua Book Company.

Wilhelm, R. (Translator). (1950). *I Ching, The Book of Changes*. Princeton, NJ: Princeton University Press.

Chapter 6

Think big

Jung's new age paradigm shift will have an ecological framework

Dennis Merritt

The fundamental problem with our species is that we do not see ourselves as being part of nature; part of the complex web of life in an integral relationship with the inorganic world. As James Hillman pointed out years ago, the pathologies of the environment are beginning to make people aware of our disconnection from nature, pathologies like the adverse and cascading effects of climate change, the growing immunity of pathogens to antibiotics, and the genocide of other species on the planet (Hillman 1992, pp. 89–130). We have the exciting challenge of needing to think big and boldly to address the truly apocalyptic dimensions of environmental disasters. Jungian psychology offers an excellent framework for doing that, for in 1940 Jung coined the terms "new age" and "age of Aquarius" as labels for the paradigm shift he saw coming in the West (Jung 1973, p. 285). I will develop the thesis that this new Age of Aquarius will have an ecological construct.

As Jungians we are adept at looking at issues from a symbolic and archetypal perspective, by definition the broadest and deepest perspective. We can see how a theme runs like a fractal from the intra-psychic through the political, cultural, and spiritual and into our dysfunctional relationship with nature. For Jungians ecology begins with the quality of our relationship with what Jung called "the little people" within, and what Richard Schwartz of Internal Family Systems called our "inner tribe" (Jung 1969, par. 209; Schwartz 1997). Hillman's ideal of psychic functioning is more like a beehive or an ant's nest (I love that as a Ph.D. entomologist!) rather than a psyche the ego attempts to dominate (Hillman 1988, p. 59). Thanks to the application of complexity theory to seminal Jungian concepts, the beehive analogy makes perfect sense to me as a scientist. We now have the mathematics for how the Self brings all elements of the psyche into relationship with each other—and potentially to the environment (Hogenson 2004, 2005). The archetype of the Self is interchangeable with the scientific concept of an organism where the mathematics of the self-organizing properties of an organism run like a fractal from atoms to the human psyche to the creation of galaxies (Ho 1998). In my writings I have made a case for Hermes as the god of complexity theory, thereby allowing us to provide a mythic and imaginal framework to the abstract world of complexity theory mathematics (Merritt 2012b). The Jungian contribution to the environmental movement and to academia will be considerably enhanced with this understanding of archetypes, including the Self as an organism.

Jung's concept of the layers of the collective unconscious is helpful in demystifying the idea of a collective unconscious and rendering it more easily to the application of complexity theory to major Jungian concepts. Imagine a mountain of many layers, representing the levels of the collective unconscious, rising up from the ocean floor with the peak of the mountain being above water representing ego consciousness. Jung thought of the family experience as being in the conscious domain as well. All levels of the collective unconscious are to be considered to be in immediate and continual interaction with each other. What Jung called a Central Fire permeates the ego and all levels (Hannah 1991, pp. 16–18). The Fire is the type and movement of energy in the universe and the dynamisms of the organism as prescribed by complexity theory.

The concept of layers of the collective unconscious is also a marvelous tool for analyzing our dysfunctional relationship with each other and with the environment. This begins at the intra-psychic level with the dream **ego's** relationship with the little people within, then attachment issues with mother and the quality of Winnicott's maturational environment coloring one's experience of the *family*. At the *national* level of the collective unconscious an American is formed by the mythic images of the rugged, independent cowboy who conquers the Wild West. At the *Western cultural* layer we have the myths of endless progress and an ever expanding GDP. Ecotheologan Thomas Berry attributed the origin of this belief in progress to the Book of Revelation in the Bible where 1,000 years of abundance and human perfection was supposed to precede the end of the created world (Ryley 1998, pp. 207–208). In the 17th century Descartes and Newton helped establish a worldview that prized thinking and rationality over all else and de-sanctified the world into spiritless matter whose movements were described by mathematical equations. One of the greatest challenges Jung gave us as modern men and women was to unite our cultured side with the *primeval ancestors* in the collective unconscious, what I like to call "the indigenous one within" at the tribal level of human relationships. Life at this level is centered around small, democratic groups with an emphasis on relationships and a sacred sense in nature. Indigenous peoples are also close to the *animal ancestor* foundation of the psyche, the bottom layer of the mountain, appearing in such forms as spirit animals, plants, weather phenomena, and landscapes. I maintain that the deepest disturbance in our collective unconscious is at the animal soul level because one species, namely, us, will be responsible for eliminating 30–50% of the approximately 10 million species on the planet. And we are decimating the basic requirements for our life as an animal: food, water, shelter, and a relatively stable climate.

Jung hammered us about the necessity of increasing consciousness. We think of this as greater psychological consciousness, but I say it is now equally important that we be aware of the uniqueness of our species in being able to generate what many are calling our current era—the Anthropocene, or era dominated by humans. Every member of every species is mainly concerned with its survival as an individual and to varying degrees the survival of other members of that species. Our species has used human intelligence to delineate the laws of the universe and bend them to the benefit of our species alone. The greater consciousness Jung called for must inevitably include a sensitive awareness of the complex inter-relatedness of everything. My thesis is that the environmental pathologies have the potential to force an ecological intelligence upon us that, if properly developed, could extend to all levels of human experience and culture, countering our egotistical and narcissistic nature. The ecological framework for the new age begins at this point.

Archetypal, mythic dimensions of our environmental problems include the attributes of the god of science and technology, Apollo, diligently being applied to satisfy the desires of the Great Mother archetype in her nourishing and protective form. She wants her children to have an abundance of food, clothing, shelter, water, and protection from diseases. The god Saturn works to satisfy her by giving us the systems and laws that have evolved to maximize the application of science and technology worldwide.

Jung cautioned us about big things, what he called the modern-day dragons and monsters in the form of big machines, big militaries, and big governments. His particular example was especially chilling. "Imagine how all the little merchants felt," he said, "crushed by the Standard Oil Trust" (Jung 1984, pp. 538, 539). We now have this problem on steroids with the corporate model gone global. It has the rights of a person and with the US Supreme Courts *Citizen's United* decision corporations can now expand their ability to have the best government money can buy. Corporations have one goal: to maximize profits for their shareholders usually assessed on a quarterly time frame. People are not part of the equation and the environment is what economists call an "external"—a resource base and a waste dump. Our planet and people's lives are now under control of the ultimate dragon, the ultimate narcissist: the abstraction and virtual reality called the corporation. Unless we change the corporate model, all else we do for people and the environment will be the proverbial rearranging of the chairs on the deck of the Titanic. This will be a huge challenge in the paradigm shift, and not by any means an easy one to accomplish.

Let's remember that these are systems created by humans and can be changed by humans. I would like to focus on two powerful replacements for our current systems: a Jungian ecopsychological framework for our educational system and a green, sustainable economic system.

I found that the integration of Jungian psychology, science, and Native American spirituality that I began to develop in 1991 with week-long Spirit in the Land gatherings fits nicely into the new field of ecopsychology. Ecopsychology began to emerge in the mid-90s. It is the study of how our attitudes, values, perceptions, and behaviors affect the environment. Its more radical dimension has as its goal a total revamping of our political, cultural, educational, economic, and spiritual systems in order to live sustainably. In my book *Hermes, Ecopsychology, and Complexity Theory*, which is volume 3 of *The Dairy Farmer's Guide to the Universe—Jung, Hermes, and Ecopsychology*, I develop the Greek myth of Hermes stealing Apollo's cattle as the mythic foundation for Jungian ecopsychology (Merritt 2012b). Hermes realm is the relational space between organisms and systems, the liminal realm of transitions and exchanges. As god of advertising, psychology, business, diplomacy, shamans, Jung, and Winnicott, I see Hermes as the god of ecopsychology.

In my book *Jung and Ecopsychology*, volume 1 of *The Dairy Farmer's Guide*, I provide a sketch of how Jungian ecopsychology could frame our educational system. We would do well to focus our attention on the younger generation because they are more attuned to the disastrous consequences of the snowballing effects of the environmental damage that our and previous generations have created. Depth psychological concepts of the shadow, anima and animus, and the stages of life would help cultivate the intra-psychic dimension. Instruction about archetypes and the evolution of the Western symbol systems as related to Christianity would be important elements in the new educational system. Age appropriate dreams, fairy tales, myths, and movies could be used to engage and educate students, especially the Hermes/Apollo myth. Stories can be integrated with scientific facts and complexity theory using Hermes as the god of complexity theory, for example (Merritt 2012a, pp. 117–124).

> I like the bold ideas of the green or sustainable economists that include wealth redistribution on a planetary level, limiting population numbers, decreasing working hours by almost half, and spreading the work hours around the planet. This allows time for workers to spend valuable hours with family, friends, hobbies, and community building activities.
>
> (Dietz and O'Neill 2013)

The archetypal framework for my entire presentation is expressed in hexagram 42 in the *I Ching*: Increase. The Chinese see this developing out a change in hexagram 12: Standstill/Stagnation, where the upper three yang (solid) lines associated with the archetypal masculine, spirit, and heaven naturally tend to move up and therefore out of relationship with the lower three yin (broken) lines associated with the archetypal feminine, earth, and the receptive, which naturally move downward. "The creative powers are not in relation" the *I Ching* says, "It is a time of standstill and decline" (Wilhelm 1967, p. 52). We can think of this as the ego in relation to the unconscious and the little people within, the have vs. the have-nots with the growing income inequality, patriarchal and colonial mentalities, and humans in relation to the environment (Figure 6.1).

Hexagram 42: Increase, develops when the lowest line of the top three yang lines of Hexagram 12 "sinks down and takes its place under the lower trigram [lower three lines]." Wilhelm's translation says of this movement:

This conception also expressed the fundamental idea on which the Book of Changes is based. To rule truly is to serve.

A sacrifice of the higher element that produces an increase of the lower is called an out-and-out increase: it indicates the spirit that alone has power to help the world (Wilhelm 1967, p. 162) (Figure 6.2).

Jung was very pessimistic about the future of humankind. "We are beset by an all-too-human fear that consciousness—our Promethean conquest—may in the end not be able to serve us as well as nature," he said (Jung 1969, par. 750). Several mythic systems foretell a dismal end for humankind, including the Book of Revelation. Jung thought his psychology was 500 years ahead of its time but I say its time is now. As a PhD biologist and environmentalist I see nothing better for bringing about a desperately needed paradigm shift than Jungian ecopsychology. We are at a Turning Point as described in hexagram 24 of the *I Ching* where like-minded people get together to bring about change, which is what this conference is about.

Figure 6.1 Hexagram 12: standstill.

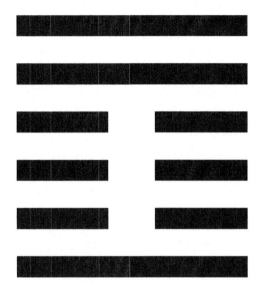

Figure 6.2 Hexagram 42: increase.

References

Dietz, R. and O'Neill, D. 2013. *Enough is Enough—Building a Sustainable Economy in a World of Finite Resources.* San Francisco, CA: Berrett-Koehler.

Hannah, B. 1991. *Jung: His Life and Work.* Boston, MA: Shambala.

Hillman, J. 1988. "Going Bugs." *Spring*, pp. 48–72.

Hillman, J. 1992. *The Thought of the Heart and the Soul of the World.* Woodstock, CT: Spring Publications.

Ho, M. W. 1998. Organism and Psyche in a Participatory Universe. In *The Evolutionary Outrider: The Impact of the Human Agent on Evolution. Essays in Honour of Ervin Laszlo.* D. Loye, ed. Westport, CT: Praeger, pp. 49–65.

Hogenson, G. 2004. What are Symbols Made of?: Situated Action, Mythological Bootstrapping and the Emergence of the Self. *Journal of Analytical Psychology* 49: 67–81.

Hogenson, G. 2005. The Self, the Symbolic and Synchronicity: Virtual Realities and the Emergence of the Psyche. *Journal of Analytical Psychology* 50: 271–285.

Jung, C. 1969. *The Structure and Dynamics of the Psyche.* Vol. 8 of *The Collected Works of C. G. Jung.* 2nd ed. H. Read, M. Fordham, G. Adler and W. McGuire, eds. R. F. C. Hull, trans. Princeton, NJ: Princeton University Press.

Jung, C. 1973. *Letters. Vol. 1. 1906–1950.* G. Adler and A. Jaffe, eds. R. F. C. Hull, trans. Princeton, NJ: Princeton University Press.

Jung, C. 1984. *Dream Analysis: Notes of the Seminar Given 1928–1930.* C. G. Jung and W. McGuire, eds. Princeton, NJ: Princeton University Press.

Merritt, D. 2011. *The Dairy Farmer's Guide to the Universe: Jung, Hermes, and Ecopsychology.* Carmel, CA: Fisher King Press.

Merritt, D. 2012a. The Diary Farmer's Guide to the Universe: Volume 2. *Jung and Ecopsychology.* Carmel, CA: Fisher King Press.

Merritt, D. 2012b. The Diary Farmer's Guide to the Universe: Volume 3. *Hermes, Ecopsychology, and Complexity Theory.* Carmel, CA: Fisher King Press.

Ryley, N. 1998. *The Forsaken Garden: Four Conversations of the Deep Meaning of Environmental Illness.* Wheaton, IL: Quest Books.

Schwartz, R. 1997. *Internal Family Systems.* New York, NY: Guilford Press.

Wilhelm, R. 1967. *The I Ching or Book of Changes.* Cary Baynes, trans. Princeton, NY: Princeton University Press.

Migration, refugees, walls, bridges

Chapter 7

The salience of borders in the experience of refugees

Monica Luci

In this chapter, I would like to demonstrate that borders have a special significance in the experience of refugees, which is, in a broad sense, characterized by their violation, at different levels, psychological, social, and political. In particular, I would like to explore the meaning, the function, and the effects of such violations, and their implications, keeping in mind the narratives of refugees who arrived from Africa and the Middle East to Europe through the Mediterranean Sea, and my clinical experience as a Jungian analyst with them. Although I do not intend to approach clinical material here, this text is informed with ideas and narratives and information collected during sessions with refugee patients.

The violation of bodies and minds

In the work with refugees, the first aspect we are faced with is the sometimes shocking impact of various forms of collective violence on their individual, interpersonal, and social life (Alberto & Chilton, 2019; Napolitano et al., 2018). The reasons to leave their country are often some form of social, political, and familial violence. Sometimes people are persecuted for their political or religious convictions or for ethnicity or family circumstances. At times, refugees are targeted because of their gender or sexual orientation. Occasionally, the violence is private, but even in such cases, it often reverberates widespread social, political, or more systemic violence.

Although the circumstances that lead to displacement vary, all of them end with an expulsion of the person from their living environment. The previous ties with family, work or school, relationships, social milieu, the natural and built environment are severed. In this banishment, there is a dimension of violence, defined or ambiguous. The etymology of violation and violence refers to *vis* = force. A force is imprinted on people's lives. This *prime mover* applies to people producing the movement that leads them to displacement, that is, to cross national borders, fleeing to migrate, seeking *asylum* or another type of *international protection* and a new place in which to live.

The relationship between state violence and the body

The relation between the state and the body is complex and ambiguous. It consists of control, protection, discipline, persecution, compassion, repression, and regulation (Cameron et al., 2013; Foucault, 1975, 1976).

According to some philosophers and sociologists, the state has a foundational relation with violence. For example, Weber (1918 [1946]) maintains that in the ideal-typical social contract that links individuals, the state is supposed to protect society from violence through law and law enforcement, and in exchange, is granted a monopoly on legitimate violence. When this contract is not respected, either because security is denied or because abuse is gross, individuals may feel entitled to resist the state or even revolt against it. Such is often the case of people that at certain point are led to seek for asylum.

Asylum seekers often bear the marks of state power and violence imprinted on their bodies. Generally, they must prove their eligibility for human and social rights and the body is often the place that displays the evidence of truth in the face of asylum determining authorities (Fassin & d'Halluin, 2005, pp. 597–598) in the asylum country.

Thus, the body is the place of an inscription of the relationship between a group and an individual. From a developmental perspective, the body is always the place of an intersubjective meeting. Since birth, it is the crossroads of relationships; the territory of the other (recognized or rejected, imposed, idealized, or denied); and the platform of our identity (cohesive or perforated). Even the most benevolent meeting of the beginnings is a meeting with another, 'M-other' and 'Fa(o)ther', someone with whom to negotiate a differentiation that helps us draw our own boundaries and make coexisting feelings of dependence, interdependence, independence, and separation. 'Facing the reality of the body thus involves a paradox: it means simultaneously taking ownership of the body, its desires and limitations, and integrating the fact that the body is the site where we meet the other, where we negotiate the meaning of sameness and difference' (Lemma, 2010, p. 175). For this reason, the body is the place where we start drawing our own self-defining borders with respect to the other, the place of identity, of how we define ourselves.

In the beginning, the infant body is an object-subject – more an object than a subject because it is exposed to the other's will and projections – with the potential to be transformed into a subject-object – a subject with residual characteristics of an object – through the development of a mind that is to some extent integrated with its body, thanks to more or less thoughtful interaction with caregivers. However, this process is never completed, and the body continues to work as an object to the subject itself and others: a disputed territory between conscious and unconscious, and between me and others in relationships.

It is now a stable acquisition of psychoanalytic thought that the mind needs other minds to process the parts of itself that are not integrated since its origin and those parts that possibly dissociate later in life. In other words, the psyche is not integrated at its origin and inherently dissociable, as Jung correctly comprehended (1920, 1928, 1948). However, such unintegrated and dissociated parts of the psyche cannot stand being left apart and spontaneously look for containers, as M. Klein (1946) and Bion (1962, 1967) and other authors emphasized, in order to work through undigested and non-transformed emotional contents. At the beginning, the body is the place of encounter and confrontation with an other, and through these initial interactions, if the caregiver's handling and holding (Winnicott, 1960) is appropriate, and the infant feels contained and thought about through maternal rêverie (Bion, 1963), its mind acquires the ability of thinking and creatively playing with reality and meanings. When unbearable affects cannot be digested by the caregiver's mind, they remain unintegrated and inscribed in the body as alien parts.

As infants, as much as adults, we need *containers* in which to deposit what our mind cannot integrate. These deposits are also functional to a possible working through of their contents, by means of others who, hopefully, can do something to facilitate our integration of those contents. These fundamental dynamics continue to function in adult life within the more complex and manifold matrix of social relationships. If dissociated parts of a psyche find similar dissociated parts in other people's psyches, they can become the basis for social bonds, and they can start looking for containers, often finding them in the body of socially weaker subjects. This is particularly akin for the emotions triggered by trauma that seek the other's body, the body of a potential victim, to find containment, the ultimate repository of their emotional deposits. This search is what creates torture victims (Luci, 2017a, pp. 156–157) and victims of other kinds of social violence (Hollander, 2010).

Somatic and psychic envelopes and trauma

The 'somatic envelope' of the self, the skin, emerges almost always as violated by situations at the limit of survival: laceration scars, burn scars, dermatological diseases, and infections resulting from the violence endured before fleeing, from poor hygienic conditions or accidents or intentional violence during travel and detention in overcrowded places, and more.

After arriving at Italian shores, a refugee patient of mine used to dream he was skinless. Heartbreakingly, he recounted a dream in which his skin had been removed by a group of people who skinned him alive, and for this reason, he could neither touch nor be touched. I would like to give theoretical substance to the idea that transformations of self, psychic and somatic, go through the skin because the skin is the root of self. The skin and the self have a mutual relationship, and this intuition can be retraced in many theories of psychic development (Anzieu, 1989; Bick, 1987; Freud, 1923; Meltzer, 1975; Ogden, 1989; Tustin, 1991, 1992).

Sigmund Freud (1923) sees the skin as a fundamental enabler of the mind's processes and a crucial constituent of the early ego. He remarks: 'The ego is first and foremost a bodily ego; it is not merely a surface entity but is itself the projection of a surface' (1923, p. 26). And in a footnote, he adds: 'The ego is ultimately derived from bodily sensations, chiefly from those springing from the surface of the body. It may thus be regarded as a mental projection of the surface of the body' (1923, p. 26). Similarly, Donald Winnicott (1960, 1975) understands the skin as an indispensable means to the infant's mind/body integration. Wilfred Bion, in his works on the 'container' and the 'contained' (1962, 1967), views the skin as the sensory-perceptual foundation of the infant's capacity for thought and thinking.

However, it was Bick's ground-breaking work on early infancy (1987) that demonstrated the importance of the surface of the body as a substratum for the genesis and structure of the self. Observing infants' behaviour and interactions, Bick came to the conclusion that they fluctuate between two primary states of mind: a state of coherence which is associated with feelings of aliveness and existence, when the caregiver is meaningfully present, and the infant will experience itself as integrated and bound and held together; and a state of in-coherence which is associated with feelings of anxiety and annihilation, when the caregiver is absent, and the infant's mind will likely be experienced as unintegrated, unbounded, and falling to pieces. Because mind and body are not felt to be in any way separate in these early months, the experience of a contained body can and will serve as the foundation for the experience of a contained mind.

If this cannot happen, then the infant fears that its self will dissolve and, ultimately, leak into a limitless space living in extreme anxiety, which results in a range of disturbed personality structures that have in common the lack of or a perforated mental skin, one experienced as precarious and full of holes.

Bick's work was further developed by her successor, the French psychoanalyst Didier Anzieu, (1989) who built a model for what he called the *skin-ego* that emphasizes the surface of the body and its role in the creation, elaboration, and organization of the mind. The skin-ego is defined by the different senses of the body. The skin, as Anzieu pointed out, is a wrapper, a container of the child's body, but it is also a border, a security barrier between the inside and the outside; it is a place of contact and exchange with the outside world.

In his unique theoretical elaboration, Ogden reworks several of Melanie Klein's key concepts, giving a new account of the development and the working of the self. Understanding the immense importance of the skin, Ogden extends Klein's developmental model by adding to her paranoid-schizoid and depressive positions a third one called the 'autistic-contiguous' position. By juxtaposing these two terms, Ogden intends to convey the fact that the infant's 'autistic' experience of the world – an exclusively sensorial experience of its surroundings, and no awareness of the distinction between its self and the world around it – is informed by a range of 'contiguous' sensory events – events that, over time, transform the infant from an insular being to an increasingly relational one.

The autistic-contiguous position is associated with a mode of generating an experience that is of a sensation-dominated sort, characterized by proto-symbolic impressions of sensory experience that together help constitute an experience of bounded surfaces (Ogden, 1989). In this position, the infant's relationship to its significant others is neither object-oriented (as it is in the paranoid-schizoid position) nor subject-oriented (as it is in the depressive position). Instead, the infant's relationship to its significant others in the autistic-contiguous position is 'sense-oriented' (1989, p. 32). Over time, the sensory impressions that are understood by the infant to begin and end at the body's surface give rise to the experience of a boundary between inside and outside, self and other. Indeed, even sensory impressions that are not straightforwardly tactile like, say, sights, sounds, and smells, tend to create for the infant a sense of boundary. In Ogden's understanding, this provides the infant with an incipient sense of groundedness, that is, with a sensory 'foundation' from which they can generate rudimentary forms of experience that will ultimately serve as the 'floor' of the infant's personality.

In adulthood, the self continues to use this mode of organizing the experience as a background of other psychic functions that are more in the foreground of mind.

The transgression of national borders

Migration routes, objectification, and confinement in closed spaces

In Africa and the Middle East and in other regions of the world, asylum seekers pass through national borders in various ways, by various means of transport, often walking, and/or putting themselves in the hands of traffickers, 'smugglers', and 'passeurs'. Initially, traffickers are often compatriots, who can communicate in local languages and recruit migrants who want to leave. At intermediate stages, they facilitate the next steps to other countries on the migration route. Sometimes, the contacts are established before the moment of departure; in other cases, they are made during the journey. The migrants must pay for many services: the transport, the advance payment that the trafficker lends them to rent a bed, the food, the bribe to the police at the various checkpoints, etc. This often results in building up a debt towards the trafficker whose sum is not ever known. When it is not possible to continue the journey because of financial shortage, people will have to work. These moments are dramatic for exposure to a high level of violence by the employers, police, and, in unstable political contexts by different kinds of groups: a real business that exploits foreign labour or profits through extortion and kidnapping.

In recent years, more and more migrants have been imprisoned in detention centres in Libya. Libya did not sign the 1951 *Convention Related to the Status of Refugees* and does not recognize the existence of refugees. Here migrants undergo torture and truly inhuman and degrading treatment. Some detention centres are state-owned; others are run by rebels or traffickers. Here people are forced to live in overcrowded, dirty cells, without light, in unhygienic conditions, without proper food and subjected to daily beatings, torture and constant humiliation in order to extract money from their families. When this is not obtained, they are sold as slaves and employed in forced labour.

A question that arises is about the psychological meaning of this confinement and disproportionate violence perpetrated on migrants enclosed in these prisons where violence, murders, and extortions are on the daily agenda. If, as an adult, someone wants to 'skin us alive', the experience forces us to relate to a persecutory object that will result in our not being able to get rid of the grip of this persecutory bad object, and leaves us with the need to match with an ideal good object that will guarantee us the loving gaze of the other to shield ourselves. This splitting is the typical dynamic left as in-heritage of relational trauma in 'victims'. Or when the relationship is filled with interpersonal hostility and the body is the receptacle of the 'bad', 'appalling' and unacceptable parts of the other – a possible way to survive is 'to skin the other alive', that is to supplant it, 'becoming' Other. These are the kinds of dynamics we tend to find in 'perpetrators'.

In a country in the grip of chaos, divided into two and more pieces, as a matter of fact with no state, in which the ferocious violence of armed gangs and corruption are spread everywhere, there is no shortage of unbearable and unthinkable bundles of anxiety. In this context, migrants lend themselves to be used as 'objects', as concrete containers in which to put and store the most disturbing and immediately, bodily felt clots of anguish (the Other). Unbearable dread is felt as 'other within' (Kristeva, 1982), which urges to be extruded in order to restore a sense of self. For this purpose, a minority group or a group with a minority status is exploited as the Other, someone in whom to evacuate formless dread via repetition of the initial trauma and intrusion into bodily boundaries, to give pre-symbolic form to the dread that is evacuated there. This guarantees some safety from unbearable otherness. These dynamics are what creates the *abject*. Julia Kristeva (1982) develops a notion of abjection that contains both corporal and pre-objectal aspects and provides an understanding of the dynamics of social oppression. She

conceptualizes abjection as an operation of the psyche through which subjective and group identity are constituted by excluding anything that threats
one's own (or one's group's) borders. In *Powers of Horror* (1982) the abject
refers to the human reaction to a threatened breakdown in meaning caused
by the loss of the distinction between subject and object or between self
and Other. The fear is caused by the breakdown of any distinction between
ourselves and the world of dead material objects (1982, p. 207). In Libya this
degradation of migrants to objects is done at the hands of criminal groups
with the complicity of the civilian population.

For Anzieu, 'There is no group without a common skin, a containing envelope, which make it possible for its members to experience the existence
of a group self' (1990, p. 97). The group is seen metaphorically as a 'body'
with an *esprit de corps*, providing a skin for individual members (1984). Anzieu proposes that the achievement of belonging in a group happens when it
overcomes its anxieties about fragmentation, often by exporting those anxieties in the direction of others. This is what gives a group its sense of being a
body that is not dismembered. The primal phantasy of a group as a mother's
body, previously elaborated by Bion in his Kleinian review of *Experiences in
Groups* (1961), is re-elaborated by Anzieu. On the one hand, there is nurture
and a physical experience of bonding and safety; on the other hand, a terror
of rejection and disapproval with frightening inner consequences of loss or
fragmentation of what holds firm internally and in the group (Anzieu, 1984,
pp. 118–119). The population in Libya is clearly in the grip of fragmentation
and anxiety of final disintegration as a large group. Lack of political consen-
sus among the various political actors, and their inability to resolve regional
differences through peaceful national dialogue resulted in two parallel civil
wars raging in the east and west of Libya and recently burst out in the most
ferocious way. The Civil War has been fuelled by detrimental foreign intervention, while the local actors have been justifying their conflicts under
banners of fighting 'terrorism' or standing up to a 'counterrevolutionary
forces' (Martinez, 2014). In this framework, migrants, once made Other and
objectified at the hands of their exploiters, are the perfect containers for all
the abject that circulate in the country.

After detention in Libya, for those migrants who survive, there is the
Mediterranean Sea. Libya nowadays has many actors involved in trafficking human beings. This has led to a sharp drop in prices and quality of the
means of transport to cross the Mediterranean Sea. Often, in order to be
able to pay for travel or simply because they are forced to do it, migrants
lead the boats without any experience, increasing the risk of drifting or
wrecking, also due to the high number of people present and the conflicts
between different players in sea. More and more often, now that atrocities
have intensified in Libya and European countries are in the grip of their internal anti-immigrant nationalisms, it happens that these boats are detected
by the Libyan coast guard who takes them back to its shores where the hell

starts again, for some people several times. At other times, these boats are intercepted by ships that come to rescue, before or after a shipwreck. Rescue or recapture depend on many variables, mainly the fate and the politics on immigration of European nations bordering the Mediterranean Sea.

The Mediterranean is a concave space, a space that allows reciprocal mirroring between cultures and countries, not shaped for rejection. In addition, the sea confronts us with our vulnerability and obliges to solidarity as the Law of Sea provides. However, from time to time, countries on the Mediterranean Sea close their ports, and stiffen their borders through national politics or outsource them: for example, in Greece with the 2016 EU-Turkey agreements aiming at discouraging refugees to enter EU; in Italy with the 2017 Italian-Libyan Memorandum of understanding to combat illegal immigration and human trafficking; with United Kingdom leaving the EU; Hungary raising its barbed wire and carrying its anti-immigration reasons at the European Court of Justice (with Slovakia); with Spain, the only European country with a border in Africa, that surrounds its border by triple 10-metre fences and moats, protected by frontier guards. At the same time, the debate within Europe is always on the table, and many projects for vulnerable asylum seekers continue to be financed. Discourse about human rights, rescue operations, their failures and scandals, sea tragedies, reception policies, and political debates about migrants appear in the newspaper headlines, TV talk shows, social networks, national political meetings, etc. And the populist and extreme right parties raise their barricades and evoke their ghosts in many countries. The transgression of national and European borders is a concern for public opinion and politicians.

Threatened identities in the Mediterranean: lessons by refugees

Once a week, I facilitate an empowerment group for refugees who survived torture. During one of these sessions, a spontaneous discussion developed. The members coming from African countries, the majority in this group, commented how African group identities have been profoundly altered by the arbitrary divisions of borders of the colonial period and how their own education, now purely Western, ignore local traditions. To these participants, it was very clear that by dividing people and imposing its education, Europe is still controlling the social and political life of African countries and can still exercise its influence and concern for its economic interests in the area. A cogent political analysis that implied that personal and collective identities are intrinsically connected to a group's living space, and that dividing that space and the ethnic groups living in it, implies controlling that space and those groups.

People create an identity by positioning themselves relative to other people and by giving to these relations a meaning that tends to be stable in time. For Leon and Rebecca Grinberg, identity is 'born of the continuous interaction among spatial, temporal and social integration links' (Grinberg & Grinberg,

1989, p. 132), where spatial links confer a sense of cohesion to the self, temporal links establish continuity of a sense of self over time; and social or relational links between self and other establish a sense of belonging via processes of projection and introjection. An identity guarantees the being, a person or a group, in the flux of time by linking past social relations with those in the present and in the future. All these 'constructions' allow interrupting the permanent change of social relations thus creating a shared sense of sameness (an identity) in which persons, groups or societies can see their own image reflected, despite possible internal multiplicity. If others coercively introduce new social relations that disruptively change this sense of continuity of a group, its members' identity and sense of belonging will be affected, as will the group's ability to function as a whole, producing culture, rules, and organization.

The implication of group participants was that aggressive European politics had moved their boundaries, initiating violent processes in many countries. Kast (2002) writes that the first important function of aggression is that of moving boundaries. The line that we draw with respect to our neighbour is precisely the space we claim. Europe claimed a big space in the XIX and XX centuries in other continents, especially in Africa and Middle East. If the other completely (and traumatically) invades my space or if I pervade the other's space, the tension between me and the other is completely cleared, and then aggressor and victim are bound in an enduring bond. We were or still are their aggressors (and saviours) transgressing their group borders. Conversely, at individual level, for asylum seekers, the State from which they flee is to some extent an aggressor who transgresses their personal boundaries (inflicting wounds to their bodies and minds) and our State a potential saviour (when it recognizes the right to asylum). We have a bond to them which is not accidental, but historical. In this sense, what we have done politically and economically to them is coming back.

The Western concept of 'national community' was imposed on African ethnic groups, and new countries were created with territorial borders that were not perceived as such by many of the old identities that continued to persist, often across the borders. However, specific social groups (or tribes, as invented by the West) who obtained power in the new states used such a power in order to gain access to resources that traditionally belonged to other groups. In this perspective, the migrants' transgression of national borders, arriving in Europe and claiming asylum, appears as the return of a European ghost. The etymology of the term 'asylum' (a-sylon) refers to a space that is 'not violable', a space protected by boundaries, which is evocative of a previous transgression.

Madsen & van Naerssen (2003) notice that identities are not static but continuously (de- and re-) constructed; this implies a continuous process of bordering and 'othering' of us/them (van Houtum & van Naerssen, 2002). On both sides of a border, countries have identities that correspond to 'imagined communities' and nations or states are a significant cornerstone of these identities, that are made through different instruments, among which are rituals, symbols, the construction of a heroic past. This is not only the result of top-down processes generated from formal institutions of the state, but a construction by people who are not merely passive receptors, but who play active roles in bordering and constructing identities. Social networks of parents and friends and colleagues with diverse structures and varying degrees of hierarchy and equality participate actively in this process and are important agencies for identity construction: families, local communities, religious institutions, etc. National identity is always significant, but its importance varies at different stages of a country's history, and territory may have different roles in it. During the colonial period, when nationalism was at its high point in Western Europe, national and territorial identities were of greater importance in the daily life of people than they are in today's era (Madsen & van Naerssen, 2003).

Today, the EU is a supranational entity with a common past and a weak present based primarily on institutions and economics, with loose social bonds among its members. Its identity is multicentre, not based on territory but on functional and partially overlapping 'areas' and a few founding values (Luci, 2018). However, proponents of the EU have not succeeded in creating a strong sense of pan-European identity that supersedes the identities of its member states. Those national identities are tenacious and vary tremendously, ranging from relatively open ones that could accommodate diverse populations to others that create deliberate barriers to the assimilation of immigrants. The European identity needs something that goes beyond the sense of shared interests and abstract reciprocal solidarity (Fukuyama, 2018, p. 153). Collective identities are linked primarily to individuals in concrete interaction situations, emotional ties such as the sense of pride and shame become an important mechanism for reproducing such identities. Social psychology holds that the more loose and indirect social relations are, the more important become *social carriers* – objects that store the emotional and narrative meaning of collective identities (Eder, 2009, p. 5). In this sense, asylum seekers may have become our [European] *social carriers,* storage points of generalized emotions, positive and negative that are moving the boundary of our national identities (both through threat and empathy) enabling us to recombine them on the basis of a self-image as humans with respect for human rights, and also able to defend self-interest and possibly reject external threats, or contain disruptive internal pressures. If this is true, it also means that migrants, both those admitted into our protection and those painfully remaining outside it in a space of violability, are substantially contributing to building the European Union.

Conclusion

Borders have a special significance in the experience of refugees at different levels: individual (physical and intrapsychic), social, and political. The salience of borders emerges from this analysis of the self and its intimate connection with the environment that sustains it and aims to inform it. The violation of bodies and minds and the rupture of the links with the living environment characterize the experience of asylum seekers and expose their bodies and minds to severe exploitations in exchange for a salvation hope. The search for migration routes by individuals breaches national borders through illegal crossings and implies for them new adversities, challenges, and social risks. For asylum seekers, their seeking protection also implies a painful reworking their own self and identity, which tends towards a future reconstruction of a new order of connections between the self and a new social/interpersonal and natural/built environment. However, during the journey, this search is profoundly marked by the suffering determined by violent encounters with others who bear their own wounds and psychic needs and are often inclined to search for concrete containers for their anxiety, finding them in asylum seekers' bodies. These bodies, often already degraded to being an object (of violence) by others, become the currency of exchange and compensation for perpetrators' own suffering, and containers of bundles of anxiety. They are transformed into social *abject* (Kristeva, 1982), imprisoned, isolated, and sealed off in horrible detention conditions in which even the last drop of energy is extracted from them through extortion of money, forced labour, rape, organ harvesting, etc., before ejecting them to the sea on precarious boats.

The painful events at sea, the shipwrecks, the rescues, deaths, and the related debates that take place in European politics among states and within institutions on the subject of migrant rescues at sea (and their distribution among European countries) belong to the confrontation of Europe with itself, with its past ghosts, and its own identity. If we consider this phenomenon not accidental for Europe, but as something endowed with historical meaning, we can read more clearly these debates and fears and the closure of nationalist policies that the phenomenon of refugees raises in Europe.

Borders are challenged by asylum seekers that struggle to find a place and space in a new environment, a new self, new connections between themselves and the natural and social environment, and a new identity for both social actors implied in this play, a new fabric of social ties, customs, laws, belongings, and a new 'social skin'.

All these levels imply individual and social dimensions in which the self and identity are transformed through these crossings and shifts of borders.

References

Alberto, C., & Chilton, M. (2019). Transnational Violence Against Asylum-Seeking Women and Children: Honduras and the United States-Mexico Border. *Human Rights Review*, 20(2), pp. 205–227. doi:10.1007/s12142-019-0547-5.

Anzieu, D. (1984). *The Group and the Unconscious*. Boston, MA: Routledge & Kegan Paul.

Anzieu, D. (1989). *The Skin Ego: A Psychoanalytic Approach to the Self*. New Haven, CT: Yale University Press.

Anzieu, D. (ed.) (1990). *Psychic Envelopes.* London: Karnac Books.

Bick, E. (1987). The Experience of the Skin in Early Object Relations. In M. Harris (ed.), *The Collected Papers of Martha Harris and Esther Bick.* Perthshire: Clunie Press, pp. 114–118.

Bion, W. R. (1961). *Experiences in Groups.* London: Tavistock.

Bion, W. R. (1962). *Learning from Experience.* London: Heinemann.

Bion, W.R. (1963). *Elements of Psychoanalysis.* London: Karnac.

Bion, W. R. (1967). *Second Thoughts: Selected Papers on Psychoanalysis.* London: Karnac Maresfield Library.

Cameron, A., Dickinson, J., & Smith, N. (eds.) (2013). *Body/State. Gender in Global/Local World.* London: Routledge.

Eder, K. (2009). A theory of collective identity. Making Sense of the Debate on a "European Identity." *European Journal of Social Theory,* 12(4), pp. 427–447. doi:10.1177/1368431009345050.

Fassin, D., & d'Halluin, E. (2005). The Truth from the Body: Medical Certificates as Ultimate Evidence for Asylum Seekers. *American Anthropologist,* 107(4), pp. 597–608. doi:10.1525/aa.2005.107.4.597.

Foucault, M. (1975). *Discipline and Punish: The Birth of the Prison.* New York: Random House, 1979.

Foucault, M. (1976). *The History of Sexuality, Vol. 1: An Introduction.* New York: Vintage Books, 1990.

Freud, S. (1923). The Ego and the Id. In J. Strachey et al. (Trans.), *The Standard Edition of the Complete Psychological Works of Sigmund Freud,* Volume XIX. London: Hogarth Press.

Fukuyama, F. (2018). *Identity: Contemporary Identity Politics and the Struggle for Recognition.* London: Profile Books.

Grinberg, L., & Grinberg, R. (1989). *Psychoanalytic Perspectives on Migration and Exile.* New Haven, CT: Yale University Press.

Hollander, N. C. (2010) *Uprooted Minds: Surviving the Politics of Terror in the Americas.* New York: Routledge.

Jung, C. G. (1920/1969). The Psychological Foundations of Belief in Spirits in *CW,* vol. 8.

Jung, C. G. (1928/1966). The Relations between the Ego and the Unconscious, in *CW,* vol. 7.

Jung, C. G. (1948/1969). A Review of Complex Theory, in *CW,* vol. 8.

Kast, V. (2002). *Abbandonare il ruolo di vittima. Vivere la propria vita.* Roma: Ed. Koiné.

Klein, M. (1946a). Notes on Some Schizoid Mechanisms. In M. Klein (ed.), *Envy and Gratitude, and Other Works 1946–1963.* London: Vintage, 1997, pp. 1–24.

Klein, M. (1946b). Notes on Some Schizoid Mechanisms. *International Journal of Psychoanalysis,* 27, pp. 99–110.

Kristeva, J. (1982). *Powers of Horror: An Essay on Abjection.* New York: Columbia University Press.

Lemma, A. (2010). *Under the Skin: A Psychoanalytic Study of Body Modification.* London: Routledge.

Luci, M. (2017). *Torture, Psychoanalysis & Human Rights.* London and New York: Routledge.

Luci, M. 'Crossing physical borders and the making of identity: The case of Europe.' IAAP-AJAS Conference, *Indeterminate States: Trans-Cultural; Trans-Racial; Trans-Gender.* Goethe University, Frankfurt am Main, Germany 2–5 August 2018.

Madsen, K. D., & van Naerssen, T. (2003). Migration, Identity and Belonging. *Journal of Borderlands Studies*, 18(1), pp. 61–75.

Martínez, L. (2014). Libya, from Paramilitary Forces to Militias: The Difficulty of Constructing a State Security Apparatus. Policy Alternatives Arab Reform Initiative. Available at: https://archives.arab-reform.net/en/node/598.

Meltzer, D. (1975). Adhesive Identification. *Contemporary Psychoanalysis*, 11, pp. 289–310.

Napolitano, F., Gualdieri, L., Santagati, G., & Angelillo, I. F. (2018). Violence Experience among Immigrants and Refugees: A Cross-Sectional Study in Italy. *BioMed Research International*, 2018, 7949483, 8 pages. doi:10.1155/2018/7949483.

Ogden, T. (1989) *The Primitive Edge of Experience.* New Brunswick, NJ: Jason Aronson.

Tustin, F. (1991). *The Protective Shell in Children and Adults.* London: Karnac.

Tustin, F. (1992). *Autistic States in Children Revised.* London: Routledge.

United Nations, *Convention Relating to the Status of Refugees.* Adopted on 28 July 1951 by the United Nations Conference of Plenipotentiaries on the Status of Refugees and Stateless Persons convened under General Assembly resolution 429 (V) of 14 December 1950. Entry into force: 22 April 1954, in accordance with article 43.

Van Houtum, H., & Van Naerssen, T. (2002). Bordering, Ordering and Othering. *Tijdschrift Voor Economische en Sociale Geografie*, 93, pp. 125–136. doi:10.1111/1467-9663.00189.

Weber, M. (1918[1946]). Politics as a Vocation. In H.H. Gerth & C. Wright Mills (Trans. and ed.), *From Max Weber: Essays in Sociology.* New York: Oxford University Press, pp. 77–128.

Winnicott, D. W. (1960). The Theory of the Parent-Infant Relationship. *The International Journal of Psychoanalysis*, 41, pp. 585–595.

Winnicott, D. W. (1975). Primary Maternal Preoccupation. In D. W. Winnicott (ed.), *Through Paediatrics to Psycho-Analysis: Collected Papers.* London: Hogarth Press, pp. 300–305.

Chapter 8

Getting on better with prejudice

Begum Maitra

> Jung, in other words – ... – is a magnet for many of our contemporary preoccupations; above all, how we have come to believe that we need to believe in something (or someone) in order to have good-enough lives.
>
> (Phillips 2004)

Our best selves, we imagine, must surely be free of prejudice. The Second 'World War'[1] marked sweeping changes to many of the old hierarchies based on markers such as nationality, race, class, and gender, but there is little to suggest that it displaced the old prejudices these relied on. We might say that efforts to uproot or eradicate prejudice – say, against women, or 'racial' groups, or to soften national prejudices against old enemies – have not lived up to our early optimism. If anything, we might wonder whether seeking to eradicate prejudice 'once and for all' is more likely to provoke other prejudices, in disguises that make them harder to object to meaningfully. Regenerating mythic monsters, and what is needed to defeat them, hint at the nature of what we fear and the categories we use to disguise which interests are being protected. If Hercules needed the assistance of his nephew, Iolaus, and a special technique (burning each monstrous neck cut to prevent its regeneration) if the Hydra was to be defeated what might we learn from a comparable Indian[2] myth. (Here we run into one of the prejudicial consequences of writing in English. Seeking to fit other cultural ways of engaging with the world within the limits and possibilities of this language presents the writer with an uncomfortable choice in which making easy sense to the English reader might well be less desirable. The risk of presenting the non-European as 'exotic', however unpleasant, might be preferable to that of homogenizing important differences.) The *asura Raktabija* (literally, blood seed) regenerated with each drop of blood that fell to the earth and was immune to the power of the male gods. It needed feminine *Shakti* (literally, power) to adopt a new and transgressive form – naked *Kali* with the devouring mouth and tongue that needed to be contained once the danger was averted. The Indian myth emphasizes not just the limits of male heroism but also the costs of counter-terrorism which, whatever its justification, cannot simply be tidied away as 'collateral damage'. The impossibility of separating good and evil, angels and demons, into tidy water-tight categories reappears frequently in Indian myth. That this remains part of a living tradition of thought must suggest a function more vital than mere cultural embellishment. Indeed, it must raise the question why the ambiguities of myth have succumbed, even in cultures that claim their roots in ancient Greece, to the totalizing dualism of Christian categories. The answer lies, perhaps, in the accidents of history. To European commentators, goddesses were already suspect, and a naked devouring one was quickly demoted to demoness or, no less ambivalently, to 'Terrible Mother' by Erich Neumann. This venture into comparative mythology reveals the cultural biases and preferences of this writer; while wishing to appear congenial as I write about cultural prejudices I must emphasize that there are few 'culture-free' zones.

This chapter continues an exploration that began with a paper presented to a Jungian gathering in 2017, developing into a publication (Maitra 2019) that examined how prejudice is transmitted in Jungian trainings through an overwhelming preoccupation with European traditions, and a reluctance to question European exceptionalism. As Jung wrote 'I could not help feeling superior because I was reminded at every step of my European nature. That was unavoidable: my being European gave me a certain perspective on these people who were so differently constituted from myself' (in Dalal 1988, p. 270). Even if not openly dismissive of other traditions of thought Jungian trainings treat these as essentially much less important, if not irrelevant. This chapter explores recent developments within Jungian circles to demonstrate something of the difficulties in addressing prejudice through institutional reform. As the daily news – of resurgent nationalisms, or the normalization of right-wing politics – must remind us Jungians are not alone in wishing to cling to a fading European supremacy, although we might wonder why questions of prejudice elude 'depth psychologists' as easily as they do those presumably less 'deep' in their thinking.

An Open Letter in the *British Journal of Psychotherapy* in late 2018 from a group of clinicians and academics (many reputed to have long campaigned in this area) was a notable beginning to just such a process within the Jungian institution, and we will consider in some detail the tensions it sought to address. First, most obviously, are tensions seething in its title – *Open Letter from a group of Jungians on the question of Jung's writings on and theories about 'Africans'*. This mysterious emphasis on 'Africans' is widened in the body to include 'persons of African and South Asian Indian *heritage*, as well as other *populations of colour* and *Indigenous peoples*' (BJP 2018, emphases mine). As one of the signatories to this letter who is not 'African' (and cannot help wondering at the specificity of 'South Asian Indian'), this seems to me an unfortunate emphasis on a narrow preoccupation. The differences being emphasized, whether dressed as 'race' or 'heritage' (whose only virtue lies in emphasizing social transmission rather than biology), or 'populations of colour' (to circumvent the negative connotations of 'non-white'), fails to ask why we remain quite so transfixed by colour? Does it advance our interest in the current plight of populations formed by particular sorts of historical suffering? And what must we make of the scare quotes around 'Africans' in the title, and does singling out that continent reveal something about the preoccupations of the Letter? It might seem as though instruments ('heritage', colour, claims of indigeneity) shaped for other battles fought elsewhere – for example, to be adequately represented; to receive state recognition of collective 'needs'; to name oneself in ways that reveal, or undo, historical oppressions – have unthinkingly slipped into this 'new' enterprise, that is, our interest in how prejudice persists unchallenged in Jungian institutions.

Samuels (2019) gives some of the background to explain the emphasis on 'Africans', scare quotes, and all. The possibility, he writes, of a statement such as this Letter was first raised by him in a meeting in South Africa. (So much for the physical reality of the African continent.) 'The question has been raised as to why the focus is on persons of African heritage and only passing mention is made of other populations of colour and Indigenous peoples. The reason' Samuels writes 'is that it was felt that such a focus was precisely what was needed'. But what the emphases on focus, precision, and need do is distract attention from the unsatisfactory nature of this as explanation as though precision could trump the focus on whose need was at stake. As unsatisfactory as Samuels (2019) must have found the decision of the IAAP Congress 'that it was not the time to issue such a statement' in 2016. Like so many 'decisions' made by committees, elected or self-styled, both responses are seemingly impatient with the diversity of opinions they hope to represent. What such institutionally approved reckonings of focus and timing are being less than transparent about are exactly how vested interests work as prejudices to simplify incommensurable histories of suffering and need.

Given that the Open Letter relies heavily on Farhad Dalal's critique (1988) of Jung's colonialist and racist bias, how have changing popular and academic discourses in the intervening decades influenced the Letter's approach to institutional prejudice? When not quoting Jung (whose own terms blur, history, religion, state and colour – from black man; negro[3]; Elgonyi; Pueblo Indians; Indians; Hindu; oriental; and so on), Dalal refers to 'black' and 'white' in the terminology of the 1980s, and to the 'non-European' because, he emphasizes, the category is implicit in Jung's separation of Europeans from all others (Dalal 1988, p. 265). Dalal's interest in his detailed and closely argued critique lay in the peculiar and racist illogic of Jung's claims to scientific discovery, and in the explicit equation he made between the modern black, the 'prehistoric human', and the white child. He questioned

the 'selective blindness' of a Jungian community that continued nevertheless to extol Jung as 'the great equaliser and the great unifier'. 'It is this',
Dalal emphasizes,

> that constitutes the racist core of Jungian Psychology on which all else is
> based. The equations are where he begins; these are the ideas and beliefs
> that he accepts without question. ...On the whole it will not be neces-
> sary to interpret passages to find the 'hidden meaning' in his words.
> Given that the words speak for themselves, it is curious to note the se-
> lective reading of Jung that has taken place.
>
> (Dalal 1988, p. 263)

What has changed in the ways in which we might read Dalal's critique today,
given the identity wars and shifting power relations that have influenced the
Open Letter's framings of 'Africans', colour, heritage, and indigeneity? Has the
growing concern with group identities, the anxious re-naming to capture some
essentialized detail, or advantage of positioning helped or hindered attempts to
influence institutional change? We could imagine that an 'identity' politics in-
flected by a hierarchy of suffering (which was worse – anti-semitism or racism,
the Holocaust or slavery, Jung's influence or wider European attitudes) could
leave its victims too deeply and exclusively marked by their injury, and pitted
against each other. It would be an error however to underestimate the sensibil-
ities of those who feel the urgent need to police these changing terminologies
themselves as though to defend real boundaries against future re-traumatizing.
Does such identity politics lock us into an exaggerated anxiety about prejudice
itself? In this writer's experience Dalal's paper was almost entirely unknown to
the Jungians she encountered; being faced with Dalal's examples from Jung's
writing evoked shock and surprise (and possibly disbelief) in them. Some ob-
jected at how offensive Jung's language was to contemporary readers; very few
expressed any curiosity about the intentions embedded in that language, and
whether contemporary Jungians might continue to underestimate the complexity of other cultures, their ways of life and their richest ideas, and to perpetuating racist bias today.

The British academic Stuart Hall (2017) warned about the disarming se-
ductiveness of the signifier 'ethnicity'. This was a suspiciousness he shared
with movements for racial justice in the United States where the liberal discourse of cultural pluralism had repeatedly excluded citizens of African
descent. His influence, along with that of other British thinkers from the
Caribbean, led to the rejection of 'multiculturalism' by British antiracist
movements of the 1970s on the grounds that it deflected attention from 'structural inequalities' faced by those from the former colonies of Britain. In the
minds of many black British thinkers this turned cultural meaning-systems
as the rationale for a more pluralistic approach into a 'soft' option, almost

feminine in comparison with the militant muscularity the black American movement so dramatically presented. This logic, of feminizing those one would persuade of their lack of some essential virtue, is reminiscent of the logics of colonial[4] persuasion. Rand and Wagner (2012) discuss the British strategy of 'racializing' what they extolled as martial qualities, and equated with masculinity, in those Indian groups (Gurkhas in Nepal, Sikhs, and Pathans from Punjab and the North-West Frontier of India) that had served British interests in the Indian uprising of 1857. In *The Martial Races of India* British Lieutenant-General MacMunn wrote in 1933:

> to understand what is meant by the martial races of India is to understand from the inside the real story of India. We do not speak of the martial races of Britain as distinct from the non-martial, nor of Germany, nor of France. But in India we speak of the martial races as a thing apart and because the mass of the people have neither martial aptitude nor physical courage … the courage that we should talk of colloquially as 'guts'.
>
> (quoted in Rand and Wagner 2012)

That these sentiments are echoed almost exactly by Jung may merely reflect the ideas that held sway across Europe, perhaps even among the Swiss who had no direct colonial interests like the British. Jung's own admiration for all things English is well known (Phillips 2004) – '… in many ways it is an advantage to have been imprinted with the English national character in one's cradle. You can then travel in the most Godforsaken countries and when anybody asks "Are you a foreigner?" you can answer, "No, I am English"' (CW, vol 10, 1964, p. 487, para 921). But what shall we make of Jung's insights into Indian 'mentality' (CW, 10, p. 521, para 995) inferred rather bizarrely from a jumble of impressions of their costumes and customs. He too found manliness in the North Indian (in the same Gurkhas, Sikhs, and Pathans), against what he saw as 'effeminate and babyish' (even disgusting in its resemblance to an 'overgrown diaper') in the costume of what he calls 'the Hindu'. Is this preoccupation with a precarious masculinity at constant risk of being overcome by feminization merely an influence of Western culture? Or should we be concerned about the lack of intellectual ('scientific') rigour as he leapt from unsubstantiated assertions (about 'matriarchal trends' in southern India) and personal opinions (their 'essentially unwarlike dress') to hold forth disparagingly on the 'pacifist mentality of the Hindu' man.

It is to this racist illogic of Jung's claims to scientific discovery that Dalal also wishes to draw attention:

> As the scientists measured the femur and the weight of the brain, *Jung presumed to 'measure' the psyche's 'maturity'*. His fundamental error was in thinking he could do this … His methodology follows logically from

the *a priori* acceptance of the supposed conclusions of the investigation: i.e. the various equations of black and white. In other words
his investigative edifice is a tautology. He has two laboratories, the
first one being the psychoanalysis of the European. Jung presumed
that the data he gathered from the European unconscious gave him
information about the black conscious. As he discovered more about
European children and their faculties so he presumed to discover
more about nonEuropeans and their faculties. The second labora-
tory was Jung's bed. As he dreamt and discovered more about his unconscious and his 'primitive' aspects, he presumed he discovered the
thought processes and the emotional life of the modern primitive, i.e.
the non-European. ... Nowhere does he give a reason or proof of the
alleged connection.

(Dalal 1988, p. 273 emphasis in the original)

Jung offers little evidence also when borrowing Levy-Bruhl's notion of 'participation mystique' among primitive peoples other than to inform us that
he discovered it 'in the modern Negro, or the modern Indian' (Dalal 1988,
p. 275).

The Open Letter presents, as it were, an up-to-the-minute list of positions that might be taken on prejudice and we find it unambiguous about
the explicit and implicit, 'inner' and 'outer', harm caused by the *de facto*
institutional and structural racism ... present in Jungian organizations'.
Given that such public declarations might have become obligatory since the
MacPherson report (1999) exposed the widespread institutional, and structural, racism within British public institutions how might we tell genuine
conviction from rhetoric? Too facile a confession must surely fail to clear the
penitent's conscience, or to persuade the victim of the possibility of change.
Change must be premised at the very least on a sufficiently complex understanding of the 'structures' that must be undone, and of the privileges that
as a result will undoubtedly be lost to some. Admittedly, those details may
be outside the scope of a Letter intended, perhaps, to launch a shot across
the bows of 'Jungian organisations'. However, as those opposing entrenched
interests know well there may always be a reason for it not being the 'right
time or place' for change.

In its curiously worded wish 'not so much to chastise Jung' we could wonder whether the Letter slips into revealing an ambivalence, perhaps the wish
to chastise him (even if a little less than it hopes to achieve some other more
general wish) as if in acknowledgment of the gravity of the injury Dalal, for
one, is charging him with. But it almost immediately reduces Jung's responsibility to the 'largely uncritical embrace' of the prejudices of 'his time' –
that scapegoat that would carry the blame for him. Or perhaps we should
not chastise him 'so much' but distribute it among his followers, but there
too for a curiously limited responsibility – 'the harm that has ensued in

these 30 years' since the paper by Dalal. It is as if to say that 'analysts, clinicians and academics' might be forgiven for their uncritical embrace of Jung's prejudices until Dalal (the non-European) pointed these out to us. Urged 'to acknowledge and apologize for these offensive attitudes, and their potential harm and confusion' the reader might wonder at the progressive diminution of the scale of injury – from actual to potential harm, to attitudes, and confusion, subtly turning the victim (levelling charges of racism if not proposing chastisement) into the aggressor – wrong-minded, maliciously accusatory, and unjustly punitive; the angry black person with the chip on their shoulder, no less!

Of such fumbling the British scholar Christopher Ricks wrote 'Sometimes the public conscience hastens to catch prejudice not in a definition or in an argument but in a metaphor; yet the metaphor then has a way of so fumbling as to let the suspect escape'. About good intentions, he observes wryly –

> You are to think well of it, not think well about it. Which is one of the things meant by prejudice, that you are to know in advance just what is expected, and that you will not devote any scrutiny to whether the judgement offered has truly been made good
>
> (Ricks 1988/1994, pp. 78–79).

What we know in advance and may not wish to scrutinize is the state of play, the 'considerable intense and fractious discussion' within the International Association of Analytical Psychology that opposed the Open Letter before its publication (Samuels 2019), and continues its objections after. The Oxford Reference dictionary (Hawkins 1986) describes rhetoric as 'the art of speaking or writing impressively, language used for its impressive sound (often with an implication of insincerity, exaggeration, etc.)'. What are we – readers of Jung – letting ourselves be persuaded by when we accede to language that sounds impressive while saying very little. For Christopher Ricks it 'is intimate with the prejudicial; both are endemic; the healthy as well as the morbid tissues are built upon both …' (Ricks 1988, p. 13).

Wishing neither to chastise Jung, nor to apologize for his ideological errors, the Letter has another suggestion – to encourage a more inclusive approach by recruiting more 'students, clinicians and scholars of colour' to train, and to engage in research, presumably in the hope that this would change attitudes more organically from within. While this must meet with the approval of those who believe that a combination of 'representation' and 'positive action' might turn around deeply entrenched oppositions to change, this is not a hope backed by much 'evidence'. As the Black Lives Matter campaign painfully highlights in the United States (where some of these ideas originate) the increasing representation of African Americans in professional and public life has not assured more equitable life circumstances for most African Americans. Nor indeed does this generalize to other disadvantaged minority groups. Let us also consider the sort of caché the term 'people of colour' has acquired. Cleansed of its associations with slavery and apartheid, miscegenation, 'passing', and all the associated history of pain, the emphasis on colour has re-entered polite discourse in altered guise. Or perhaps this signals the increasing hybridity of those who might have once rallied under a 'black' flag – both those who might trace some heritage from 'Africa'[5], and all those others without African heritage – with a shift in focus from policing entry into 'white' groups (the 'one drop rule'; unease about 'passing') to questions of identity and loyalty. The official terminology in Britain remains 'black and minority ethnic', obscuring with a faux innocence important historical differences between groups that continue to profoundly influence their life-chances, while artlessly including within this overarching term migrant groups of varied European extraction. (Perhaps it is really economic status we are referring to since the economic elite of any colour do not seriously influence the statistics or fortunes of 'minority' groups). Given how inaccurate these appellations – white and black – are in real skin terms it is worth considering why we have acceded to the naïve categorizations imposed by first impressions of the most obvious and visible feature, of skin colour. Long used to distract from more relevant characteristics (cultural productions; naturally occurring traits of value) colour has dominated imaginations on both sides, causing pervasive psychological harm. This history of denigration and exploitation is 'managed' to some extent by the re-naming mentioned, and by hi-jacking and inverting the derogatory power of other terms (black, nigger, bitch); we might underestimate the risk, even as knowing and self-conscious perpetrators of that particular joke, of perpetuating the rage and pain we hoped to avert.

Can students bring that much-desired freshness into hide-bound academic traditions? Personal experience suggests otherwise. It would have been impossible to reject the charge of assessors of my first-year essay as a Jungian trainee – namely, that I had used my 'fine intellect' to 'pad it out'. My essay on suicide as sacrifice examined a South Asian patient whose psychotic breakdown triggered by profound anxieties about religious law, community expectations, and envy had led him to make a suicide pact. It may have been arguable (although not, I think, by a trainee) that the mythic and cultural material presented, although dismissed by the examiner as 'interesting reading in as much as some of the myths and stories are not familiar in the West', was exactly what was at issue. From numerous such experiences I gathered the impression of an utter indifference to what may have been central to my patient's experience, and that I might have demonstrated access to this, marginalized as we both were by a Jungian audience who claimed superior understanding of elevated matters of the spirit, and of 'India', based on Jung's own limited experience (Sengupta 2013) and uncertain extrapolations. Professional trainings are inevitably a form of indoctrination, even if willingly entered upon, tying successful graduates[6] into systems of prestige and forms of practice, social networks, and financial considerations that few might feel able to jeopardize. It makes the invitation to 'students of colour' to enrol, without first ensuring that those training them are sufficiently trained to avoid those same biases that we are so concerned not to accuse Jung himself of, an extraordinarily specious act.

Are forms of evidence or argument shaped by culture too? I have long wondered at my preference (like the prevailing Indian fondness for illustrative anecdotes) for the specificities of case examples when making clinical arguments, rather than for rules abstracted from data and rationales presented elsewhere, by experts who are inevitably unavailable to consider the unique combination of factors at play in a case at hand. It was with some delight that I discovered a discussion of ancient Indian traditions of rhetoric in the *Nyāya Sutrās*[7], and their comparison with the Aristotelian systems they pre-dated. Lloyd (2007) notes that colonial approaches to Indian knowledge systems frequently dismissed these as solely spiritual and having little real contribution to logic or rhetoric. However, he warns, contemporary interpretations are no less at risk of misrepresenting these sources given the 'post-colonial unease' of contemporary academics in India that prevents its inclusion in mainstream education on the grounds that this could smack of 'revivalism'.

> ... our assumptions about what rhetoric is, what it is not, and what terms it should use, have all been dictated by the essays and dialogues of Aristotle, Plato, the Sophists and others. As a result, already *Nyāya* has been dismissed as inferior, unsystematic, and non-syllogistic...
>
> The danger now is that we would once again miss *Nyāya*'s importance and absorb it into existing theoretical concepts, perhaps as simply a type of arguing from signs, an existing inferential model, or as a relative of the epicheirema, a Greek model of argument ...
>
> (Lloyd 2007, p. 35)

There is a pressing need to look for non-European sources if we are to grasp how culture is implicated in the very models of reasoning and inference, a task that must be central to the possibility of any psychoanalytic conversation between different cultures. In Lloyd's account these Indian forms of rhetoric differ by being more crucially dialogic, more essentially linked to example, both positive and negative. In contradistinction to what British philosopher Stephen Toulmin (quoted by Lloyd) describes as 'a subjective/objective split that has called into question even the possibility of objectivity' in 'the West', in *Nyāya* ' ... the subjective and objective are both verifiable inter-subjectively, our perceptual abilities are basically seen as reliable, and collectively – through our perceptions, arguments, and inferences – we may be relatively assured of the world we live in' (Lloyd 2007, p. 36). It would be difficult to summarize in the space permitted here the complexity, the similarities, and differences, of even these two systems, but as the foregoing discussion demonstrates, these must be crucial to our understanding of which arguments seem persuasive across cultures, and which do not. For example, an argument by simple Aristotelian enthymeme (in which one premise is not explicitly stated) might state 'the Iraq war is just because it promotes freedom'. Those who share this cultural style assume what is missing, namely, that 'wars to encourage freedom are just', or even, that freedom can be imposed (on a defeated enemy!). In *Nyāya* examples would be required for and against both premises, with motivation, and morality, and agreed upon by both arguers. The goal of *Nyāya* 'is 'fruitful' argument by presenting a glimpse of sharable truth. Its approach 'specifically reasons from enthymemes based in particular cases and underscores how different examples lead to different conclusions' (Lloyd 2007, p. 31).

Let us take the briefest example of a British adolescent referred to a London child mental health clinic for 'aggressive' behaviour at school. Since the child refused to comply with adult expectation, such as the requirement to attend treatment sessions set by the clinician, her mother attended instead in the hope of picking up pointers she could use at home. The clinician heard how the mother had survived quite extraordinary adversity in her own life – ranging from childhood sexual and physical abuse, peer and intimate partner violence, educational disadvantage, and prolonged economic hardship. In her determination to invent for her daughter and herself the sort of home and family life she had never had, this mother had cut herself off from her family of origin and distanced herself from the cultural community that had colluded in her suffering. It hurt and puzzled her when her child seemed to prefer the 'lower mentality' of that same community, the sexualized language, the easy recourse to threat, violence, and criminal activity.

In recent years intersectionality has been much talked about as a concept that illuminates the dilemmas of these particular populations simultaneously handicapped by multiple disadvantage and adversity. 'Of course', writes Samuels (2019) in a way that must, paradoxically, suggest uncertainty, 'as the current term "intersectionality" implies, all prejudice and discrimination against specified groups of people is, at some level to be linked'. Perhaps this is what feminist scholars Phoenix and Pattynama (2006) meant by 'everyone is talking about intersectionality', and for it being hailed by some as the most important theoretical contribution made by women's studies. The history of the concept and surrounding debates reveal other sorts of potential prejudice. Kimberlé Crenshaw's use of the metaphor of intersections/crossroads within the frame of US feminist jurisprudence in 1989, and the 'genealogical roots in the activism of African American (lesbian) feminists' of the term (Lewis 2009) – does not immediately establish its relevance to our focus on institutional prejudice in Jungian thought. This is not to underestimate what intersectionality draws attention to – 'the relationships among multiple dimensions and modalities of social relations and subject formations' (McCall 2005), and its ability to expose institutional forms and practices that make some social subjects and social processes invisible. However, to do so it needs to locate its argument in particular historical, ideological, social, cultural, national contexts.

Expressions of solidarity with African American lesbians and feminists apart, we must consider whether US histories of race, gender and sexuality are the most useful starting point for British, or indeed any other, society where minorities struggle to make their concerns visible. For some scholars the problem of intersectionality as theory lies in its basis in identity categories. Social life is too irreducibly complex, overflowing with multiple and fluid determinations of both subjects and structures, making of fixed categories 'simplifying social fictions that produce inequalities in the process of producing differences' (McCall 2005, p. 1773). A categorical approach is, however, most useful when the subject is multigroup, and the method is systematically comparative. For example, it could help us grasp how multiple minority groups negotiate with dominant society, and with each other, to compete for resources, making alliances, fixed or fluid, with some groups and 'in competition' with others, and in response to local circumstances. The complexities within single groups, single categories, or both, requires an 'intracategorical' approach, that is single-case intensive rather than comparative and comes a little closer to the individual focus of psychoanalytic practice. For a wider application of psychoanalytic theory (and for changes in training) we must first include an understanding of how the construction of categories (that are essentially fluid – such as 'race', gender, sexuality, social class) and their overlapping, intersecting features are shaped by, and shape in turn, those macro-structures specific to a regional, national, or political context.

For Mohanty (1984) the distance between academics in the West and their subjects elsewhere arouses concern about a sort of discursive colonization that appropriates and codifies 'scholarship' and 'knowledge' about women in the Third World by using analytic categories which take as their referent matters of interest only to feminists in the United States and Western Europe. For example, she writes –

> An analysis of 'sexual difference' in the form of a cross-culturally singular, monolithic notion of patriarchy or male dominance leads to the construction of a similarly reductive and homogenous notion of what I call the 'Third World Difference' – that stable, ahistorical something that apparently oppresses most if not all the women in these countries.

There is no universal patriarchal framework, she continues, which this scholarship

> attempts to counter and resist – unless one posits an international male conspiracy or a monolithic, ahistorical power hierarchy. There is,

however, a particular world balance of power within which any analysis of culture, ideology and socio-economic conditions has to be necessarily situated.

(Mohanty 1984, pp. 333–334)

The usual stance on cultural difference in psychoanalytic trainings assumes that the circumstances of the individual client provide sufficient contextual material for the therapeutic focus required for individual growth. Any cultural detail is to be understood using the same universal thinking about archetypal meanings that apply to all other clients, from any other world of cultural meanings. More recent attempts to consider what are referred to as 'cultural complexes' seek to address cultural differences but fail to sufficiently widen (and deepen) the frame of what counts as culture. Singer and Kimbles (2004) wonder why, despite Jung's own interest in the collective and active exploration of diverse cultures, his 'complex theory' had never been systematically applied to the life of the group, and its expression in the individual psyche. A central difficulty lay, they believe, in the tendency for 'collective life' to fall into the Jungian shadow. 'Clearly', they write, although it seems far from clear to this reader, 'a substantial part of Jung's genius was his sensitivity to the perils of the individual's falling into the grips of collective life. Like all who lived through the 20th century', they assert again, apparently with little suspicion that this could scarcely apply to the entire world,

> Jung witnessed the terrible side of collectivity. Beginning with the deadening effect of collective religious life on his father's spirit, Jung went on to dream and then see the map of Europe and much of the rest of the world bathed in blood, violence, and terror ...
>
> (2004, p. 4)

It seems clear by now that we are again in the territory of a rhetorical argument that erases the experience of those multitudes who have had vastly difference experiences of collective life, and who have very different understandings of why Europe, and elsewhere, might have been bathed in blood, without in any way converging with Jung's, or Singer and Kimbles', understandings of history or culture.

Would it influence our approach to the mother in the earlier case example if we were told she had migrated from the Caribbean islands? Would we then read her experience differently – relying perhaps on all-too-familiar accounts of the lives of immigrant women in Third World poverty, or well-known tropes of black families fragmented and dehumanized by slavery, and its normalization in sexual and physical violence? Mohanty warns about a homogenous notion of the oppression of women that produces the 'average third world woman' – who 'leads an essentially truncated life based on her feminine gender (read: sexually constrained) and being "third world" (read: ignorant, poor, uneducated, tradition-bound, domestic, family-oriented, victimized, etc.)' (Mohanty 1984, p. 337). It is difficult to see how the particular obligations of individual psychoanalysis, whatever the personal sympathies and views on inequity or activism held by the analyst, could justify anything other than the most careful, continuing, and un-prejudged attention to the client before them.

In an essay titled 'Prejudice' Christopher Ricks draws together the reasons why it may be intrinsic to the most basic mental functions we share. His vantage point as a literary critic permits him to explore the multiple alternative positions and half-uttered prejudices that literature (and literary essays) dare in ways forbidden to anthropologists, and psychoanalysts. These observers of others' lives must tread more cautiously, attempting to limit the amount of intrusion into that delicate balance between participant and observer, the real and the imagined, individual and group intentions. Each realm – literary criticism, anthropology and therapy – provides opportunities for the exploration of the multiple, overlapping, contradictory, and near inexhaustible possibilities of meaning that attend social lives. About why prejudice is quite so elusive, Ricks writes:

> The word 'prejudice' or prejudiced' itself has a way of being prejudicial. Of demanding in advance a bullying superiority over any counter-term which might be mustered; and this prejudicing of the issue is compounded by the increasing propensity of the word to suggest prejudice *against* much more than prejudice *for*. 'A feeling favourable or unfavourable ...': but the word has come to have its own prejudice or bias.
>
> (Ricks 1988, p. 81, emphases in the original)

Conclusion

Pre-judgement, as we know, is part of how perception itself works. Mary Douglas wrote:

> In the normal process of interpretation, the existing scheme of assumptions tends to be protected from challenge, for the learner recognizes and absorbs cues which harmonize with past experience and usually ignores cues which are discordant. ... If every new experience laid all past interpretations open to doubt, no scheme of established assumptions could be developed and no learning could take place.
>
> (Douglas 1999, p. 109)

When Fanon wrote of the child crying 'Mama, see the Negro! I'm frightened!' (Fanon 1986, p. 112) he was calling attention to the act of categorization that perception entails, even in this case in what we assume is the freshness, the first-timeness, of a child's perceptions, given the categories of a society that predicates so much on some markers and not others. To perceive is to ignore.

Prejudice is one of those subjects that defies a tidy conclusion, or a rational programme of progressive correctives building cumulatively to a state of ... – what? What it is we might be (being) if we weren't prejudiced? Christopher Ricks considers, and rejects, impartiality and conviction, to emphasize other elements – a willingness to rectify our view in the light of new evidence; a particular kind of scepticism that includes the habit of examining evidence; and a capacity for delaying decision to allow for these possibilities. But the first step must be a willingness to consider the prejudgement in our most valued beliefs, especially those that benefit us, while excluding or profoundly damaging others. Why have Jungians been so little perturbed by what Jung's writings reveal about the extremity of his racialized and belittling views of non-Europeans? Has our habituation to the 'marketing' ideologies of our capitalist societies blunted us, as we pride ourselves on our higher purpose, to how we have slipped into competitive turf wars with other Jungian and psychoanalytic schools, promoting – whether for prestige or financial gain – expensive training, therapy and supervision courses, or into unabashed self-promotion as though merely responding to 'unmet need' in parts of the world less fortunate than we believe ourselves to be? A 21st-century civilizing mission based on European ideas that have not faced critical evaluation for global relevance must surely flout those ideals of freedom, equality, and the rights of choice we congratulate ourselves for promoting. It is this faith in the superiority of our sources (and a curiously exclusive and repetitive reliance on ancient Greece above all other civilizations), a sort of Western parochialism that, while necessary once to shore up the self-aggrandizing needs of colonialists, can scarcely be justified any longer.

Notes

1 Continuing to refer to the events of 1939–1945 in Europe in this way demonstrates the ways in which European exceptionalism continues to make claims that originated in a colonial past. Despite marking a watershed point in the histories of Western states its benefits, and costs, could scarcely be described as equally apportioned, or relevant, to the 'world'. It is to this prejudice – the uncritical universalization of European/Western interests – that I wish to draw attention.

2 The mythic imagination of the populations of the subcontinent contains influences brought by trade, and invasions, from ancient Sumer onwards, and from both east and west. The categorization of this syncretic agglomeration into 'Hinduism', and 'Hindu' mythology by colonial administrators triggered a long-continuing and essentially pointless debate about what is or is not authentically 'Hindu'.

3 His use of 'nigger' in one instance (CW, vol 18, p. 286) was defended by the editors of the Collected Works as a term that 'was not invariably derogatory in earlier British and Continental usage', adding that it was 'definitely not' so in this case. How did they know, we might ask!

4 Colonialism may not be quite as far in the past as some might believe. Three dozen new states in Asia and Africa achieved autonomy or outright independence from European rulers only as recently as between 1945 and 1960. (Office of the Historian at https://history.state.gov/milestones/1945-1952/asia-and-africa, downloaded on 24.5.19.)
5 Although that might include the entire sum of humanity.
6 Ironically, it is the unsuccessful – who qualify for entry but not for full membership – who may tell us more about why indoctrination fails.
7 The *Nyāya* school of Hindu philosophy (composed between 6th century BCE and 2nd century CE) contains five books of 528 aphoristic sutras that deal with reason, logic, epistemology, and metaphysics.

References

Dalal, F. (1988) Jung: A racist. *British Journal of Psychotherapy*, 4: 263–279.

Douglas, M. (1975/1999) *Implicit Meanings. Selected Essays in Anthropology.* London: Routledge.

Fanon, F. (1986) *Black Skin, White Masks.* London: Pluto Press (Original work published 1952).

Hall, S. (2017) *The Fateful Triangle. Race Ethnicity Nation.* Cambridge, MA: Harvard University Press.

Hawkins, J.M. (1986) *The Oxford Reference Dictionary.* Oxford: Oxford University Press.

Jung, C.G. (1964) The Swiss Line in the European spectrum. Vol 10. *Civilization in Transition.* The Collected Works of C.G. Jung. Bollingen Series. Princeton, NJ: Princeton University Press.

Lewis, G. (2009) Celebrating intersectionality? Debates on a multi-faceted concept in gender studies: Themes from a conference. *European Journal of Women's Studies*, 16, 203.

Lloyd, K. (2007) A rhetorical tradition lost in translation: Implications for rhetoric in the ancient Indian *Nyāya Sutras. Advances in the History of Rhetoric*, 10, 1, 19–42.

MacPherson of Cluny, Sir William. (Febuary 1999) *The Stephen Lawrence Inquiry: Report of an Inquiry.* London: The Stationery Office. Accessed on November 12, 2013 at http://www.officialdocuments.co.uk/document/cm42/4262/4262.htm.

Maitra, B. (2019) With respect to prejudice. *Journal of Analytical Psychology*, 64, 2, 189–205.

McCall, L. (2005) The complexity of intersectionality. *Signs*, 30, 3, 1771–1800.

Mohanty, C.P. (1984) Under Western Eyes: Feminist scholarship and colonial discourses. *boundary 2*, 12, 3, On Humanism and the University I: The Discourse on Humanism. Spring-Autumn, 333–358.

Neumann, E. ([1951], 1963 2nd ed.) *The Great Mother.* Bollingen: Princeton University Press.

Open Letter. (2018) The Authors(s). *British Journal of Psychotherapy.* BPF and John Wiley & Sons Ltd.

Phillips, A. (2004) A Man in Two Minds. Books, The Guardian, 17 January 2004.

Phoenix, A. and Pattynama, P. (2006) Editorial: Special issue. *The European Journal of Women's Studies*, 13, 3, 187–192.

Rand, G. and Wagner, K.A. (2012) Recruiting the 'martial races': identities and military service in colonial India. *Patterns of Prejudice*, 46, 3–4, 232–254.

Ricks, C. (1988/1994) *T.S. Eliot and Prejudice*. Faber and Faber Ltd.

Samuels, A. (2019) Notes on the open letter on Jung and 'Africans' published in the *British Journal of Psychotherapy* in November 2018. *Psychotherapy and Politics International*.

Sengupta, S. (2013) *Jung in India*. New Orleans, LA: Spring Journal Books.

Singer, T. and Kimbles, S. (2004). *The Cultural Complex: Contemporary Jungian Perspectives on Psyche and Society*. Hove and New York: Brunner-Routledge.

Section 4

Histories and futures

Chapter 9

Environments of the self, world crises as initiation, and the telos of collective individuation

Scott Hyder

> Although the mind cannot apprehend its own form of existence, owing to the lack of an Archimedean point outside, it nevertheless exists. Not only does the psyche exist, it is existence itself.
> — C.G. Jung (1- Jung, 1958, p. 12)

Since 2014, under the rubric of 'Analysis and Activism,' sponsored by the International Association of Analytical Psychology and the local training societies, a small group of analysts has organized conferences in London, Rome, and Prague. Presentations highlight matters of psychological, political, and cultural importance for International Association for Analytical Psychology (IAAP) members and others concerned with and committed to the realization that Psyche must be respected and realized in the world at large and cannot be attended to exclusively between two people in the consulting room. That's a necessary and fortunate perspective, given the scale of challenges facing our world, as well as the inner and outer environments of the Self, today.

It's a monumental task, naturally, and naturally Jung's comprehensive appreciation of the scope of psyche offers us a guiding perspective for our way forward, given that,

> the 'self'...should be understood as the totality of the psyche. The self is not only the centre, but also the whole circumference which embraces both conscious and unconscious; it is the centre of this totality, just as the ego is the centre of consciousness
>
> (2- Jung, 1953, p. 41)

This commitment has a long lineage throughout history. Considering the title of the original presentation proposed to address 'relationships of resonance and dissonance in thresholds of crises and consciousness at scale as initiations to greater integrity in being humans in the world,' hopefully a cursory historical and psychological review may help clarify this unwieldy subject somewhat for the interested reader.

Historical and psychological background

Metaphorically, the linguistic paternity or maternity around the mantra 'thinking globally and acting locally' may be a matter of some dispute, but Patrick Geddes (1854–1932), a Scottish biologist, sociologist, pioneering town planner and social activist, was an early and seminal advocate (Shabecoff, 2003, pp. 86–87). Promoting approaches resonant with, rather than aggressively counter to, the environment, Geddes wrote:

> 'Local character' is thus no mere accidental old-world quaintness, as its mimics think and say. It is attained only in course of adequate grasp and treatment of the whole environment, and in active sympathy with the essential and characteristic life of the place concerned.
>
> (Geddes, 1915, p. 397)

Over a century after Geddes' vision of sustainable planning for cities, symbolically our collective egos, only marginal realization of the ideal exists in urban, let alone global spaces. In terms of discrete human lifetimes, psychological collective change often seems excruciatingly slow. Recognition of and even potential solutions to a problem provide no certainty of problematic resolution. Numerous stages of denial and resistance seem necessarily to precede any healing of the wounded whole. Paradoxically, we might be obliged to adopt both a humbler and more urgent attitude simultaneously in the face of intransigence and opposition in the world, as with ourselves. The subtitle of Geddes' Cities in Evolution contains the 'study of civics,' offering insight that solutions seldom come in external fixes of our cultures but only through internalized attitudes of common interests and responsibilities shared proportionately among fellow citizens. As US cities, states, and businesses now strive to reach or better the Paris climate accords limiting CO_2, deliberately overriding federal policy regression, perhaps deeper collective changes are indeed emerging.

Resonating with dissonance between theoretical awareness and practical applications, a quarter century ago, late, great, iconoclastic Jungian analyst and Archetypal Psychology founder, James Hillman, wrote a book: *We've Had a Hundred Years of Psychotherapy—And the World's Getting Worse.* Significantly, as most analysts can attest, issues plaguing individuals who enter into depth analytic process often don't improve but even appear, or become, worse during beginning stages of work. From that vantage, that a century of psychotherapy has not magically transformed worldly woes should hardly be surprising; conditioned patterns of abuse, repression, oppression, and trauma have manifested over millennia. Unfortunately, the patterns repeat themselves even today. Undeniably, changes within therapeutic approaches addressing psyche and its ills within individuals and collective are certainly warranted and necessary. Further, Hillman's central critique of status quo psychotherapeutic attitudes and procedures is essential: psyche is not limited within one's skin but exists throughout the world in all experience, including but not limited to our narrow sense of an embodied self (Hillman and Ventura, 1992, p. 3).

This recognition and a concomitant resolve to related action are vital in any depth process of healing collective psyche and the tormented world that suffers through abuse and neglect within and around ourselves. Symbolically amplified local and global environments of the Self exist personally and collectively. They extend in conceptually distinct but practically interwoven systems or fields of mutual health and mutual dis-eases, psychologically, politically, educationally, economically, and ecologically. If the approaches are not mutually supportive and consistent in demonstrating integrity as concerns a practice of wholeness in the context of all 'other' disciplines, then ethical integrity is also wanting.

Space, time and tolerance thresholds permit only a cursory review of selective 'outer' crises confronting us. Each can be readily researched; many are already oppressively familiar to most of us. Beyond numbers are lives and deaths of countless beings.

American Museum of Natural History released a six-plus minute video, showing human population growth and migration upon a spinning Earth. Set to soothing music, text declares that over 200,000 years were required to reach a population of 1 billion, only 200 years to reach 7 billion. Less than a decade later, we are now at or near 8 billion. If the biological concept of 'carrying capacity' only kicks in once resources have been exhausted, we may not rest easy, despite experts' predictions of a leveling off of population sometime soon (American Museum of Natural History, 2016).

Elizabeth Kolbert, chronicling modern climate change and extinction, notes that during the past 50 years the planet's human population has doubled. She cites Robert Watson, chairman, United Nations-backed Intergovernmental Science-Policy Platform on Biodiversity and Ecosystem Services, 'What's at stake here is a liveable world.' Summarizing findings, upwards of a million species are likely to become extinct, many within decades. The 300 plus member panel list habitat destruction and overfishing as principle causes of decline in biodiversity. Climate change itself, however, is increasingly seen as a 'direct driver,' exacerbating impacts of other 'drivers,' and its effects are accelerating. Essential pollinators like native bees but also bats and birds are in decline in many regions, despite three-quarters of all food crops and nine-tenths of all flowering plants requiring pollination. One probable culprit is growing use of synthetic pesticides which don't discriminate between useful and unwanted insects. Shockingly, the very chemicals designed to thwart crop failures may pose one of the greatest dangers in creating them. Watson wrote that 'we cannot solve the threats of human-induced climate change and loss of biodiversity in isolation. We either solve both or we solve neither' (Kolbert, 2019, pp. 23–24).

Encroaching global desertification and chronic flooding can be traced to global climate change, due greatly to human activity, especially fossil fuel consumption. Many other mass effects result, including ocean acidification, catastrophic extinctions, ensuing conflict and suffering around the globe (Kolbert, 2014, pp. 101, 113–114, 123–124). Often liminal hostages of climate catastrophes, 2018 saw the forced migration of over 70 million people, doubling over the last 20 years, according to the UN Refugee Agency (UNHCR, 2019).

Fossil fuels provide nearly 80% of global energy used by humans, similar to mid-1980s proportionally. Because energy use has nearly doubled, amounts of coal, oil, and natural gas burned now have almost doubled. Cars, planes, refineries, and power plants currently produce about 36 billion tons of CO_2 annually worldwide (10- Kolbert, 2017, p. 64).

Estimated economic cost of our addiction to status quo resource consumption is about $4.3 trillion per year. In 2015, pollution alone caused the deaths of roughly 9 million people, a number 15 times greater than the number of those dying through all violence worldwide, indeed, more than those succumbing to AIDS, malaria, and tuberculosis combined. Over 90% of pollution-caused deaths occurred in low- and middle-income countries, with India atop the list of polluting countries, where around 2.5 million people died from pollution-linked diseases in 2015, about a quarter of all deaths in India that year. One encouraging statistic that bears replication elsewhere is that since 1970, every dollar spent on curbing pollution has returned about $30 to the US economy (Lancet, 2015).

Plastic pollution is found in more than 60% of all seabirds and in 100% of sea turtle species, mistaking plastic for food. Every year, 8 million metric tons of plastics enter our ocean on top of estimated 150 million metric tons presently circulating the planet's marine environments (Ocean Conservancy, 2017).

In 2016, approximately 40.3 million people, including 10 million children, were victims of modern slavery worldwide. Among them, 24.9 million people across the world were trapped in forced labor, 15.4 million girls were in forced marriage. In terms of forced marriages, included for the first time in worldwide statistics, money and debt were deemed to be principal causes of exploitation (Kelly, 2017).

Deep Trauma of collective psyche will not heal without a global 'truth and reconciliation' process, akin to Nelson Mandela's process of rehabilitation in South Africa. Only an authentic, resolute trans-disciplinary attitude and approach to chronic suffering will permit global healing, health and wholeness. Restitution of integrity is the goal of our species, and, like the resolution to confront a one-sided view of Psyche, this goal was envisioned if not fulfilled long before us today. However simplistic or obvious the observation, we exist within but one world, an interdependent and ultimately coherent whole, however incoherent human attitudes and behaviors might be within and toward this global reality. Historical precursors proffer deep roots and profound sources of inspiration in our contemporary individual as well as our collective quest for meaning and direction as a whole, psychologically, spiritually, educationally, economically, ecologically.

We do not need to reinvent the wheel, but our responsibility and obligation may be in further imagining cycles of life more spherically. Psyche is, was, and will ever be multi-dimensionally present. An attitude and consequent behavior as a species in accordance with such an awesome reality might give us pause, as well as greater purpose, for the continuing encounter we are privileged to have with life. The goal is not merely adaptive survival but an environment of thriving. Not only re-evaluation of one-sided values of profit and loss is required. Only restored relationships of humility, limits, respect, and responsibility toward Psyche's responses within and beyond ourselves can redress disease spiritually and environmentally. Our own further evolution and that of countless other species upon the planet, providing time and opportunity allow such opportunity, rests upon a fundamental re-orientation of contemporary attitudes and behavior in the world.

Inner and outer environments are inextricably linked, but variably interwoven. Recognition, and more crucially integration and embodiment, of this insight will result in profound implications for the planet, our own and other species, in turn. It is not fatuous or extravagant to posit that life grounded in meaningful values of social and environmental integrity would result in fewer wars, less crime, superior mental and physical health, and greater well-being overall. Have we not imagination and will to co-create such a world?

Analytical Psychology can offer valuable insights and mirroring to developing collective awareness, precisely in so far as we offer perspectives into depths of the unconscious on both individual and collective levels. The shadow of the tribe is no less potentially destructive to culture as a whole than are personal and collective shadow to the individual personality. While most species engage in hierarchies within their own kind, even as we do, 'modern' human beings abstract ourselves beyond all other species. This fundamental delusion of inherent separation, superiority, and immunity is dangerous, destructive, and ethically indefensible, as environmental symptoms bear witness throughout the world.

Drawing from the deep well of Psyche, Analytical Psychology can offer a taste of the water of life. A restoration of emotion and differentiated feeling values, as well as the necessity of bridging the irrational and rational aspects of self, are vital for an arid, parched collective consciousness. But to do so, obviously the discipline must also recognize our own shadow of biases, pretensions, defenses, power drives, inevitable ignorance, and limits.

Collective individuation

'Collective individuation' is an oxymoron I had once presumed to be my own invention. Jung coined the term in addressing Erich Neumann's summary of a manuscript, encouraging Neumann to expand his reflections on Jacob and Esau. Jung wrote:

> Jacob is the quintessence of the Jew and therefore a symbolic attempt at a collective individuation, or rather at individuation on a collective level [....] a symbolic exponent of folk psychology.
>
> (Neumann, pp. xx–xxi)

Here, I am adopting and amplifying the conceptual gem into a more general sense of humanity's purpose and ultimate goal—our telos. Our own species' mission is to differentiate processes and stages which serve—from those which undermine— the uncertain and precarious evolution of 'collective individuation,' and to live accordingly. However improbable or conceptually contradictory the notion of an individuating collective may seem, just such an evolution of consciousness on a species-wide level may be not only desirable but also essential, existentially speaking.

Discrete issues of species extinction, abuses, trauma, gender, race, capitalism, slavery, pollution, mental illness, and other environment of the Self abound. Each merits discrete attention. However, we must cultivate and strengthen awareness of an encompassing, shockingly unconscious, speciocentricity, i.e., the collective narcissism of humankind that threatens homeostasis on Earth altogether. While mutual activism reinforces holistic consciousness and transformation, the adage that 'a house divided against itself must fall' should alert us to the dangers of power complexes within competing activisms whose demands for exclusive interest of the part risk undermining, even collapsing, the whole.

Pernicious disinformation specializes in splitting manipulations, pitting people against each other, weakening the fabric of the whole; factional what-aboutisms can negate concerted action altogether. Richard Stengel's *Information Wars: How We Lost the Global Battle Against Disinformation & What We Can Do About It* illustrates governmental strategies of abusive emotional, tribal exploitation to corrode democracy, and further interests of totalitarianism (Stengel, 2019). As stated, manipulated or not, even authentic, fervent champions of one cause over all others can prove injurious to the whole, if a narrow prejudice of particularism evinces contempt toward all others while demanding respect and sovereign status for itself. Nonetheless, the forest we would save is indeed made up of individual trees, and we must beware of proto-fascist bulwarks which would silence the unique voice challenging systemic abuses and wrongdoing of policies and governments designed to defend the whole. Testimonials to the personal courage, as well as to personal threats and costs, involved in such courageous undertakings are revealed in Tom Mueller's Crisis of Conscience: Whistleblowing in an Age of Fraud (Mueller, 2019).

Relationships between humans, as well as relationships between us and the world, are infinitely complex and multi-faceted, with dissonances and resonances wherever we look. The 'cognitive dissonance' that we consider ourselves good and caring beings, even as our actions collectively endanger many environments of the planet and Self altogether is only one example confronting us individually and collectively. Thus, in terms of activist enterprises, since complexes can render each of us relatively thin-skinned and bone-headed, vulnerable and retributive, the challenge before us inevitably, painfully, and perpetually, calls our own wounds and shadowy narcissism into question, even as we address what we might consider ignorance and arrogance of our kind. Collective individuation, then, must occur in individuals and groups before manifesting globally.

As Marie-Louise von Franz stressed:

> [U]ltimately the Self ... orders and regulates one's human relationships, so long as the conscious ego takes the trouble to detect...delusive projections and deals with these inside himself instead of outside. ...[I]n this way...spiritually attuned and similarly oriented people...create a group that cuts across all the usual social and organizational affiliations....The consciously realized process of individuation thus changes a person's relationships....[F]amiliar bonds such as kinship or common interests are replaced by a different type of unity—a bond through the Self.
>
> (von Franz, 1964, p. 221)

Such an admonition clearly is warranted and hardly to be taken for granted for champions of any cause. Purposeful existence and meaningful engagement with challenges threatening both ourselves and so much of the living planet can only be addressed if we envision and enact as an evolving collective; this requires personal evolution, personal individuation — the psychic hygiene of shadow assimilation. Again, personal individuation and collective individuation are interlinked, interdependent.

Along with modest hope and grand aspirations for a 'consciously realized process of individuation' among humankind, differentiating and thereby changing collective relationships and behavior, von Franz warns against believing that,

> [...] there will not be collisions of opinion and conflicting obligations, or disagreements about the 'right' way, in the face of which one must constantly withdraw and listen to one's inner voice in order to find the individual standpoint that the Self intends one to have.
>
> (von Franz, 1964, p. 223)

We cannot expect universal concord or unanimity, even if we must wary of mutual competition and contempt.

Jung wrote of the essential link of heart and mind for well-being, as well as the pathological, pathogenic splitting that occurs when they are divorced from each other:

Ideas are not just counters used by the calculating mind; they are also golden vessels full of living feeling. 'Freedom' is not a mere abstraction, it is also an emotion. Reason becomes unreason when separated from the heart, and a psychic life void of universal ideas sickens from undernourishment (Jung, 1950, p. 310).

Mythologist Joseph Campbell prophesied, 'The only myth that is going to be worth thinking about in the immediate future is one that is talking about the planet...the planet, and everybody on it' (Campbell, 1988, p. 41). Thirty years later, that immediate future is now!

As Chief Sealth (Chief Seattle), a 'First Nations' representative, warned:

> Whatever befalls the earth, befalls the sons of the earth. Man does not weave the web of life, he is merely a strand in it. Whatever he does to the web, he does to himself.'
>
> (Macy, 1998, p. 200)

Indeed, whatever befalls the earth and the sons of the earth befalls equally the daughters of the earth; we are all implicated, none is immune, and none is superior to another. Thankfully, daughters and sons alike are indeed calling out to careless elders across the planet.

A Sufi teaching tale provides a metaphor of our common plight with the Earth, while underscoring failings of a despotic, unrelated extraverted thinking-sensate orientation divorced from the values of feeling and holistic appreciations of intuition regarding the ultimate significance and nature of the matter in question:

An ancient and valuable fragile Chinese vase had been found by the villagers. There was an argument in the teahouse as to its exact capacity.

During the wrangling, the Mulla entered. The people appealed to him for a ruling.

'Simple,' said Nasrudin. 'Bring the vase here, together with some sand.'

He had the vase filled with layer after layer of fine sand, packing it down with a mallet. Ultimately it burst.

'There you are,' —he turned to the company triumphantly— 'the maximum capacity has been reached. All you have to do now is to remove one grain of sand, and you will have the precise amount needed to fill a container like this' (Shah, 1971, p. 184).

Having previously addressed challenges of the biological term of carrying capacity with population limits linked to resource depletion, we must likewise be mindful of our own limited psychological capacity to carry awareness with insufficient rest and resources of heart and mind. Merely enumerating, let alone tending to our many ills, can be overwhelming and exhausting. Reflective activism, in distinction to reactive activism, will help to nurture and heal rather than squander our efforts, squabbling among ourselves as to the pre-eminent issue or outrage of the day. Let's bear in mind Jung's admonition: 'insights do not come... easily; they are gained only through the severest shocks' (Jung, 1954b, p. 195).

Jung's observations for individuals apply to the collective and global illnesses of our times. In addressing psychic disturbances, he noted the:

> teleological aspect of fitness in biology, which in the psychic realm would have to be formulated as meaning. In psychic disturbances....
> [(t])he general rule is that the more negative the conscious attitude is, and the more it resists, devalues, and is afraid, the more repulsive, aggressive, and frightening is the face which the dissociated content assumes.
>
> (Jung, 1967, p. 342)

However, as Jung writes, 'Every form of communication with the split-off part of the psyche is therapeutically effective' (Jung, 1967, p. 335). May we take heart, therefore, in encountering and confronting troubling, dissociated contents in our global culture, however frightening they are in fact. In relation to current 'presenting issues' for global analysis, the trials, tribulations and existential threat presented in our time actually represent a critical initiation into meaning, heart and integrity in and of all functions and senses, without which we may not have gained either right or wisdom to survive. Jung noted:

> The totality images which the unconscious produces in the course of an individuation process are similar 'reformations' of an a priori archetype (the mandala). [(T])he spontaneous symbols of the self, or of wholeness, cannot in practice be distinguished from a God-image. Despite the word... ('be transformed') in the Greek..., the 'renewal' of the mind is not meant as an actual alteration of consciousness, but rather as the restoration of an original condition, an apocatastasis. This is in exact agreement with the empirical findings of psychology, that...there is an ever-present archetype of wholeness which may easily disappear from the purview of consciousness or may never be perceived at all until a consciousness illuminated by conversion recognizes it....[(and]) the original state of oneness with the God-image is restored. It brings about an integration, a bridging of the split in the personality caused by...instincts striving apart in different and mutually contradictory directions. The only time the split does not occur is when a person is still as legitimately unconscious of his instinctual life as an animal. But it proves harmful and impossible to endure when an artificial unconsciousness—a repression—no longer reflects the life of the instincts.
>
> (Jung, 1959b, p. 40)

Our 'artificial unconsciousness,' including the artifice of willful ignorance, belies an artificial consciousness, bereft of solid ground, integrity and an ethic of belonging. As we hurtle now headlong into Artificial Intelligence, our common ground as human beings —and our common psychological language— must be rooted in a biocentric orientation, a wholistic attitude of interwoven relationships as one species, sharing a common lineage, however differentiated and unique our individual cultures have become. Individually and culturally, we can be equal in worth, dignity, and integrity, even if we are different in material and psychological ways. Unless we cultivate both common ground and mutual respect in our attitudes and behavior, our split from integrity will prove our undoing.

The 70th Gospel of Thomas, resonates with Jung's conception of the ambivalent Self, addressing a fundamental relationship and responsibility toward the telos of self-actualization with individual and collective implications: "'When you bring forth what is in you, what you have will save you. If you do not have that in you, what you do not have in you will kill you'" (Gathercole, 2014, p. 475).

Do we lack potential creative forces and shadow confrontation needed toward a dynamically sustainable, thriving, world? How have these been thwarted, suppressed, or perverted, turning demonic and destructive due to misunderstanding, indolence, denial, or short-sighted exploitation of egocentric will? Can we hold and transform destructive dissonance through a process of humility and imaginal growth in consciousness? Not imagining, not doing, and not being so leads to both ecocide and, as David Wallace-Wells documents in *The Uninhabitable Earth; Life After Warming*, to suicide, perhaps collectively but certainly individually. Remembering earlier considerations of informational carrying capacity and psychic hygiene, Post Carbon Institute's Richard Heinberg depiction of a colleague's suicide reverberate: 'I sometimes call it toxic knowledge….Once you know about overpopulation, overshoot, depletion, climate change, and the dynamics of societal collapse, you can't unknow it, and your every subsequent thought is tinted' (Wallace-Wells, 2019, p. 207).

Fortunately, Jung repeatedly made the case for a healing archetypal predisposition, amplifying cross-cultural history of redemption motifs, Christian and otherwise. The telos, or goal, of a restoration of wholeness can be seen throughout the ages in different myths, as well as in the individuation process, the meaningful myth of Analytical Psychology, which is the great work of individuals as well as of humanity as a whole. Our quest is in rediscovering, recovering, that myth of wholeness today. As Jung wrote, 'Life is teleology par excellence; it is the intrinsic striving towards a goal, and the living organism is a system of directed aims which seek to fulfill themselves' (Jung, 1960, p. 406).

Jung's researches demonstrate this goal in hero-myths of rebirth, offering restitution of what had been lost, an apocatastasis (Jung, 1954, p. 245). The process manifests in myths of Holy Ghost and the 'Father,' analogously in physics with proton and electron formation of positive and negative charges promoted by primordial energy (Jung, 1958, p. 187); of Epimetheus, Prometheus, and Messias (Jung, 1971, p. 271); of Christ and the phoenix (Jung, 1963, p. 336); and of Demeter and Kore, whose relationship transcended finite time of existence with immortality, and about whom Jung noted:

> Demeter and Kore, mother and daughter, extend...feminine conscious both upwards and downwards. They add an 'older and younger,' 'stronger and weaker' dimension to it and widen out the narrowly limited conscious mind bound in space and time, giving it intimations of a greater and more comprehensive personality which has a share in the eternal course of things....The individual's life is elevated into a type, indeed it becomes the archetype of woman's fate in general. This leads to a restoration or apocatastasis of the lives of her ancestors, who now, through the bridge of the momentary individual, pass down into the generations of the future. An experience of this kind gives the individual a place and a meaning in the life of the generations, so that all unnecessary obstacles are cleared out of the way of the life-stream that is to flow through her. At the same time the individual is rescued from her isolation and restored to wholeness. All ritual prescription with archetypes ultimately has this aim and this result.
>
> (Jung, 1959a, p. 188)

The theme manifests in the Gnostic archetype of Anthropos, which we may hope and help to preside prudently over our epoch in the Anthropocene, a term coined and published by frustrated Dutch chemist and Nobel laureate winner, Paul Crutzen, in 2002 (Kolbert, 2014, pp. 107–108). Jung wrote:

> Because the microcosm is identical with the macrocosm, it attracts the latter and thus brings about a kind of apocatastasis, a restoration of all individuals to the original wholeness. Thus 'every grain becomes wheat, and all metal gold,' as Meister Eckhart says; and the little, single individual becomes the 'great man,' the homo maximus or Anthropos, i.e., the self. The moral equivalent of the physical transmutation into gold is self-knowledge, which is a re-remembering of the homo totus.
>
> (Jung, 1967, pp. 284–285)

Jung makes it clear that for individuation to occur with our participation, consciousness must confront the unconscious, an action that is not possible through logic but that is dependent upon symbols which make the irrational union of opposites possible, leading to the realization of the self or whole human being (Jung, 1958, p. 468).

Elsewhere, Jung elaborates:

> Now, all these myth-pictures represent a drama of the human psyche
> on the further side of consciousness, showing man as both the one to
> be redeemed and the redeemer. The first formulation is Christian, the
> second alchemical. In the first case man attributes the need of redemp-
> tion to himself and leaves the work of redemption, the actual...opus, to
> the autonomous divine figure; in the latter case man takes upon himself
> the duty of carrying out the redeeming opus, and attributes the state of
> suffering and consequent need of redemption to the anima mundi im-
> prisoned in matter. In both cases redemption is a work.
>
> (Jung, 1953, p. 306)

While none dare be so bold as to assume that (s)he might force a redemption
to take place, an attitude of humility is to be remembered, by even the most
devout of Christians who, as a part of God's world, can hardly be content
with the laissez-faire attitude or passive role regarding a multitude of crises
of human rather than divine cause. In both cases, work is implied, and there
are no free rides to spiritual oneness or psychological health. Responsibility
is a prerequisite in relation to any redemptive process which is, sooner or
later but in the main, a struggle of life and death... for rebirth.

The apocatastasis is now and ever-present. The archetypal potential for
restoration, renewal, and redemption individually, collectively, and globally
is not owned or controlled by creed, nation-state, corporation or religious
order. Jung elaborates:

> The old master saw the alchemical opus as a kind of apocatastasis, the
> restoring of an initial state in an 'eschatalogical' one ('the end looks to the
> beginning, and contrariwise'). This is exactly what happens in the individ-
> uation process, whether it take the form of a Christian transformation ('Ex-
> cept ye become as little children'), or a satori experience in Zen ('show me
> your original face'), or a psychological process of development in which the
> original propensity to wholeness becomes a conscious happening.
>
> (Jung, 1959, p. 169)

For Jung, and for the purpose of our gambit against despair, it is useful to
keep in mind the changeable nature of the self, mirroring humankind's own
experience,

> for the self is not just a static quantity or constant form, but is also a
> dynamic process. In the same way, the ancients saw the imago Dei in
> man not as a mere imprint, as a sort of lifeless, stereotyped impression,
> but as an active force.'
>
> (Jung, 1959b, p. 260)

Likewise, in providing a central myth that unites aspects of both right-wing conservative nostalgia for some inkling of 'good old days' which actually may never have existed except in potential, as well as left-wing progressivism of universal rights and environmental restoration without sanctimony, the 'psychopompic' value of the apocatastasis archetype is apparent. It does not force people into a transformation that is foreign to their nature but promises restoration of what was lost—or remains latent, potential, yet undeveloped (i.e., 'in the shadow')—within relationship to one's own being. Adolescent, activist, and psychopomp, Greta Thunberg, evokes something of this 'original face,' profound, simple, straightforward, without guile, speaking truth to power, while summoning the whole of humanity to empowerment.

And where is psyche?

Given Jung's citation regarding self and psyche at the beginning of this chapter, along with Hillman's challenge against reductive 'inner-only' psychology, where in the world is psyche? Rather where is 'psyche in the world' today? If the world is psyche, and psyche is everywhere in the world, what can we say of the environments of psyche, except that only a myth imagined and modeled as a fundamental unity of the world embracing all differentiation can best offer such a conversion for survival and thriving? A thriving humankind will hinge less upon insights and incidence of singular genius than upon a coherent worldview, with corresponding governance, economic, ecological, and educational systems in mutual relationship. Such a relationship is at once with ourselves, each other, the planet, as well as with the deep Self, Psyche ever-evolving within and through us and the all.

Human population and concomitant anthropogenic threats are overwhelmingly 'to scale' in the world. Our challenge now is in manifesting ourselves and our impact to scale in ways ever more consciously, conscientiously, politically, and with increasing psychological differentiation as a species and collective. Analytical Psychology can help to us to mature as a species, navigating between the Scylla of myopic, one-sided rationality, at one extreme, and at the other extreme the Charybdis an all-consuming whirlpool of irrationality; between these destructive extremes, the entire spectrum of the trans-rational nature of the Self beckons us to further development and exploration.

Indeed, Analytical Psychology bears tremendous responsibility and potential to give expression to the spirit of time within the unconscious, pushing to be born in our age and our species. Jung encourages such optimism in the face of surrounding obstacles such as complacency and apathy, as well as deliberate opposition from status quo interests of exploitation, declaring:

> Nor is the striving for self-knowledge altogether without prospects of success, since there exists a factor which, though completely disregarded,

meets our expectations halfway. This is the unconscious Zeitgeist. It compensates the attitude of the conscious mind and anticipates changes to come.

(Jung, 1964, p. 303)

Encouragingly illustrative of such success, a current exhibition exemplifies this propitious attitude for collective challenges. Smithsonian National Museum of Natural History in Washington, D.C. now hosts an exhibit called 'Deep Time,' redolent with meaning and symbolically resonant with the Hydra-headed crises confronting us globally. Conceived by Siobhan Starrs, the exhibition was chaired by a woman for the first time in Smithsonian Museum's history, and contains texts written entirely by women as well, extending the conscious determination of the institution to reflect an orientation other than traditional male-dominated dissemination of cultural and factual relevance with regard to our species.

Philanthropically underwriting $110,000,000 renovation of Smithsonian and the exhibition, was one of the Koch brothers, infamously conservative pharaohs of fossil fuel extraction who likewise fund climate change denial through pseudo scientific obfuscation around CO_2's role in global warming. Here, however, the late David C. Koch exercised no influence on exhibit content or vision. Whether ironic anomaly or marking a sea change, the exhibit courageously speaks truth to power, addressing climate change and the very anthropogenic nature of our current environmental crises which the status quo supporting funder officially disputed and denied while alive (PBS Newshour, May 31, 2019).

This exhibition combines elements essential to meaningful contributions of Analytical Psychology in future. The depth of conception illustrated in encompassing deep time, as well as the role of environment and economic considerations within the contemporary fossil fuel age framed in an educational setting serves as a psychopomp and mentoring example to our own discipline of the analytical psychology of the Deep Self.

There are other reasons to hope, believe, do and be: paradigmatic syntheses of education, ecology, and economics are exemplified in pragmatic steps toward a union of theory and practice worldwide. Reforestation 'at scale' is occurring, despite discouraging news from the rainforest in Bolsanaro's Brazil. In 2016, 50 million seedlings were planted in India, and in 2019 Ethiopia bested the count with nearly 350 million tree seedlings planted, each within a day. Competition can serve the whole, when instinctive drives channel collective rather than individual welfare alone, manifesting a threshold of transformation (BBC News, London, July 29, 2019).

According to Science magazine, massive global tree restoration could cut the atmospheric carbon pool by a quarter, mitigating climate change as societies wean from fossil fuels, without disrupting agriculture or encroaching on urban areas (Bastin et al., 2019, pp. 76–79).

While not all are equal in quality or effect, numerous programs exist to mitigate the carbon footprint of air travel. Planting trees globally, one organization with proven carbon offset credentials is: myclimate.org. (Foundation myclimate, 2019).

Further demonstrating that at least some humans have and do bring forth that within which creatively and spiritually can save, confronting and transforming shadow of collective destructivity into mutually supportive environments and educational opportunities, massive volunteer efforts in Mumbai cleaned polluted beaches over a three-year period. Sea turtles, absent 20 years, again nested in 2018, and hatchlings made their way to sea, restoring the cycle of millennia (smithsonian.com, March 29, 2018).

As daunting a prospect as it seems, and indeed truly is, our collective situation mirrors individuals coming into depth process work only after all else fail. Crises are at, even beyond, 'scale.' Both personal and collective ego, feeling defeated, bereft, and alone must then finally yield to Self as source and primal psychopomp of restoration.

Jung's prescience anticipated and enhances ecological movements, seeing individuation, as rooted within nature as a whole, amplifying and grounding our purpose and development within the resonant context of environments of the Self on multiple dimensions. Here, we must assume our own responsibility in the manifold and mutual relationship, owning the challenges confronting us from within and without:

> The self does not become conscious by itself, but has always been taught, if at all, through a tradition of knowing....[I]t stands for the essence of individuation, and individuation is impossible without a relationship to one's environment...
>
> (Jung, 1978, p. 167)

This is the primordial and pre-eminent truth we must integrate. Consequent reflective attitudes and activism must follow needs on collective as at individual levels. Through an ever differentiating practice of acceptance of limits and responsibility of effects in equal measure, we may begin to express and experience an eventual reconciliation, potential redemption, and dynamic healing and wholeness with the anima mundi. The soul of the world depends upon it, as does much of life and ourselves, breathing, vital, yet hardly assured participants of the world soul ultimately, despite presumptions of pre-eminence and self-absorbed preoccupation atop a self-styled pyramid of sentience on the planet.

Only then— only now, on the brink of annihilation even— might we survive painful crises of coming to consciousness, living in reciprocity and respect with the unconscious and the whole of life, healing and becoming whole ourselves. Only then, only now, may we learn to realize the potential of thriving through arduous initiations of collective individuation toward greater integrity in being more fully human as human beings in the world.

References

American Museum of Natural History. (2016). "Human Population through Time," YouTube video published and released. November 4.

Bastin, J.F., et. al. (2019) "The Global Tree Restoration Potential." *Science*. Vol. 365, no. 6448, pp. 76–79.

BBC News. (2019). "Ethiopia 'Breaks' Tree-planting Record to Tackle Climate Change," London, July 29.

Campbell, J. (1988). *The Power of Myth*. New York, NY: B. S. Flowers, Ed., Doubleday.

Foundation myclimate, (myclimate.org). (2019). Zürich, Switzerland.

Gathercole, S. (2014). *The Gospel of Thomas: Introduction and Commentary*. London and Boston: Brill.

Geddes, P. (1915). *Cities in Evolution: An Introduction to the Town Planning Movement & to the Study of Civics*. London: Williams & Norgate Publishers.

Hillman, J., and Ventura, M. (1992). *We've Had a Hundred Years of Psychotherapy--And the World's Getting Worse*. San Francisco, CA: Harper.

Jung, C.G. (1950). *The Symbolic Life Development of Personality*. Collected Works, Vol. 18. Bollingen Series XX. (translated by R.F.C. Hull). Princeton, NJ: Princeton University Press.

Jung, C.G. (1953). *Psychology and Alchemy*. Collected Works, Vol. 12. Bollingen Series XX. (translated by R.F.C. Hull). Princeton, NJ: Princeton University Press.

Jung, C.G. (1954a). *The Practice of Psychotherapy*. Collected Works, Vol. 16. Bollingen Series XX (translated by R.F.C. Hull). Princeton, NJ: Princeton University Press.

Jung, C.G. (1954b). *The Development of Personality*. Collected Works, Vol. 17. Bollingen Series XX (translated by R.F.C. Hull). Princeton, NJ: Princeton University Press.

Jung, C.G. (1958). Psychology and Religion: West and East. Collected Works, Vol. 11. Collected Works of C.G. Jung Series (translated by R.F.C. Hull). Routledge, NY: Routledge & Kegan Paul LTD.

Jung, C.G. (1959a). *The Archetypes and the Collective Unconscious*. Collected Works, Vol. 9i. Bollingen Series XX (translated by R.F.C. Hull). Princeton, NJ: Princeton University Press.

Jung, C.G. (1959b). *Aion*. Collected Works, Vol. 9ii. Bollingen Series XX (translated by R.F.C. Hull). Princeton, NJ: Princeton University Press.

Jung, C.G. (1960). *The Structure and Dynamics of the Psyche*. Collected Works, Vol. 8: Bollingen Series XX (translated by R.F.C. Hull), Princeton, NJ: Princeton University Press.

Jung, C.G. (1963). *Mysterium Coniunctionis*. Collected Works, Vol. 14. Bollingen Series XX (translated by R.F.C. Hull). Princeton, NJ: Princeton University Press.

Jung, C.G. (1964). *Civilization in Transition*. Collected Works, Vol. 10. Bollingen Series XX (translated by R.F.C. Hull). Princeton, NJ: Princeton University Press.

Jung, C.G. (1967). *Alchemical Studies*. Vol. 13. Bollingen Series XX (translated by R.F.C. Hull). Princeton, NJ: Princeton University Press.

Jung, C.G. (1971). *Psychological Types*. Collected Works, Vol. 6. Bollingen Series XX (translated by R.F.C. Hull). Princeton, NJ: Princeton University Press.

Kelly, A. (2017). *The Guardian*. London: September 19.

Kolbert, E. (2019). "Climate Change and the New Age of Extinction." *The New Yorker.* Vol. XCV, No. 13, May 20.

Lancet Commission on Pollution & Health. (2015). Global Alliance on Health and Pollution, New York, NY.

Macy, J. (1998). *Coming Back to Life: Practices to Reconnect Our Lives, Our World.* Philadelphia, PA: Molly Young Brown, New Society Publishers.

Mueller, T. (2019). *Crisis of Conscience: Whistleblowing in an Age of Fraud.* New York, NY: Riverhead Books.

Neumann, E. (2019). *Jacob & Esau: On the Collective Symbolism of the Brother Motif.* Edited and foreword by Erel Shalit, translated by Mark Kyburz. Ashland, NC: Chiron Pub.

Ocean Conservancy. (2017). Washington, DC.

PBS Newshour. (May 31, 2019). "Show at Smithsonian's Renovated Hall of Fossils: Dinosaurs Are Just the Beginning." https://www.pbs.org/newshour/show/at-smithsonians-renovated-hall-of-fossils-dinosaurs-are-just-the-beginning.

Shabecoff, P. (2003). *A Green Fire: The American Environmental Movement.* Washington, DC: Island Press.

Shah, I. (1971). *The Pleasantries of the Incredible Mulla Nasrudin.* New York: E.P Dutton & Co., Inc.

smithsonianmag.com, Smithsonian Institute, Washington, DC, March 29, 2018.

Stengel, R. (2019). *Information Wars: How We Lost the Global Battle Against Disinformation & What We Can Do About It.* New York, NY: Atlantic Monthly Press.

The UN Refugee Agency, United Nations High Commissioner for Refugees, Geneva, Switzerland. (2019): www.unhcr.org.

Von Franz, M.L., Jung, C.G. et al. (1964). *Man & His Symbols.* New York, NY: Doubleday & Co.

Wallace-Wells, D. (2019). *The Uninhabitable Earth; Life After Warming.* New York, NY: Tim Duggan Books.

Chapter 10

The Japanese psyche reflected in the suppression and transformation of "Hidden Christians" in feudal Japan

Yasuhiro Tanaka

Muromachi period in Japanese history

Katsuro Hara, an outstanding historian of the late 19th century in Japan, described the Muromachi period (1336–1573) as "Japan's Renaissance." We may say that, having broken away from the formerly strong influence of Chinese culture, Japan-specific culture was first firmly established in the Heian period (794–1185), in a manner that was well expressed as "Japanese spirit imbued with Chinese learning (和魂漢才)," but subsequently dissipated by the *samurai* (warrior) culture of the Kamakura period (1185–1333). After this suspended animation, it was revived and achieved fruition in more sophisticated forms in the Muromachi period, in which we can find individuals who were recognized as "great masters" in many cultural fields, such as Zeami (世阿弥) in *sarugaku* (猿楽; one of the original forms of noh), Sesshu (雪舟) in landscape painting, Ikkyu (一休) in Zen Buddhism, and Isho (惟肖) in poetry.

Together with this cultural flowering, political collapse had surely progressed; the administrative power of the Ashikaga shogunate (*bakufu*) had gradually weakened. We might say that successive Ashikaga *shoguns* had become not leaders of warriors but rather just excellent and representative men of culture in Kyoto where the shogunate was based; a typical example is Yoshimasa Ashikaga (1436–1490), the 8th shogun, who built Ginkaku-ji Temple in Higashiyama. During the rule of Yoshimasa in this manner (1449–1473), the Onin War (1467–1477) finally broke out due to the struggle for succession in the family of one of the strongest provincial governors (*shugo*), in which the capital burned during over a decade of urban warfare.

Through this vicious war, Kyoto was shuttered and scorched and the shogunate emerged mortally wounded, but still managed to limp along ineffectually for over a century; no effective central government existed.

The first encounter between Europe and Japan

Consequently, the trend of *gekokujo* (下克上; an inverted social order when the lowly reigned over the elite) proliferated nationwide, driving Japan to its *Sengoku* Period (Period of Warring States).

It is said that in 1543 a Chinese ship carrying Portuguese passengers was caught in a storm and drifted to the island of Tanegashima, located in the southern part of Japan. They were the first Europeans to land in Japan. Guns were also first introduced to Japan at that time. The warring lords, of course, were strongly interested in these weapons which became known as "Tanegashima" and soon started to be manufactured in Sakai, the largest commercial city, and other places; firearms proliferated rapidly and fundamentally changed the tactics in war.

In 1549, that is, six years after the arrival of guns in Tanegashima, Christianity was introduced into Japan by missionaries' visits to Japan. The first missionary was Portuguese, Francisco de Xavier (1506–1552), one of the founding members of the Society of Jesus.

At that time, Europe had already entered the age of discovery leading eventually to the age of colonialism. As is well known, Spain and Portugal led this thrust, based on their agreed "demarcation." Christian societies including the Society of Jesus took on an important role not only in proselytizing but also in diplomacy and trade.

Francisco de Xavier had been in Japan for about two years, endeavoring to make converts first in some provinces in Kyushu, then in Suo Province. He moved to Kyoto in 1551, but his activities there were not successful due to the above-mentioned political instability and the presence of well-established Buddhist sects. One episode gave an example of his difficulties; although he felt at first that the people in Japan well accepted his preaching about "Deus," he noticed only one year after the commencement of his missionary work that his interpreter, Yajiro, had been translating "Deus" as *Mahavairocana* (大日; Great Sun).

After his departure from Japan, other Jesuits engaged in missionary work in Japan. In 1563, Luis Frois (1532–1597) also came to Japan as a Jesuit missionary. Since he had a talent for writing, he left a lot of documents relating to Japanese people, culture, and history. *The First European Description of Japan, 1585* was a collection of his early written documents relating to Japanese clothing and food, religious faith and practice, weapons and warfare, disease and medicine, writing and books, plays and dances, including descriptions of musical instruments. After this, he wrote a great work, *History of Japan (Historia de Iapam)* which started with the arrival of Francisco de Xavier in 1549 and ended with some descriptions from around 1593. This book includes many character sketches of the warring lords including

Nobunaga Oda and Hideyoshi Toyotomi, with whom he met and talked privately.

Luis Frois' descriptions of Japan seem largely objective, though we still find some exaggerations and over-generalization of particular instances. However, some of the Jesuit missionaries had discriminatory views on Japan and Japanese people[1]. For example, Lorenzo Messia and Francisco Cabral reported to their headquarters in Rome that the Christian faith of the Japanese was so superficial that ordination was totally impossible, Japanese people were in general arrogant, greedy, unprincipled, and conscienceless, and there was no trusting relationship even within their families because they believed that they should not open their mind to others, which was even a virtue for them.

These missionaries, like Messia and Cabral, neglected the cultural differences between Europe and Japan. However, at that time these kinds of prejudiced views on the citizens of countries that should be colonialized were widely held, even among missionaries, rather than being personal opinions. It was commonly considered that the West should enlighten and civilize them with its advanced culture because they were uncultivated and living in the darkest ignorance. However, such views were considered normal in this era, the 16th century. Just so. Therefore, I tend to think that it was not discrimination in the narrow sense, since they did not know Japan and Japanese people, just as we did not know European people and Christianity.

On the other hand, European colonial politics in Japan proved markedly different from those in South America. Spain and Portugal did not exercise armed force to bring Japan under their control, due to Japan's geographical and political conditions. The main policy was based on missionary-mediated trade and proselytization.

How was Christianity welcomed and suppressed in Japan?

Spain and Portugal allowed trade with Japan only by Christian missionaries. As described above, at that time, Japan entered its *Sengoku* Period (Period of Warring States), in which the warring lords wanted to enrich themselves and import necessary commodities including guns through trade with European countries (and indirectly with China). Thus, the warring lords had to communicate with the missionaries to commence and develop trade with these foreign countries. This is a pragmatic reason why Christianity was welcome to Japan; it spread quickly and widely together with the "Tanegashima" guns.

Moreover, during this long period of warring states, as Tetsuro Watsuji (1889–1960), one of the established Japanese philosophers, pointed out in his essay, "Buried Japan: Its ideological context around the arrival of Christianity," we can find many stories, such as "Reality of Kumano-gongen shrines" or "Origin of Itsukushima-jinja shrine," describing a "suffering God" or a "surviving God," in which feelings of people in general were well reflected at that time[2]. They had been exposed to the fires of war again and again; many warriors died in the battles continuously occurring in various regions. The whole of Japan was seeking "help" in this period. This is a social-emotional reason why Christianity was welcome to Japan.

As Hayao Kawai, the first Jungian analyst in Japan, pointed out, we can say from a certain viewpoint that the Period of Warring States was very fortunate timing for Christianity to be introduced into Japan in the sense that, since the trend of *gekokujo* entailed the destruction of the former social order, it was the age in which the Japanese could, or had to, become most self-assertive on the collective level. As Kawai said, "Japanese ego was most exalted… Japanese most asserted their own ego in the Period of Warring States," so this psychological trend could fit with the Western individualistic culture including Christianity, which could reasonably and scientifically explain how the world was arranged and constituted. This is a psychological reason why Christianity was welcome to Japan.

We call this era "the century of *Kirishitan* (Christianity)," which lasted from the arrival of Xavier in 1549 to the enforcement of the closed-door policy by the Tokugawa shogunate in 1639. As Shusaku Endo, a famous Catholic-Christian novelist in Japan, has commented, the age of *Kirishitan* was one in which Japan collided with the West most violently and for the first time in its history.

Of course, after the closed-door policy had been in place for 250 years, in the Meiji period, too, Japan collided with various aspects of Western culture, but we could describe this collision as adoption of things that were convenient for us with our very effective ingestion ability, or adapting some cultural aspects from the West into something comfortable for us, thereby skillfully avoiding things unfamiliar to our senses, as expressed in the phrase, "Japanese spirit imbued with Western learning (和魂洋才)" used to describe this period.

In that sense, we may say that, in the age of *Kirishitan*, Japanese were really "baptized" by Christianity, the most unfamiliar, distant, and one of the severest religions for them. On the other hand, due to the above-mentioned reasons, Christianity was accepted quickly and widely in Japan. A report written by a missionary in 1591 stated that there were already 30,000 Christians in the Kyushu region at that time. Another list from 1591, after the anti-Christian edict issued in 1587 by Hideyoshi Toyotomi, reported that there had been 217,500 Christian converts since Christianity's arrival in 1549, and another said that 240 churches had been built and 250,000 people had been baptized in the same period. Moreover, according to a report in 1603 when the Tokugawa shogunate was already established, there were 300,000 Christians, 190 churches, and 900 persons in charge of propagation of the faith.

In this way, the number of *Kirishitan* had increased *explosively* to "300,000" in Japan; although there are various theories about this, it is generally said that the total estimated population of Japan in around 1,600 would have been only 12,000,000 persons. However, this strong influence of Christianity made the rulers, Hideyoshi Toyotomi and Ieyasu Tokugawa, anxious and suspicious, because (1) they feared that they may lose control to the lords and the people due to their belief; (2) they suspected that Christianity may destroy something traditional and chthonic in Japan because there were many cases of *Kirishitans* with their religious leaders organizing subversive activities toward Buddhist temples and Shinto shrines in the provinces; (3) they expected that the European countries might eventually use military force to colonialize Japan after Christian propagation and education.

As shown in Figure 10.1, Christian propagation was tacitly permitted even after the Anti-Christian edict issued by Hideyoshi Toyotomi in 1587 and the establishment of the Tokugawa Shogunate in 1600. However, it was seriously suppress after the Anti-Christian edict was issued by Ieyasu Tokugawa in 1613. The regulations against *Kirishitans* were progressively strengthened after this, and Bureau for the Investigation of Religion was ultimately established in 1635.

During this period, many *Kirishitans* and missionaries were martyred and apostatized in Kyoto, Nagasaki, and Edo. The number of martyrs, who were allowed to die only after being put to various relentless tortures, was estimated to reach tens of thousands. The Shimabara Rebellion could be regarded as an insurrection against this through persecution, in which about 37,000 rebels died to hold the Shimabara Castle. After this rebellion, there were many raids (*Kuzure*) resulting in mass arrests of hidden Christians.

1549	Arrival of Xavier, introduction of Christianity	
		official approval of propagation
1587	Anti-Christian edict issued by Hideyoshi Toyotomi	
		tacit approval of propagation
1613	Anti-Christian edict issued by Ieyasu Tokugawa,	
	after which many Christians were martyred in Kyoto, Nagasaki, and Edo	
1635	Bureau for the Investigation of Religion was established	
1637	Shimabara Rebellion, after which there were many raids (*kuzure*),	persecution
	meaning mass arrests of hidden Christians	
1858	while maintaining the suppression policy, the shogunate permitted	
	churches for foreigners	recommencement of propagation
1865	Hidden Christians found by Father Petitjean	
1873	Removal of official bulletin board for anti-Christian edict	

Figure 10.1 Abbreviated chronological table of *Kirishitan* (Kawai, 2013).

In this way, the first violent collision with the West from the 16th to 17th century was not metaphorical but a true one involving a lot of bloodshed.

What kind of transformation occurred in "*Kakure Kirishitan* (Hidden Christians)" under the suppression policy?

The above-mentioned absolute suppression forced *Kirishitan* devotees to choose among the following three alternatives: (1) martyrdom, (2) apostatizing, and (3) pretending to apostatize. (2) and (3) were called "*Korobi* (conversion)," and the *Kakure Kirishitan* (Hidden Christians) are the descendants of the communities who maintained the Christian faith in Japan as an underground church during the time of persecution (3), which lasted from about 1614 until 1873, and who then chose not to be reconciled with the newly returned Catholic missionaries (Turnbull, 1998).

In this sense, as Kentaro Miyazaki (2001) pointed out,

> the *Kakure Kirishitan* today do not hide themselves and are not Christians any longer. Their faith is one of the typical ethnical religions which has been fermented in Japan's traditional climate of religion for a long time and thus completely merged into the religious life of chthonic people
>
> (p. 5)

Only a limited number of *Kakure Kirishitan* communities continue to exist in Nagasaki prefecture. The number of the believers is steadily decreasing due to the lack of successors following the aging and depopulation of these communities.

During the period of persecution, their ancestors became *Danka* (supporters) of some temples and trampled on a plate with a crucifix or another Christian symbol every year in order to prove themselves to be non-Christians. They had been totally separated from authentic Christian guides; there had been no Padre in Japan for about 250 years. Moreover, none of the *Kakure Kirishitan* communities ever communicated with each other because they were afraid of mass arrest (*Kuzure*).

Under such circumstances, each *Kakure Kirishitan* community developed its own religious customs including baptism, every day service, funeral rituals, annual events, and so on, in their own way. In general, it could be regarded as a syncretism and eclecticism between Christianity, Shinto, and Buddhism, which should be evaluated as "the typical ethnical religion" in Japan. Here I will just briefly explain as examples their Bible, "*Tenchi Hajimari no Koto* (The Beginnings of the World)," and their prayers, "*orasho* (oratio)."

"*Tenchi Hajimari no Koto*" was discovered by Koya Tagita, a private researcher of *Kakure Kirishitan*, in 1931. It was recited by a 91-year-old man as a descendant in one of the *Kakure Kirishitan* communities and later, he found a copy kept by Zenjiro Shimomura, which was made only in the Taisho period (following the Meiji period), though it is said that it was established in the second half of the 17th century. The reason why it had been only recited for a long time is certainly that it was very dangerous for them to keep it in written form under the suppression policy, but partially that they did not want to reveal themselves, or their own belief, as *Kakure Kirishitan*, as shown by the fact that they did not want to return to the Catholic Church even after the restart of propagation in Meiji period. Without Koya Tagita's effort to establish a relationship of trust with the people actually living as *Kakure Kirishitan*, it would have not become public at that point. As a parting address for him in 2009, one of the eldest of the *Kakure Kirishitan* who had a close relationship with him said, "He was a true benefactor to bring our *Kakure* belief into the world."

In any case, there are various points of difference from orthodox Christianity in their Bible, "*Tenchi Hajimari no Koto* (abbreviated as *Tenchi* below)." Here I would like to draw attention to the following three points: (1) God, (2) the Redemption, and (3) the Trinity.

God was called "*Deusu* (でうす)" in *Tenchi*, as they simply adopted the sounds of the word, "Deus," which probably implies a distinction from "*Kami* (神; Gods)" in Shinto and "*Hotoke* (仏; Buddhas)" in Buddhism. However, in this story, "*Deusu*" was depicted as "the Lord of Heaven and Earth," "the Parent of Creation (including human beings)," and "Something like the Sun," not as transcendental Absolute, in *Tenchi*. The relationship between "Deusu" and man was basically a parent-child one; "Deusu" generously accepts men's sincere apology for their sinful worship of "*Rushiferu* (Lucifer)" during His absence. "Deusu" said to men that those who were exiled from "*Paraiso* (Paradise)" to the Earth because of their sin of eating the forbidden fruit and thus repenting for their sins while dedicating eulogies, "Continue to dedicate *orasho* (oratio) of repentance for 400 years, then I will return you to "*Paraiso* (Paradise)."

In this way, "*Deusu*" was depicted and interpreted as a generous God who thoroughly helps men who regret and repent for their sins, despite their betraying Him. As Hasegawa (2014) mentioned, there we may observe a parent-child relationship, or a "call and response relationship." In that sense, we can say that, for the *Kakure Kirishitan* who had to pretend to worship "*Hotoke*" in order to hide their own belief, a "forgiving God" was by all means necessary for them.

The Redemption of "*Iezusu* (Jesus)" was described in *Tenchi* as follows: the King *Yoroutetsu* (Herod), heard that a baby destined to become "*Oshu* (Lord)" will be born. Herod thus intended to kill the baby in order to protect his own position. Since it was difficult for him to find "*Iezusu* (Jesus),"

Herod killed 44,440 infants in his land. "*Iezusu* (Jesus)" suffered because of this and practiced asceticism very intensely. Then the voice of "*Deusu*" addressed him, saying, "Face death for the impassive afterlife of the murdered infants." Then, *Iezusu* was crucified and killed by a blind man.

As can be seen, there was no conception of the original sin in the *Tenchi*, but "*Iezusu* (Jesus)" was crucified to stop the King's brutal and reckless behavior. As Miyazaki (1996) wrote, we may interpret that the *Kakure Kirishitan* believers needed the figure of a God who sacrifices *even* His own son for the innocent children who were killed without any sin in order generously to help *even* sinful *Kakure Kirishitan*.

Similarly, In *Tenchi*, the Trinity consists of the Father, Son and Spirit. The text runs: "Father *Deusu* is *Pateru* (Pater), *Oshu* Jesus is *Hiryo* (Filho), and Mother *Maruya* (Maria) is *Suherito-Santo* (Espírito Santo), and at the same time, *Deusu* is a union." *Kirishitan* worshipped "*Maruya* (丸や; Mary)" as the Holy Spirit, although this was *undoubtedly* heterodoxic and pagan with regard to Christian orthodoxy.

However, *there is no doubt* that "*Biruzen Maruya* (Virgin Mary)" was the most important figure in their belief, which was well shown by the fact that

Figure 10.2 Virgin and child.

about one third of *Tenchi* is devoted to "*Maruya* (Mary)." *Kakure Kirishitan* respected and followed "*Biruzen Maruya* (Virgin Mary)" as a model for pious believers, as a familiar to them existence of "mother," and as an object of veneration as the "Savior's Mother" (Figure 10.2).

Particularly in the second half of *Tenchi*, "*Iezusu* (Jesus)" was described as the "Son of God" and "*Maruya* (Mary)" as "Christakos," not as Theotokos (Mother of God). *Tenchi* tells us that "*Deusu*" summoned Jesus and Mary from heaven and proclaimed what their roles on earth shall be: it was as if they were three different hypostasises on earth, but "*Deusu*" gave Mary a role of commission and Jesus a role of assistance after their ascension to heaven, with which the three divine hypostasises were eventually united, finally forming the Trinity in the *Kakure Kirishitan* version.

On the other hand, "*orasho* (oratio; prayers)" is not a text like *Tenchi* but prayers that *Kakure Kirishitans* chant in their everyday life, rituals, and religious gatherings including "*gyōji* (event)" and "*matsuri* (festival)." Their "*orasho*" is classified broadly into two: "*denshō no orasho* (traditional prayers)," "*orasho*" being the word generally used among the *Kakure*, and derived from the Portuguese word for prayer, and "*sōsaku no orasho* (original prayers)," "*orasho*" being original creations of the *Kakure* themselves.

The *sōsaku* category includes the two hymns, "*uta-orasho* (song prayers)" composed by the Kakure themselves. One of the *Kakure* communities in Ikitsuki Island maintains the tradition of "The song of San Juan-sama (Saint John, another name of *Nakae no Shima*)," which is traditionally sung at their festivals. The verses are as follows (Miyazaki, 2001):

> The spring water before us
> The tall rocks behind us
> The waters of the sea around us.
> This spring the cherry blossoms will fall
> Spring will come again
> And the flowers will bloom.

These two verses *as a pair* describe the view of the martyrs on *Nakae no shima* and the traditional Japanese allusion of transient human life with the short-lived flowering of cherry blossom in the eternity of time's passage. In that sense, we may say that the first one is spatial and of close-range view and the second one is temporal and of wide vision.

Nakae no shima is a very small desert island adjacent to Ikitsuki Island where many of their ancestors were martyred under the severe suppression policy of Tokugawa Shogunate. It was believed that, among these martyrs, John Sakamoto, John Jirōemon, and John Yukinoura Jiōzaemon, that is, "three Johns" were martyred one after another in *Nakae no Shima* from May to July in 1622. "San Juan" linguistically means Saint ("Santo" in Portuguese) John (Figure 10.3).

Figure 10.3 John the Baptist.

In this way, not only in the *Kakure* of Ikitsuki Island, but also in other *Kakure* communities, martyrs were worshipped as ancestral spirits, or taken care of as their ancestors. Also, they believed that holy water should be drawn in such a sacred place as *Nakae no shima*, which are deeply connected with martyrdom. Thus, this drawing of water itself was regarded as one of their important religious events. In this aspect, too, their belief was quite different from the Christian tradition. Since these songs were composed in the middle of the 17th century, we may assume that they had become syncretized, or assimilated, with the chthonic ancestor worship and Shinto tradition at a very early age of being separated from the European Christian missionaries.

Aside from these "*uta-orasho*," although it would be possible for them to understand its meaning, those who chant Japanese "*orasho*" in their religious events do not try to do that at all; they just concentrate on how they could recite it and chant it rapidly and fluently. Their Latin "*orasho*" is no other than a spell for them, but exactly for this reason, it is believed to have supernatural and mystical power within itself.

Some lessons from Japanese religious psychology: oneness of eclecticism and syncretism

Eiichi Kajita (2014), famous Catholic-Christian professor of educational psychology in Japan, depicted certain phases in Catholic Christianity: "customs," "belief," "service," and "metanoia." In this schema, "belief" and "service" are supported by each other and both are alined with "customs"; "metanoia" should be joined in with those three phases.

However, as shown above, being totally different from Catholic Christianity, *Kakure Kirishitan* could primarily be regarded as "customs" that they have inherited in particular regions from their ancestors, where the phases of "belief" and "service" were not so emphasized. This inevitably entailed less tendency toward (individual) "metanoia." In this sense, we may say that what was the most important for them was a sense of solidarity; *we* have all been believers and have been sharing our ancestral "customs" *within* this community. Also, what was most fearful for them was being isolated in their community; therein we could easily and clearly see what is called "companion consciousness" which is quite *different* from "individual consciousness." That is because the *Kakure* as individuals do not need to understand the meaning of rituals including "*orasho*"; without such individual understanding, the meaning is internalized in the rituals themselves. As Jung quoted from the Talmud, "The dream is its own interpretation..." (*CW* 11, par. 41), as "customs" inherited from their ancestors, the rituals are their own interpretations.

This tendency was noticed also by Christian missionaries at that time. As mentioned above, some of them attempted to respect it as a cultural difference, but others despised it as a proof of un-civilized and un-individualized Japanese people.

As Hayao Kawai (1996) succinctly described the state of Japanese psyche behind such a tendency, based on Buddhist thoughts:

Human beings in Buddhism...exist in relationship. When taken out of relationship, a person loses "self-nature" and thus ceased to exist. Not having "self-nature," how can the person have eachness (selfness)? We have considered the ideas of the Arising of True Nature[3] and also Interdependent Origination[4]. Accordingly, if one tries to respect one's own eachness, one has to be aware of others before contemplating her/his own "interdependence." ... In fact, in such relationship, one can indeed realize one's eachness, but I would like you to pay attention to the different way of thinking which lies behind this view (p. 108).

Thus, we should not regard the religious state of the *Kakure Kirishitan* just as a specific one, even though their history and experiences as described above could be evaluated as special, being violently suppressed under the national policy for about 250 years and being totally separated from Christian orthodoxy in Europe, thereby having no other choice but to develop their own belief in their own way. Rather, as many researchers pointed out, because of *Kakure Kirishitan*, we can observe some general characteristics of Japanese religious psychology, or a prototype of Japanese way of digesting foreign cultures.

I tend to think of this as the oneness of eclecticism and syncretism. As referred to the Meiji period above, I depicted the collision between West and East as somehow eclectic, i.e., the adoption of things that were convenient for us, with our very effective ingestion ability, or adapting some cultural aspects from the West into something comfortable for us, thereby skillfully avoiding things unfamiliar to our senses. This eclectic attitude could be observed in the *Kirishitan* thought of that time, particularly in their lesser attention to, or their escape from, Jesus as the Son of Man, or the Trinity, which can be regarded the core of Christianity, although the Trinity is in part described in *Tenchi* as mentioned above. Rather, they thought predominantly of "Deus" as the absolute, returning to "*Paraiso* (Paradise)" as their salvation after death, and "Virgin Mary" as a symbol of motherhood and forgiveness.

Of course, we can also find a syncretic attitude in the *Kakure Kirishitan*, as shown in the quotation from Miyazaki, "Their faith is one of the typical ethnical religions, which has been fermented in Japan's traditional climate of religion for a long time and thus completely merged into the religious life of chthonic people." There has been a systematic harmonization, or a syncretization, of their belief with Shinto, Buddhism, and other chthonic beliefs.

In that sense, we may say that the *Kirishitan* first adopted something necessary and removed something, for them, unnecessary from Christianity half-unconsciously, and then merged such Christianity, reformed systematically and seamlessly by themselves with their daily-life religious activities, although there was certainly strong external pressure on them to do so at that time.

This oneness of eclecticism and syncretism is typical not only in the *Kakure Kirishitan* but also generally in the Japanese way of digesting foreign cultures.

Shusaku Endo as a Catholic-Christian novelist described Japan as a "swamp" in which Christianity as a tree could not take root into the soil. However, as Kawai said, there is a totally different way of thinking that lies behind each culture including religion; we must know that there are kinds of plants that grow only in "swamps."

If we were to take lessons from the history of *Kakure Kirishitan*, which express well the characteristics of Japanese religious psychology, they would relate to the necessity and importance of "religious diversity" or "cultural pluralism." As mentioned above, in the 16th century, Spain and Portugal did not exercise armed force to bring Japan under their control, due to Japan's geographical and political conditions. This was just at the political level, but at the level of culture, or psyche, it is quite certain that Catholic-Christian societies wanted to enlighten, or conquer, Japan based on their intolerance, self-righteousness, and Euro-centrism of that time. Kajita (2014) called this the "Subjugation of Psyche."

At the second Vatican Council, as recently as in the first half of 1960s, Roman Catholic religious order renounced its self-righteous and self-absolute stance that the Catholic church is the sole holder of truth, end engaged in respectful conversations with other Christian denominations, Judaism, Islam, Buddhism, Hinduism, and so on, thereby returning to Jesus' teaching.

More than 400 years have passed since the first encounter between Europe and Japan in 1543.

This shows us that it takes a long time to establish the horizon, or cultivate the ground, where different cultures can allow for each other's differences, and to communicate with each other, if only a little.

However, we may also say that we psychotherapists attempt to do a similar kind of complex and difficult work, when spending a lot of time in our consulting rooms, we gain a psychological understanding of our clients (as the other), through our own psychology.

Notes

1 Alessandro Valignano, as an Italian inspector of the Society of Jesus in the East Indian region, had a positive idea for the initiation and ordination of Japanese, but thought that, for their education, it should take much more time because they had long been polluted by pagan culture and separated from Euro-Christian culture.

2 In addition, *Mappo* negated the possibility of being saved in this life and the trend for wishing for attainment of heaven or Jodo upon death was growing and this led to the growth of the Jodo belief which worshipped the *Amida Nyorai* as its savior.

3 Kawai explained it, "The world of the Principle, which is itself absolutely emptied and hence infinitely potential, self-divides into innumerable phenomenal forms, the world we call 'reality.' The Principle manifests into the phenomena. This kind of manifestation of the Emptiness Principle is predicated in Hua-yen philosophy as 'the Arising of True Nature (性起)'" (p. 100, my bracketed).

4 "All things continually and simultaneously manifest themselves together as a whole. The philosophy of the Hua-yen calls this ontological reality 'Interdependent Origination (縁起).' As no 'individual' can exist in itself alone, it exists by the support of everything other than itself. Through everything, one indivisible Principe exists—in short, the Mutual Interpenetration of Phenomena and Phenomena" (p. 102, my bracketed).

References

Endo, S. (1992). *Century of Kirishitan* (in Japanese). Tokyo: Shogakkan.

Frois, L. (2015). *The First European Description of Japan, 1585.* London: Routledge.

Hara, K. (2010). *Reflections on Ashikaga Shogunate* (in Japanese). Aozora-buko (electric library). https://www.aozora.gr.jp/

Hasegawa, E. (2015). The Theological Mind of Nagasaki Hidden Christians: A Study of Their Biblical Stories (in Japanese). *The Journal of J. F. Oberlin University. Studies in Humanities*, Vol. 6, 15–35.

Kajita, E. (2014). *Thoughts of Fucan Fabian* (in Japanese). Osaka: Sogensha.

Kawai, H. (2008). *Buddhism and the Art of Psychotherapy.* Texas: Texas A & M University Press.

Kawai, H. (2013). Process of Transformation seen in Mythology of Kakure Kirishitan (in Japanese). *Kokoro no Saishu-kogi* (Last Lecture of Psyche). Tokyo: Shincho-sha.

Miyazaki, K. (1996). *Faith of Kakure Kirishitan.* Tokyo: University of Tokyo Press.

Miyazaki, K. (2001). *Kakure Kirishitan.* Nagasaki: Nagasaki Newspaper Office.

Turnbull, S. (1998). *The Kakure Kirishitan of Japan: A Study of Their Development, Beliefs and Rituals to the Present Day.* London: Routledge.

Watsuji, T. (2015). *Buried Japan: Its Ideological Context Around the Arrival of Christianity* (in Japanese). Aozora-bunko (electric library). https://www.aozora.gr.jp

Chapter 11

History, the orphan of our time, or the timeless stories that make up history

Heba Zaphiriou-Zarifi

> The salvation of this human world lies nowhere else than in the human heart, in the human power to reflect, in human meekness and human responsibility.
>
> (Havel, 1990)

This chapter is dedicated to the memory of Vaclav Havel whose courage, integrity, and moral values make him a symbol of resistance, and an incorruptible defender of human dignity.

A short version of this chapter was presented in Prague in December 2017 at the International Conference on *Analysis and Activism III: More Social and Political Contributions of Jungian Psychology*, and it is within this context that this chapter is to be understood.

The year of the conference coincided with the centenary of the 1917 Balfour Declaration. This prompted me to study the history of the latter, which unilaterally withdrew from Palestinians their inherent rights over their native land, turning Palestinians into a non-people, wanderers in their own homeland, forming today's 'Palestine problem'.

Prologue

I would like to invite readers for the sake of dialogue to let go of what they already know or may feel strongly about the Palestinian/Israeli issue: to open wide their hearts and listen to a history too readily ignored or dismissed. To pay heed to the stories that give life its deepest significance, in the hope that a greater understanding might lessen the sterile, meaningless suffering: 'ours', and that of 'others'.

This is an invitation to hear my contribution as arising from 'the other' point of view, the view that is dimly heard or read about, if ever, in the mainstream news and media. It is the side of the story that Theresa May, now Boris Johnson, Donald Trump and most Arab governments ignore or dismiss. This is a window from another perspective, of a Palestinian point of view, to give voice to the oppressed. One cannot emphasize enough how central and problematic is the issue of erasing the other's point of view, especially in regard to Palestinians' ownership of land and history. Yet the silenced have a voice and a haunting song to sing about a future waiting to be lived.

It is never my intention to provoke division or racial antipathies, to entice hatred or blame, but to kindle the flame of awareness, and to encourage understanding about the neglected living conditions of those whose humanity has been denied, the forsaken people of the Holy Land.

The vicissitudes of history have already seen other people deprived of state and sovereignty. This condition is not exclusive to the Palestinian people, but what makes Palestinian history unique and unparalleled is the terrible negation they have suffered through the establishment of a new 20th-century state in their homeland, but without them and against them. Their tragedy lies in the successive occupations and colonizations that have been imposed upon them since the time of the fall of the Roman Empire thus crushing their every right to sovereignty, defeating any positive solution to the orphaning of their history. Whatever legal and political movement they upheld to create a state where they could be free citizens of the world, they were utterly denied. The tragic history of Palestine is not that of a people who enjoyed political sovereignty and lost it, but that of a people who never had one. This categoric dismissal is what makes their history so tragic but also uniquely important. Perhaps it is timely to remind everyone that Palestinians are conducting one of the last anti-colonial struggles in our 'liberated' world today. I hope that by shedding the light of consciousness, something, however small, might change for the better in an unjust and unequal situation. I hope you will appreciate this chapter, not as contributing to an imbalance, but as an attempt to restore an authentic balance. Raising consciousness about the plight of the rejected Palestinian people and its need for correction is ultimately conducive to peace.

'The Line Dividing Good and Evil Cuts Through the Heart of Every Human Being' (Solzhenitsyn, 1974)

Nearly two decades ago I participated in a katabatic-anabatic initiation ritual with a Jungian group of embodied women. I chose to sacrifice what is for me of the highest value, the most precious and beloved, yet sacrificed for the foundation stone of 'what is to come' to use Jung's words. I am the heir to the keys and the deeds of my family home and land in Palestine, whose ancestral owners died in exile. I chose to sacrifice that home to give home to the European Jewish family who is living now in my home. The family has 'settled' in our house, and decades later are still using our furniture, sleeping in our bedsheets, and eating from the orchard trees of our garden. I am exiled and barred from returning to our home, and a European Jewish family has made our home their own.

Sacrifice is not destruction, nor is it an act of giving up, or giving away, it is giving: a giving of oneself, and from oneself, entirely, without any expectation of return. To sacrifice my home (the etymology is *sacre fare*) is to make it sacred. I sacrificed preciousness for love in community with the other. Sacrifice is an act of love. Sacrifice is made on the breath of becoming. By sacrificing I chose life, though the experience was of death. It was perhaps the most painful choice I ever had to make, but I made it for life: mine and that of the other, and for the dead. To symbolize the bitter-sweet sacrifice, and in the conscious-presence of the participants, I gave my shawl to an Israeli-Jewish woman, and wrapped it around her shoulders. It was made of the most precious material and richly coloured, embroidered, and gifted to me by my mother. In return she gave me a pink silk scarf.

Theft does not give rights to a land which is not one's own. Neither does it fill one's emptiness. Israel has not sacrificed any of its covetous ambition for Palestine's present right to exist. Emptiness cannot sacrifice, only fullness can. I have sacrificed my home, because it is mine to give.

I can never forget the pain endured, nor can I soothe the pain that throbs within me as I write about the sacrifice that has cost me everything. To bare one's heart and to expect nothing in return is to surrender, for knowledge of the heart bequeaths deeper insight. And what I had never anticipated were the gifts that appeared unexpectedly from nowhere. A few months later, Palestine came back to me a thousandfold: in reconciliation work I undertook with bereft Palestinian and Israeli families, with female Jewish patients whose psyche needed a safe home to trust, and several male patients whom in some way or another had meaningful connections to Palestine. It also came back to me through Palestinian music whose resonance goes on forever. The immanent-transcendent quaternity of a Quartet instilled new spaces of silence between the notes reaching Palestine in rippling waves of eternal harmony. To be consoled with music is healing, like pouring olive oil on the wound. Transmuted in the cauldron of suffering, the orphaning of our history has metamorphosed here into musical form. Everything muted transfigures into music, and the white pain of suffering becomes a cry coloured with dignity. There are quantum links between people and their geography, a 'correspondence principle' that cannot be severed.

For future peace to exist in the Holy Land based on a new foundation a mutual sacrifice must occur. At the very least, recognition of the sacrifice made by one for the sake of the other must be acknowledged.

The history of a people 'who love their home and hearth'

There are many beginnings to Palestine, and a narrative of Palestine's early history is not here to compete with the foundational claims of Zionism, but to empirically clarify the deeply rooted connection that Palestinians have to their homeland. Their bond to land and culture is that of people planted, like their ancient olive trees, for hundreds of years before the modern notion of nation-state nationalism was born in the 9th century.

Herodotus, the Ancient Greek historian known as the Father of History, first coined the Greek word '*Philistoei*' for Palestine, to describe the people he visited in the 5th Century BC living in that region, as *Philo-Hestia* (Φιλυ-Εοτίυ): the 'people who love their home and hearth' (Herodotus, pb2013; Herodotus, pb2018). This root-word later became *Philasteen*, Arabic for Palestine.

The region Herodotus outlined as 'Palestine' in 5th Century BC is roughly the same as historic pre-1948 Palestine, an area extending from Phoenicia to the border of Egypt.

He says, in the context of the Persian invasion of Greece:

> The Phoenicians and the Syrians of Palestine have prepared 300 ships [...] This nation, according to its own self-description, has long lived on the Red Sea, where they still reside.
>
> (Zakariyeh, 2005)

First documented in the late Bronze Age, about 3,200 years ago, 'Palestine' was continuously used from 450BC until 1948AD to refer to the land stretching between the Jordan River and the Mediterranean Sea (Masalha, 2018). 'Based on this, Roman Palestine was not an invention of Rome. Rather it was adopted from a status quo that existed at least as early as the twelfth century BCE' (Zakariyeh, 2005, p. 86).

An Israeli archaeological study has proved that the Biblical text is not a historical work, thus casting doubt on the historical accuracy and familiar accounts of many received Biblical assumptions. In their work, Finkelstein and Silberman present their findings, based on dozens of archaeological digs in Israel, Jordan, Egypt, Lebanon, and Syria, that:

> The key early books of the Bible were first codified in the seventh century BCE, hundreds of years after the core events of the lives of the patriarchs, [when] the Exodus from Egypt, and the conquest of Canaan were said to have taken place
>
> (Finkelstein and Silberman, 2002)

They discover no evidence for the Exodus, for Joshua's conquest of Canaan, or for the vast united monarchy of David. Their work effectively rescues the Bible from the 'concretisation' of metaphoric language, and from the widespread tendency among Jews and Christians alike to read the Bible literally. We discover that the Biblical saga differs dramatically from the results of careful scholarly studies.

Religious texts made literal concur with the rewriting of history for political and ideological ends. In the process, this thwarts any possible opening towards new insights and unifying conclusions, abducting religion for political aims.

Historic Palestine has always been the locus of strategic crossroads between both Eastern and Western civilizations. Palestine demonstrated a true example of diversity and has been a melting-pot of ancient cultures. It was never historically inhabited by one people, but by a mixture of many peoples, for 'we were many on this land' (Ezekiel 33:24).

Today's Palestinians are descendants of the Canaanites, who are the fathers of the Judean and the Palestinian branches, also of the Greeks, Romans, Arabs, Crusaders, Mongols, and Turks (Menuhin, 1965); a vivid example of the integration of the many into one. It is worth noting, according to several scholars, that there is more Hebrew blood in present Palestinians than in today's Jews (Rodinson, 1967).

Several pernicious myths have been spun, both as a result of omission or state-managed commission, revolving around a spindle of disaffected knowledge. Is it true that European Jews came to an empty, un-inhabited land, a 'terra nullius' to establish their state? This is but one of these fables that turns the murky waters of history into muddier trenches. Even in the book of Genesis we learn Abram discovered the 'Promised Land' was already inhabited. He travelled through the land as an immigrant. Abram did not possess the land, nor did he own any of it, instead he made a deal with a local for a cave in which to bury his wife, Sarah. 'I am a foreigner and stranger among you. Sell me some property for a burial site here so I can bury my dead' (Genesis 23:4 NIV). He also met other people with kingdoms of their own such as Melchisedek, King of Salem (which was an ancient Middle-Eastern town) who blessed him and gave him wine and bread. 'Abram travelled through the land as far as the site of the great tree of Moreh at Shechem. At that time the Canaanites were in the land' (Genesis 12:6 NIV).

The need to return to a mythic past in order to create a founding myth of belonging is inevitably a movement towards fascism. Origins are made of a plurality, and the over-simplification of ethnicity ineluctably induces the inclusion of the one and the exclusion of the other. The genealogy of a 'pure' race insinuates a nostalgic view of origins. Effectively, identities have a multiplicity of beginnings; moreover, they are a becoming. 'We are what we have become' (Sanbar, 2017) is a constructive view of identity, integrating differentiation into a teleological development, providing a panacea to the divided self. However fictional and unfounded is *Eretz Yisrael*'s founding biblical myth of origins its expansionism: 'from the Euphrates to the Nile', can no longer go unquestioned (Genesis 15:18 NIV).

Now this religion happens to prevail
Until by that one it is overthrown,
Because men dare not live with men alone
But always with another fairy tale. (Al-Ma'ari)

The Balfour Declaration – a Faustian pact

The length of this publication does not allow a thorough study of the historic context that has set the backdrop to the Balfour Declaration. Nevertheless, it is worth noting a few points.

Historical facts, grounded in historical dates, root our history in time. They function as pointers, highlighting the difference between historic events and revisionist fabrication, between reality and fictional beliefs, between scholarly evidence and paranoia.

The orphaning of Palestinian history is a betrayal of 'historic' promises made to Palestinians, and a refusal to take responsibility for it. It is an amputation of Palestinians from their historic motherland, and an aggressive policy to keep them banished without any political procedures to enable them to return to her. While the colonial-occupation is unremittingly stealing Palestinian land and resources from under her natives' feet, her history is removed from collective knowledge. The orphaning of Palestinian history is the silencing of a nation's soul longing for *communitas*. It is a condition of enforced fixity, an immobilization into a long-lasting state of exclusion. Except for the very few, the West has abandoned Palestine as has the East. Palestine has been coerced to become the shadow of it-self denuded of its intrinsic identity and thrown into despair. Imprisoned and enslaved is the condition of the orphaned Palestine under military occupation.

Likewise, by dismissing academic history, as per the one-sided 1917 Balfour Declaration, now amplified and mirrored by the recently voted Israeli Basic Nation-State Law declared in 2018, it only serves to fortify and further a century of injustice. Ottoman and British imperialism were morphed into Israeli colonialism.

These 'isms', like ghosts unyielding to death, unwilling to be sacrificed, feed on frozen beliefs and regressive ideas furthering deception in place of imaginative resolution (Jung, 1956). They are the restless revenants hovering about, unable to find their end, stubbornly re-enacted, though in a slightly different garb, but similar to unredeemed ghouls, they return to haunt our history like ghosts in the nursery.

In order to comprehend the intractability of 'complex' history, an indepth study must delve into past deadlocks, not to turn the clock back, but to examine where the course of history was tied in knots. Denying Palestinians their rights is to be possessed by them, for the unresolved Palestinian 'problem' is and will always remain the Israeli-Jewish problem. Therefore, an honest study of the crucial watershed in Middle-Eastern history must be given a chance to disentangle the threads of injustice and to open a pathway to peace. This requires the courage to face shame and dishonour and to take responsibility for divisive if not racist policies where the advancement of one people's fate is to the detriment of another.

The 1917 Balfour Declaration was a fatal deed in the long chain of Great Power exploits against the Palestinian people. It paved the way for devastating events to both peoples as the Zionist movement came to persecute the Palestinians, who became the secondary victims of European persecution of Jews. This has turned two people destined to live together fatally against each other, yet ironically at once highlighting them both.

I do not need to describe the complex and painful history of the Jewish people that climaxed in the 20th century with the catastrophic destruction by some Europeans of European Jews. It is not the subject of this chapter. Yet it remains central to the core conflict played out in the Middle-East over the land of Palestine. Denying Palestinians their right to self-determination is underpinned by the need for these particular European countries to wash their hands of their crimes towards the Jews. By removing themselves from the triangulation of responsibility, they have indirectly precipitated the Israeli-Jews into becoming the persecutors of the Palestinians. By laying blame onto the Palestinians they turned them into Israel's perfect scapegoat.

In his diaries, Herzl questioned the comparative merits of choosing Palestine or Argentina as the site of the new Jewish state (Herzl, pd1978). Uganda was another option suggested by the British in 1903. In effect, there was no particular urgency for Palestine to be the sole locus for the creation of the 'Jewish' state. However, 'wherever Jews settle', Herzl argued, 'the local population would have to be removed'! He went on to elaborate a careful strategy to expropriate Palestinians under the auspices of commerce. 'We shall then sell only to Jews, and all real estate will be traded only among Jews', he plotted. Israel Zangwill, a close associate of Herzl, puts it more forcefully: Jewish settlers must be prepared to drive out the indigenous population by force.

Ahad Ha'am, the founder of Cultural Zionism and of *Hebrew Monthly*, visited Palestine in 1891 and condemned the behaviour of Jewish Zionist settlers who deal with the Arabs with hostility and cruelty, trespass unjustly, beat them shamefully for no sufficient reason, and even boast about their actions. There is no one to stop the flood and put an end to this despicable and dangerous tendency (Ha'am, pb2003, p. 14).

As the Ottoman Empire crumbled, the British made three contradictory promises regarding the region's future fate: the British pledged support for an independent Arab state in exchange for Arab assistance in defeating the Ottomans. But the following year, the British and French foreign ministers secretly met to plan the partition of the Middle-East between their two Empires, under what became known as the Sykes-Picot Agreement. Palestine was designated as an international zone to be managed by a shared global regime (Barr, 2011). Yet just a year later the British were already making other 'secret' plans known as the Balfour Declaration.

The Balfour Declaration is a letter dated 2 November 1917 from Britain's Foreign Secretary Arthur Balfour to Lord Lionel Walter Rothschild (Balfour, 1917):

> Foreign Office
> November 2nd, 1917
>
> Dear Lord Rothschild,
>
> I have much pleasure in conveying to you on behalf of His Majesty's Government, the following declaration of sympathy with Jewish Zionist aspirations which has been submitted to, and approved by, the Cabinet.
>
> His Majesty's Government view with favour the establishment in Palestine of a national home for the Jewish people, and will use their best endeavours to facilitate the achievement of this object, it being clearly understood that nothing shall be done which may prejudice the civil and religious rights of existing non-Jewish communities in Palestine or the rights and political status enjoyed by Jews in any other country.
>
> I should be grateful if you would bring this declaration to the knowledge of the Zionist Federation.
>
> Yours,
> Arthur James Balfour

This pledge was made without the consent or even knowledge of the Palestinians, who at that time comprised more than 90% of Palestine's population (Khalidi, 2006; Kramer, 2008; McCarthy, 1990).

Balfour displays his racism in this statement by referring to the indigenous Palestinian population simply as 'non-Jewish', their identity irrelevant, discarded. This is further evidence as to how, unlike the Jews, they were granted neither political nor national rights. In one stroke of an over-worked and convoluted statement, Britain gifted European Jews a nation and condemned the Palestinians to national homelessness.

Nowhere in the Declaration drafts did the Zionist project mention Palestine as a refuge for the persecuted Jews; it rather commanded, as an alleged right, the building of a 'national home' for Jews (only). To fully obtain this right, meant evicting, albeit in stages, those who for centuries had already been wedded to the land. There was no mention of Jewish suffering either, only Jewish nationalism. As regards the 'existing' Palestinian population, they were not cited, nor the tremendous suffering the ethnic-cleansing programme would inflict upon them. There was certainly no mention of their legitimate right to statehood, nor even, God forbid, their inalienable right to self-determination, nor of their political rights as the custodians of the land to which they belonged.

In fact, the first draft of the Declaration spelled out explicitly the Zionist settler-colonial agenda in Palestine. Too frank to be published, the draft was drastically amended to conceal more than it revealed (Andersen, 2017). There is no mention of the Palestinians as a people in any version of the multiple drafts. Wiped out of existence, the Palestinians simply vanished in the eyes of the conspirators.

Since childhood, Arthur Balfour had been steeped in a literal rather than metaphorical approach to Bible-reading. The messianic heroism of 'saving' the Jews by restoring them to the Biblical era was tethered to his Protestant idealism, conflated in his mind with another grandiose dream of 'allowing Britain the honour of righting this wrong' (Dugdale, 2010, pp. 195–196). Little did he know that he was reproducing on 'another' the very same thing he was heroically fixing, colluding entirely with the Zionist 'reconstruction' of Palestine, worded as it was in a convoluted draft that carried his name. This 'hellish web of words', (Jung, 2012, p. 300) spun with snags and catches, ensnaring history in diabolical knots, took a century before their real intention was finally exposed to the West. The difficulty of untying the knots of treachery remains a responsibility Britain has towards resolving the orphaning of Palestine, owing them at least an apology, if not repair. The crafted Faustian pact was and will always remain a British legacy of deceit.

The 1948 Palestinian Nakba – the ethnic cleansing of Palestine

Without a fundamental historical understanding of the manoeuvres around the Balfour Declaration and the racism that paved its inception, the calamitous *Nakba* and the ethnic cleansing of Palestinians will meet no pressure for any honourable recognition or resolution. For without morality there is no politics, and Palestinian history will remain the orphan of our time.

The ongoing *Nakba,* the Palestinian tragedy of 1948, remains the longest unresolved refugee crisis of our time and, since 1967, the Israeli military occupation has been the second-longest in modern history, after Tibet.

David Ben Gurion, the first Prime Minister of Israel, in conversation with World Jewish Congress President Nahum Goldmann, showed prescience when clearly stating some of these facts:

> If I were an Arab leader, I would never sign an agreement with Israel. It is normal, we have taken their country... there has been anti-Semitism, the Nazis, Hitler, Auschwitz, but was that their fault? They see but one thing: we have come, and we have stolen their country. Why should they accept that?
>
> (Goldmann, 1978, p. 99)

These historic facts concerning Palestine have been subjected to drastic erosion by the corrosive 'facts on the ground', such as the systematic construction of Israeli settlements on dwindling Palestinian soil, facilitated by economic power, complacent world politics, and military might.

The Zionist project in Palestine from the outset was colonialist in essence and in practice. While colonialism has collapsed as a global phenomenon, in Israel it has deteriorated into what many would describe as apartheid, where Palestinian rights under international law are severely violated in the Occupied Territories, or ignored in Israel with grave consequences for democracy and peace (Davis, 2003; White, 2009; Zreik, 2004).

Israel has no compunction in denying equal rights to the residents of the country they have forcibly and unilaterally annexed. It is unbearable to see a people so steeped in their own history behave with such ruthlessness towards the people in whose homeland they live. The *Nakba* is the ongoing tragedy of Palestine. The tragedy of Israel is its blind state of denial.

The Israeli Basic Law

The contentious Basic Law, passed on 19 July 2018 enshrines Israel as a 'Jewish' state: 'the one and only state of the Jewish people'. It emphasizes the Jewish character of the state, to the detriment of its so-called democratic character, and erases Arabic, the language of 20% of its population, by imposing Hebrew on the original natives of the land. The Law thus on the one hand, entails the exclusion of the autochthone Palestinian citizens in the state that occupies them, and on the other hand, implies *ipso facto* that world Jewry, whatever their nationality, are undeniably entitled to what is utterly denied to the natives of the land, re-enacts the 1917 Balfour Declaration, and condemns Israel to be officially an apartheid state with Jewish supremacy over millions of ruined Palestinians: Muslims, Christians, and Druze alike. Indeed, a number of Israelis themselves worry about the future prospects for any genuinely democratic Israel that denies citizenship to a significant portion of the population (Schoken, 2019).

So, what now? How will the Israeli extreme right implement a strategy towards a final solution? By continuing the usual arbitrary legal procedures, land seizures, intimidation, oppression, and pressure by force against Palestinians?

By declaring the whole of Jerusalem the capital of Israel, (thereby removing East-Jerusalem as the capital of Palestine) Trump has destroyed any viable prospect of peace. His modestly named 'Deal of the Century' is rather the 'steal' of the century thus igniting a tremendous fear of extinction, threatening the elimination of one people to sanctify the sole existence of another.

Israel receives well over 3 billion dollars every year in direct foreign assistance, and the US injects more money into Israel than into any other country in the world (Mearsheimer and Walt, 2007). In 2018 Trump completely stopped any Palestinian financial aid, thus enabling a further punitive regime of control, imposing intense poverty on the occupied Palestinian population, subjugating them into total submission. Another American 'saviour' has landed on the map of Palestine, a commentator retorted, to solve severe issues of injustice and enslavement, with US-dollar injections, treating the Palestinian issue as a mere lack of investment!

Israel, with the help of the US, is doing all it can to become legitimate. But an apartheid state will never simulate assimilation or uphold morality. Israel owes its existence, not to Europe, but to Palestine and the Palestinians, sacrificed for Israel to exist. Palestine is the Via Dolorosa through which new lines in the sand are cut for the mastery of the Middle-East, but this time dictated by the victims of previous empires, now creating its own on the back of the Palestinians.

An unpleasant remaining issue for Israel is how gradual and public will be the ongoing expulsion and, ghettoizing of Palestinians into dis-connected Bantustans. Israel will shift blame, and shame Palestinians for not abiding by Israel's wilful imposition of power, banking again on victimhood to victimize Palestinians further. Israel runs no risks, despite protests. It knows that critical international opinion carries little weight in global Realpolitik. Israel knows it can get away with crime!

Today's Israeli government is one of the most right wing, xenophobic, and overtly racist governments. Its manifesto explicitly rejects even the idea of a Palestinian state. This leaves only one conclusion: the comatose peace-process was but a hypocritical charade. It is all process and no peace, giving Israel the concealment it needs to pursue its colonial project over the entire land of Palestine (Shlaim, 2017).

Since the establishment of the Israeli State in 1948, the state has ambitiously grown an empire, simulating typical colonialist policies, not dissimilar from other historical imperialist takeovers, except for its anachronism. A Jewish Journalist remarked: 'Increasingly, Israel is behaving more like some of the fundamentalist and corrupt Arab States' with indiscriminate human rights abuse and torture, as has been thoroughly documented.

Israel's panoptic surveillance system has become yet another lethal weapon at hand. Hundreds of young Palestinians are arrested and imprisoned based on Facebook posts. Criminalizing Palestinians online extends Israeli occupation to the digital sphere. What would the UK seem like if every other youth posting dissent were imprisoned? The sentence is disproportionate for such 'crimes', some incarcerations lasting for more than a decade. Obliterating dissent by extreme means of intimidation aims at totally silencing Palestinians.

The new historians of the indigenous people of Palestine

Hikayat Filasteen: *women's stories under occupation*

Palestinian history, however denied, is redeemed by the stories that bring the orphan back into the family of compassionate beings.

Palestinian women are generally the storytellers. Embroidery is one of their arts, storytelling another. They carry the nation's memory, in songs and stories, rooted in the landscape to which they belong. Like their dresses, sewn in thread and colour, they carry their stories, as once they carried their water jars proudly balanced on their heads, their long gowns swaying with the movement of their gait.

> '*Ya hamila al jarra min wen, min wen?*'
> 'O water-bearer, from where?
> Do you carry your jar of earthenware?
> O let your glances stray
> This way,
> This way.'

History may well be re-written by the victors and historical facts utterly perverted; nevertheless, eyewitnesses' stories, like testimonies, remain the mirrors of our time.

Our stories carry water to the thirsty by bringing the well of faith within reach. Emptiness is a condition of fullness, and Palestinians, like Job, shrunken to the marrow, have emptied their cup of hope for outside help. But love refills the empty cup with inner hope. All the evils of Pandora's box have been poured out in Palestine, but hope remained contained in the box. Palestinian women carry the 'jar of earthenware', which at a glance is filled with hope.

The baby is also a prisoner: the story of Suad

> The Meek shall inherit the Earth
> (Gospel of Matthew 5:5)

A few years ago, when Suad was two months pregnant, the Israeli occupation army detained her. She was slapped, tied up in painful postures, and constantly threatened with abortion during the interrogation, which lasted 18 hours a day, for 66 days. She was transferred to hospital, under intrusive surveillance, when she was due. Her legs were shackled, and her hands tied to the bed, were only released for 30 minutes after her C-section. Amnesty International and the UN Commission on the Status of Women reported several cases of Palestinian women giving birth in prison and their babies treated as prisoners.

Suad confided it was the story of *'Jubeinah and the Slave'* her mother sang to her as a child that gave her the strength to live with the pain of her neglected condition: more precisely the part of the story where Jubeinah's mother gives her daughter a bead of iridescent blue glass before she goes on her travels, warning her not to lose it. For Suad, this bead symbolized 'the spirit within': her faith, which she held onto, connecting her personal tragedy to that of nature herself.

Isolated with her baby in a cold prison of concrete walls and metal doors, Suad was plunged in the *solutio* of non-existence, under her jailer's power. The Spirit has to 'dissolve' the life it acts upon before it becomes regenerative. The spirit of nature came upon her in the core song of Jubeinah's story and acted upon her to be one with the bead. This song opened her soul to the numinous in return for her hospitality to the Self, providing the potency she needed to survive and to bring a balancing equilibrium to the unequal power between herself and the jailer.

She sang it to her beloved baby, with nature her witness:

> O birds that fly high on the wind
> O streams that flow low on the ground,
> Carry greetings to my mother,
> Carry greetings to my father,
> Tell them how their own dear daughter
> Now leads sheep to grass and water.

The bride from Galilee: the story of Mouna

> In a free society, if a few are guilty, all are responsible.
> (Rabbi Heschel, quoted in Safieh, 2010).

Twenty years ago, Mouna, a Palestinian with Israeli citizenship, was in her wedding gown, embellished by a headdress and veil, all embroidered in her Palestinian regional colours and patterns. On embarking the ferry from Haifa port to Cyprus where the newlyweds were heading for a honeymoon weekend, a group of Israeli security forces took them to one side, interrogating them harshly, threatening to go through every pleat and under-layer, leaving her no alternative but to take off her wedding dress and leave it behind, shattering her aspiration of travelling on the boat and arriving at her bridal room in her embroidered gown. While the groom watched helplessly, the security men unpicked the contents of his bride's small case, fingering each and every piece of her trousseau and negligées, her personal toiletries, opening and sniffing her perfume. Arriving at their hotel room, she discovered some of her trousseau had been damaged and the rest stolen.

Hearing this summary of the Palestinian experience and condition might ignite a desire in fair-minded observers to seek change. This is my only wish.

The self-immolation of Jan Palach

The shortest distance between two people is a story. So, I will begin with that of Jan Palach, a Jewish man, whose protest was a testimony to the impossibility of silencing everyone.

On the 19th of January 1969, Jan Palach set himself ablaze, in Wenceslas Square, Prague, 'not so much in opposition to the Soviet occupation', he uttered on his deathbed, 'but because... people were not only giving up, but giving in'. He sacrificed himself for freedom.

Her body, a living torch

The Story of Iman: 'No Coward Soul is Mine'.

Iman, a Palestinian mother in the Occupied Territories set herself on fire in broad daylight in the market place. Her body, like a living torch, burned in flames. Was it out of despair or a sense of betrayal, or was it a meek woman's story speaking up for a whole nation whose children have become enslaved, drinking the dregs of humiliation's cup? I imagine she simply did the only thing she could, to speak truth to power by self-immolation. Courageously, she sacrificed, making sacred her body and her story. What was the alternative to redeeming 'the other'? Either way, there is blood on the altar.

In 1989, these words commemorated the XX anniversary of Palach's self-immolation: 'We started forgetting that something has to resist even the greatest pressure, something fundamental that cannot be bought or sold, but that is absolutely essential for maintaining our human dignity' (Havel, 1989). Mirroring Palach's final words, the Palestinian woman explained: 'under occupation even decent people have been compromised'.

Coercive collaboration, or normalization with the occupier will always remain the most poisonous byproduct of military occupation. It takes extra-ordinary courage to become a living torch to raise public awareness regarding the abuse of a nation's soul. 'Give humanity dignity and trust that life will find the better way' (Jung, 1913). Palestine craves dignity.

Let us 'not be indifferent to the day when the light of the future was carried forward by a burning body'. Palestine is the Burning Bush of the Holy Land and with a cry for justice it exclaims: I am Palach, I am Palestinian.

The gift of heart: a living Palestinian heart

You shall love your neighbour as yourself

(Matthew 22:37–40)

The Chinese philosopher, Zhuang Zi, dreamed he was a happy butterfly. On waking he wondered: 'Now I do not know whether it was then I dreamt I was a butterfly, or whether I am now a butterfly dreaming I am a man' (Legge, 1913). The seat for the 'transformation of things' Zhuang Zi refers to, in most traditions, is the pulsing heart whose life does not end after death.

On a clear morning, a Palestinian young man sipping coffee in his Jerusalem neighbourhood was randomly shot dead by a settler whose crime was committed with impunity. The Palestinian's brain was irrevocably damaged, but his heart was unharmed. He was known for his kindness, a peaceful life-loving man. His wife and young children were distraught. The arbitrary murder was absurd and senseless. Before the family could even come to terms with their loss, a donor coordinator approached them for their beloved's heart to be donated. An Israeli man of similar age and blood group had a perfectly healthy brain but his heart was dysfunctional. A quick transplant with a 'beating heart' could save the Israeli's life. He too was married with young children. The Palestinian family agreed to donate the heart.

The split between Jew and non-Jew had suddenly blurred. The Israeli man needed the still-beating Palestinian heart. He was prepared to accept a transplant from a Palestinian if it would mean living longer. 'It has nothing to do with politics or war when it comes to saving a life: [whether] you are a Muslim, a Christian, a Jew, the most important [thing] is to save a life,' said the deceased donor's mother (Somerville, 2017).

The whole of Occupied Palestine is a hospital with bleeding hearts, amputated bodies, and traumatized souls, despite which Palestinians 'like to think that [they] are sound, substantial flesh and blood' (Elliot, 1942). When will the heart-felt sympathy for another's distress become undivided in the Holiest-City of Light: Al-Quds-Jerusalem? When will you love your neighbour as yourself?

Israelis have their Hamlets fighting with the ghost of the past deciphering whether they come from an evil or heavenly spirit. Palestinians have their Karamazov's suffering the murder of justice, rivalry between brothers, and condemnation for erroneous accusations. Yet both are facets of the same, despite the fact that history had them change places.

The notion of λατρεία (service), is the service due to God only, writes St Augustine in *The City of God*, 'whether we render it outwardly or inwardly; for we are all His temple'. The temple of the heart becomes His altar when it rises to Him. It is on the altar of the heart that the sacrifice is offered.

It is on the altar of the heart that the rivers flow. 'The Lord your God will circumcise your hearts and the hearts of your descendants, so that you may love him with all your heart and with all your soul, and live' (Deuteronomy 30:6 NIV). Circumcising the heart may re-awaken Jerusalem to become the City of God once again, and live.

> I have learned and dismantled all the words to construct a single one: Home.
>
> (Darwish, 2003)

A Palestinian *Hikaya* is a traditional story in prose or verse orated rhythmically like a song. Each verse is called *Beyt,* which is Arabic for 'home'. The love of home remains unwavering, like our songs in quatrain verse, is the home we inhabit.

Every Palestinian story is a Declaration unto itself: a family tree, an identity, a dialect, a bloodline, a perspective on how we struggle and how we survive.

We have a country of words, and every word is a story, and every story is chiselled on a facet of a stone. Put a stone upon a stone, and we rebuild our home. At every phase of our denied history a nation of storytellers awakens, recreating a cosmology of tales to tell. The lemon tree and the pomegranate, the fig tree and the sacred olive grove were once in our garden. Now, our Palestine is a shrinking wasteland, our history a cemetery of oppressed people battered into submission until they vanish. But all one needs to start a prairie is a clover and one bee.

I could add a hundred ancient references to the travails of the Jewish people and the travelling Ark of the Covenant. Likewise, today, centuries later, Palestinians, wherever they are and whatever suffering they endure, will always love their home as they have done continuously over the past three millennia. Palestinians remain confidant and determined that Palestine will one day resurrect. After all Palestine has already witnessed a crucifixion, a descent into hell and a resurrection on her land. 'Again, in spite of that, we call this Friday good' (Elliot, 1942).

> Here is an offering of a song dedicated to our ancient Olive Trees:
> May the fire of love for our country be an Olive Tree,
> We are on this earth like olive branches,
> We bend our forehead only to kiss the earth,
> The land is ours and the country is ours,
> Sing oh nightingale sing for the love of our olive tree.

So, may this love for our homeland make Palestine become again what it was destined to be: a Garden of Forgiveness.

Epilogue

I believe like a child that suffering will be healed and made up for, that all the humiliating absurdity of human contradictions will vanish like a pitiful mirage, like the despicable fabrication of the impotent and infinitely small Euclidean mind of man, that in the world's finale, at the moment of eternal harmony, something so precious will come to pass that it will suffice for all hearts, for the comforting of all resentments, for the atonement of all the crimes of humanity, for all the blood that they've shed; that it will make it not only possible to forgive but to justify all that has happened (Dostoevsky, 1880).

References

Andersen, C. (2017). *Balfour in the Dock.* London, UK: Skyscraper Publications.

Baerlein, H. (1909) *The Diwan of Abu'l-Ala Al-Ma'arri, Ma.* New York, NY: E.P. Dutton & Co.

Balfour, A.J. (1917). Letter to Lord Rothschild. Retrieved from https://mfa.gov.il/mfa/foreignpolicy/peace/guide/pages/the%20balfour%20declaration.aspx

Barr, J. (2011). *A Line in the Sand: Britain, France and the Struggle that shaped the Middle East.* London, UK: Simon & Schuster.

Darwish, M. (2003). *Unfortunately It Was Paradise: I Belong There.* Oakland, CA: University of California Press.

Davis, U. (2003). *Apartheid Israel: Possibilities for the Struggle Within.* London, UK: Zed Books.

Dostoyevsky, F. (1878–1880). *The Brothers Karamazov.* Oxford, UK: Oxford World.

Dugdale, B. (2010). *Arthur James Balfour 1906–1930.* Whitefish, MT: Kessinger Publishing.

Elliot, T.S. (1942). *Little Gidding, Four Quartets.* San Diego, CA: Harcourt.

Finkelstein, I., & Silberman, A.N. (2002). *The Bible Unearthed: Archaeology's New Vision of Ancient Israel and the Origin of Its Sacred Texts.* New York, NY: Touchstone.

Goldmann, N. (1978). *The Jewish Paradox: A Personal memoir.* New York, NY: Grosset & Dunlap. Translated by Steve Cox.

Ha'am, A. (2003) *Wrestling with Zion.* Boston: Grove press, pp. 14–15.

Havel, V. (21 February, 1990). *International Herald Tribune, Paris.* Retrieved from https://www.poemhunter.com/v-clav-havel/quotations/

Herodotus. (2003). *The Histories.* London, UK: Penguin Classics.

Herodotus. (2018). *Herodotou Kleio, in usum Regiae Scholae cantuariensis.* Farmington Hills, MI: Gale.

Herzl, T. (1978). *The Diaries of Theodor Herzl* (reprint). Gloucester, MA: Peter Smith Publisher.

Jung, C.G. (1956). *Collected Works Volume 5: Symbols of Transformation* (2nd ed.). Princeton, NJ: Princeton University Press.

Jung, C.G. (1913). *The Red Book: A Reader's Edition.* London, UK: W. W. Norton & Company.

Khalidi, W. (2006). *The Iron Cage: The Story of the Palestinians*. Boston, MA: Beacon Press.

Kramer, G. (2008). *A History of Palestine: From the Ottoman Conquest to the Founding of the State of Israel*. Princeton, NJ: Princeton University Press.

Masalha, N. (2018). *Palestine: A Four Thousand Year History*. London, UK: Zed Books.

McCarthy, J. (1990). *The Population of Palestine*. New York, NY: Columbia University Press.

Mearsheimer, J.J. and Walt, S.M. (2007). *The Israel Lobby and U.S. Foreign Policy*. New York, NY: Farrar, Straus and Giroux.

Mehuhin, M. (1965). *The Decadence of Judaism in Our Times*. New York, NY: Exposition Press.

Rodinson, M. (1967). *Israel, Fait Colonial?* (Israel, a colonial fact). Paris, France: pd in Les Temps Modernes.

Safieh, A. (2010). *The Peace Process: From Breakthrough to Breakdown*. London, UK: Saqi.

Sanbar, E. (2017). *Les Mots de la Radicalistion: Origine*. UNESCO conference. Paris, France. Retrieved from https://youtu.be/JUewbrhDZoo

Schoken, A. (2019). *Annul the Nation-state Law*. Haaretz. Retrieved from https://www.haaretz.com/opinion/.premium-the-unconstitutional-basic-law-on-israel-as-the-nation-state-of-the-jewish-people-1.7066214

Shlaim, A. (2017). *Quick thoughts: Avi Shlaim on Israel's New Historians, Hamas, and the BDS Movement*. Jadaliyya. Retrieved from https://www.jadaliyya.com/Details/34642.

Solzhenitsyn, A. (1974). *The Gulag Archipelago*. London, UK: Harper Collins.

Somerville, R. (2017). *Beat*. Dublin, Ireland: Lilliput Press.

Soothill, W. (1913). *The Three Religions of China: Lectures Delivered at Oxford*, translated by J. Legge, p. 75.

St Augustine of Hippo, (5th Century A.D.). *The City of God, X(3): The City of God against the Pagans*. Translation by R. W. Dyson. Cambridge, UK: Cambridge University Press.

White, B. (2009). *Israeli Apartheid: A Beginner's Guide*. London, UK: Pluto Press.

Zakariyeh, M. (2005) Maqdisi: An 11th Century Palestinian Consciousness. *Journal of Palestine Studies*, 22–23, p. 86.

Zreik, R. (2004). Palestine, Apartheid and the Rights Discourse. *Journal of Palestine Studies*, 34(1), pp. 68–80.

Chapter 12

The Golem-complex

From Prague to Silicon Valley

Jörg Rasche

The internet, man-made life, artificial intelligence, the alchemical project, the Golem – phantasm of Jewish People in the 12th or 16th century, and the unconscious reactions to the climate crisis today; to the disaster after decades of nuclear power plants and the accumulation of nuclear waste, these are different aspects of the same problem: how the collective psyche reacts and behaves under the pressure of such a dynamic (Figure 12.1).

All of us are familiar with the epidemic attraction of smartphones. Almost everybody, especially younger people, tend to endlessly hang on the umbilical cord of the internet – a *social media addiction* of global dimensions. I call this the *Golem-Complex*. We all live in the energy field of this complex.

There is no question that the internet has its merits. We all use it, it makes many things easier. It is a reality we have to live with. But it has already changed our world in an unforeseen dimension, and it changed our minds and our ways of thinking and feeling. This chapter is about the shadow side of the brave new electronic world. It is an uncomfortable reflection – it is about us.

Prague is the right place to reflect on this. In the time of Rabbi Loew (Lion), the creator of the famous fantasy being, Golem, Prague was among the cultural centers of Europe. The Golem was intended to protect the Jewish people, but eventually he became dangerous for his creator as well as for the entire society. All later technological developments carry a shadow

Figure 12.1 Emeth = Truth.

aspect of the Golem fantasy. In these critical times of our own culture, the Golem-Complex seems to have been activated. Today, we are subjects and objects of worldwide man-made web and matrix, which is already stronger, smarter and faster than we are. Many vicious circles contribute to an atmosphere of uncertainty. We are not *'living in truth'* (Vaclav Havel) but in a fog of unclear and unconscious dependencies and anonymous control. Exponentially accelerating technologies, as promoted, for example, by the *Singularity* movement, are said to be fundamentally reshaping the social, economic, ecological, biological and psychological world *now*. We are already spun into the Golem-web without being aware of it, cocooned in a spider web, and in a bubble, like an echo-space, as if a self-referential collective madness could be healed by another rootless fantasy and technique.

Cocooned in the net

I'll start with Facebook: having been established in February 2004, in 2012, Facebook already had 2 billion users. Similarly, YouTube has 1,5 billion, Instagram 700 million, WhatsApp 1,2 billion users. Shares in these companies are among the bestselling on the global market. Mark Zuckerberg began with quite a simple idea: there were lists of students at Harvard University, there were their photos, and he made a digital version of that data. Everybody wanted to present themselves as much as possible in a positive light and each reader, in turn, wanted to get an impression of the life behind the 'face' that was presented. The 'homo mimeticus,' the internet monkey, was born and peeping and imitating became the *meaning*: 'you are a product.' The business idea of Facebook, 'We want to be seen, as we want to be seen,' follows a dark image of mankind – it is basically misanthropic, but it sells. Consequently, from its beginning, Facebook showed strong shadow aspects: from disinformation, fake news, manipulation of elections, to online rape, murder and propagating terrorism. Facebook, then, connects those who superficially share the same opinion and produces a feeling of 'us' ('likes'), which excludes those with other views. It is basically antidemocratic. The so-called 'social network' creates isolated and streamlined individuals who are not aware of their facelessness. And it spreads like a virus.

C. G. Jung was one of the first thinkers who wanted to know what was going on backstage – not just on the conscious stage with us as the actors, but behind the veil, in the unconscious stream of archetypal dynamics. With Facebook (and similar other networks) it is all about self-assurance, about longing for personal identity and 'face' (persona) by mirroring others. But in fact, it produces streamlined people. It is a vicious circle. In totalitarian states such as China, the electronic Persona-Face is already a social reality for many millions of people: their online behavior, controlled by the authorities, limits or supports their access to a desired job, a flat or permission to marry. Already in 1978, Alexander Solzhenitsyn said in his famous Harvard speech that the methods of manipulating people in the Western world were much more subtle and cleverer than the brutal ways of Stalin's empire. He could not have known of the technological progress in information techniques and digital mass manipulation of today. Václav Havel, accused and imprisoned for subversive political actions, emphasized in his book *Attempt to live in Truth* (1978) that 'Freedom without responsibility is an Illusion.'

The darkening of our time

Who am I? As a student, I read the *One-dimensional Man* by Herbert Marcuse, and Orwell's *1984,* with fascination and horror. In the Berlin Jung-Institute 40 years ago, we were told that the number of borderline patients, and people with bonding disorders, was increasing. Classical neurosis became a rare occurrence in our practice as many patients were no longer able to create a proper neurosis. Today, the external world seems to reflect this inner loss. Who or what can 'I' be in a world with growing uncertainties, the global ecological crisis and the obvious impossibility to escape or change anything? What is the truth, and what is fake news? The future of our fragile Blue Planet is dark. Everywhere governments do the ugly work for shareholders of international companies, they support dictators and promote the proliferation of weapons. The global shadows of WWII and its genocides, of Vietnam and Iraq wars, are forgotten, the shadows are melting together into an unconscious dark layer around our planet. The ecological disaster seems like a response from nature to the crazy idea of an ongoing growth of industrialization and globalization. The darkening of our time leads to an unconscious collective depression, to collective borderline psychology and the danger of nuclear escapism. This danger is real! Facebook – *persona-book* – seems to provide an answer. But the Inter-network, spread around the globe, mirrors the globalized shadow. The products of Facebook are, in a way, synthetic people. Individuation would be the opposite to this. With the systematic instant gratification and its instant dopamine flash, even the body disappears, and with it the real world with its problems and challenges. Alcohol and drugs notwithstanding, up to now there has been no legal control that would protect at least the children from getting accustomed to a second-hand life. As the French proverb goes, 'Le bon dieu péches les ámes a la ligne, le diable les péches au filet' (*the good God fishes the souls with a hook, the devil with the net).*

The electronic Golem

Now I come the Golem of our time, a complex answer to the global feeling of a pending doomsday: the phantasm of Artificial Intelligence (*AI),* connected with human-like robots, or *Androids* or *Synthetic* people (*Synths*). With their Smartphones and their superhuman capacities everybody can feel that they have access to superhuman intelligence. This fantasy began in the 1950s, shortly after Hiroshima and Nagasaki. Early and in a way primal and concretistic symbolic versions of this fantasy are the so-called *Androids.* With the exponential development of information technology, it became likely that in the near future, synthetic humanlike robots will take over our daily chores; they will drive our cars; they will manage everything. We are told that we should not be afraid: the androids will be programmed only with useful and non-controversial algorithms. Therefore, they will be harmless to us – they will be ideal synthetic slaves with no human feelings. These *replicas* (replicates) would not develop human consciousness and feelings; therefore, their active time is, just in case, limited to four years, in order to *prevent consciousness proliferation.* After this time, they will be '*retired*' and renovated, *re-programmed* and *recharged* to be *sold again.* Each night they have to charge up their batteries.

In the plot episode of the recent movie series, *Humans,* by Jonathan Brackley, a family buys for house keeping a *Synth* – a robot in the shape of a young woman. For energy saving purposes, she moves in a bit of a robot-like manner, with humanlike gestures but she doesn't show any human emotions. Her name is Anita. It/she must follow the instructions from her *first priority user* (the father of the family). There are some funny, but also disturbing scenes: Synths look like humans, they are omnipresent in society. In 'Smash Clubs,' for fun, people can torture or brutally destroy the Synths who, of course, are not programmed to defend themselves. If a Synth fights back this is an *Unusual Synth Behavior,* and very dangerous for the entire system. Of course, in the movie series this is exactly what happens for the purpose of creating the plot and its thrilling scenes.

Complex and archetype

What we have to deal with is a *complex: a circular pattern consisting of problem and solution on the same level.* Psychological complexes are elements and working tools of our individual psyche – and they are also the elements of the collective unconscious. The Golem-Complex is a negative complex, and it is a vicious circle. The uniformed, streamlined minds of billions of electronic media users, interconnected on an unconscious level of their minds, in a kind of collective anesthesia, slip into the virtual world populated by synthetic beings. The ego-complex is caught and swallowed up by a bigger and stronger, autonomous, collective complex. And what is going on behind the veil of artificial confusion, on the backstage where the topical, present-day archetypes are being constellated? I suppose, behind the symptomatic level, on the pre-oedipal level, it is about an unconscious longing for orientation: the hope in the umbilical cord to the archetypal great mother/father, who will finally solve all problems: the individual problems of life, relationships, mating, work and so on, and the collective nightmare of the collapsing ecosystem. This may explain the fascination with the internet. On the primary level it is about power, Hybris and presumption. The jeopardized ego-complex identifies itself with the Self – the False Self in Winnicott's model. Artificial helpers, the products of human grandiosity and inflation will solve the problem which was created by human grandiosity and inflation, like the alchemical homunculi or the Zombie-slaves in Voodoo. But in the end, there are only algorithms that mirror and multiply our own behavior, our shadow and our illusions.

The Golem made of clay

The famous Golem narrative about an artificially made man was created in Prague around 1560. The idea, and the recipe for how to create a Golem are much older, going back to the 12th-century wise Rabbi and Cabbalist, *Elazar from Worms* (Worms is an old German city on the Rhine River). Elazar wrote extensively about the book *Jezirah* – the *Book of Creation* of the world, as based on the secrets of the *Torah*. The idea is that the Creation was already pre-figured in the letters of the Torah. Adam, and the concrete world came into existence when G-d read out loudly and recited the words of the Torah. The Chassidim of the 12th century reflected this idea carefully, and tried to adopt G-d's creativity. They collected clay, as G-d did when he wanted to create Adam. Then they made a kind of body out of clay and water (*Golem* means *body*), and began to recite combinations of the letters of *Genesis* in different, systematic ways: each time combining two letters with one of the four letters of G-d's holy name (the Tetragrammaton). While reciting, they walked around the Golem's body, until the creature began to move. Gershom (Gerhard) Scholem described the different recipes and the procedure in the paper he presented at the 1953 Eranos conference. Originally, it was obviously a ritual about G-d's name, which led to an ecstatic feeling. On his forehead, the Golem had the word *emeth (Truth)* written on it, and this brought him to life. He was able to do every kind of work, but he could not speak. He had to obey his master (in the modern language, his 'first primary user'). He grew every day and became stronger and stronger.

A later version of the legend describes the end of the Golem thus: each Friday, when Shabbat comes, all work must seize. Usually, as Shabbat entered, Rabbi Loew would take away G-d's name (the *Schem*) off the Golem's forehead and transformed him back to clay. One Friday he forgot to do this, and the assembly in the Prague synagogue had already begun to sing the Shabbat-Psalm 92 (*How great are They works, O Lord!*) when the huge Golem came in and began to destroy the house. Rabbi Loew was called to intervene. He fought with the Golem and managed to take away the *Schem* from his forehead. The Shabbat-Psalm had to be sung again as the Jews in Prague still do today – they sing it twice.

The Golem fell back to clay, and his remains were stored under the roof of the old synagogue in Prague, where they still are today! No one is allowed to climb up those stairs.

Cultural complex

A complex is usually built around an emotion and structured following an archetypal pattern. The primary affect is organized by means of memory. The patterns of this organization allow selecting input and registering and storing relevant information. The basic collective emotion behind the Golem-Complex is fear and the compensatory *power-complex*. The exponential growth of technology, which deprives many people of work, jobs, meaning of life and even of the ecological basis of health and existence, in addition to the fascinating possibilities of technology, creates an entangled field of affects. In addition to this, there is also an unconscious guilt complex about the actions of past generations who had abused and raped nature, killed many people and destroyed cultures, all in the more and more psychologically streamlined globalized world. The idea that the desolate object can be healed by the same means, namely technology, makes this a negative complex, a vicious circle. This is grandiosity and inflation. The Golem becomes a symbol for resurrection. For the Jews, suffering from pogroms in Prague and elsewhere, the Golem legend was a symbol for hope in times of the collective extinction complex. In Israel today, it is part of the popular culture.

The social media addiction may also be a kind of a failed collective initiation into a world where psyche and matter fall together, as in the quantum physics synthesis of *unus mundus,* and as is sometimes anticipated for the age of Aquarius.

Such a complex is not a solution but a trap. The activated symbolism of synthetic people again raises the question: what is humanity? What is the difference between us and the robot people we have created with their programmed behavior? Why are we addicted to the synthetic umbilical cord and the internet? Who is the master, who is the slave? Is there a master at all? This also raises the questions of gender roles: the Golem is a product of male fantasies. Real creativity would include female fantasies. *Synths* are not born. What will be the future of female creativity? Is the net female –a matrix? Is there no 'patrix' (as termed by Mary Woodman) to set the limits? How can we break through the fog of the complex if we are part of it?

Dead or truthful

I want to finish this chapter with a different ending to the story of the Golem. This is a paradigmatic version of the story, which can be related to the problematic results of technology and our lifestyle, from nuclear waste to the Facebook addiction. Jakob Grimm, one of the famous storyteller brothers, tells us that the Jews used the Golem for housekeeping and daily work. The inscription on his forehead read: *Emeth*, which means *Truth*, the magic word which is an attribute of G-d. The Golem grew from day to day. As a precaution, therefore, every evening, the Jews deleted the first letter, *Aleph*, so that what remained was just, *Meth,* which in Hebrew meant*: it is dead.* The Golem thereby collapses and is dissolved back to clay. But if a Golem grew and grew, and his master didn't pay attention to it, the time would come when the master would no longer be able to reach the Golem's forehead to remove the word written on it. In terror, he would order the Golem to kneel down and take off his master's boots so that the latter can climb on a bench and reach the magic inscription on his servant's forehead. This worked and the master was able to delete the first letter on the Golem's forehead. But, alas, the lifeless mass of the huge Golem now fell on the master and crushed him to death.

What matters is *Emeth – the Truth.*

References

Brackley, J. and Vincent, S.. (2015). *Humans.* Die komplette Staffel, DVD.

Golem – Catalogue. (2016). Jüdisches Museum, Berlin, Kerber Verlag.

Havel, V. (1990). *Versuch in der Wahrheit zu leben* (Attempt to live in Truth). Essay, Rowohlt, Reinbeck bei Hamburg.

Kurzweil, R. (2005). *The Singularity is Near: When Humans Transcend Biology.* New York: Penguin.

Rasche, J. and Singer, T. (edit.) 2016. *Europe's Many Souls. Exploring Cultural Complexes and Identities.* New Orleans, LA: Spring-Journal-Books.

Scholem, G. (1953). Die Vorstellung vom Golem. *Eranos Jahrbuch XXII,* Rhein Verlag.

Psyche in political context

Chapter 13

Psychological citizenship

A problem of interpretation

John Beebe

In April of 1934, Toni Wolff was in Great Britain, reading a lecture she had written in English to the Analytical Psychology Club of London. Drawing toward the end of her prepared remarks, she mentions that "the Protestant religion has no feminine goddess," and ventures that "maybe this fatal psychological omission of the Reformed Church is one of the reasons why the Christian Trinity symbol has become insufficient." She adds:

> In the early days of the Gnostics the Holy Spirit was of female character, it was Sophia, the wisdom. But that was thought to be a dangerous and therefore heretical, teaching. And, anyhow, we cannot go back in history. I think it likely that some such feeling of what is wrong in the psychology of men and women has prompted the German Government to pass laws "whereby man and woman should again find their correct place."[1] Maybe that by being externally limited the woman discovers her inner femininity, and thereby the wisdom of nature, which is really her prerogative.
>
> (Wolff, 1934, p. 13)

The new laws in Germany that she refers to encouraged women to stay at home and procreate, restricting them from certain kinds of professional work. Having offered this hint of her political attitude, and how at that time it was both shaping and being shaped by her psychological views, Wolff proceeds into an extended example with which she will end the lecture, which carries the title, "Some Principles of Dream-Interpretation." It is these Jungian principles, vintage 1934, that I want to examine here, because they seem to me to raise questions as to how analysts listen to the citizen in the psyche (Samuels, 2007; Singer, 2019) when he or she speaks.

I quote from Wolff's concluding remarks:

> To end, I would like to give you some dreams of a man, which to my feeling are a remarkable apperception of the principle which seems more and more the necessary one in Europe. The dreamer is a most cultured

man of about 60, and of a nationality which places him in a position whereby he is able to value objectively the general political situation. He lives in Switzerland. His great hobby has always been history and his most admired hero is Julius Caesar. Quite a number of years ago he dreamt he saw in an underground room the foot and shoe of a Roman soldier of one of Caesar's legions. The dream at this time could hardly be interpreted. But events showed where it led to. In March, 1933 he had the following dream which was really a nightmare. He was in a room. In the opposite corner stood a figure wrapped like an Egyptian mummy. But gradually the figure became alive and slowly began to move towards him. It tried to get free of its bandages, and the bearded head of a man appeared. He looked like a man who had been shut up in a dark prison for years. His eyes rolled wide and he tried to form words, but apparently he had either forgotten speech, or did not know the language of the world into which he had come back. Perhaps he was even unware of the epoch he had come back to. As he advanced toward the dreamer and stammered in wild and desperate tones, the dreamer woke in terror.

(p. 13)

"The associations," Wolff continues,

were of a historical film he had seen wherein a prince was unjustly thrown into prison, and had looked like the figure in the dream when he had finally come out. The mummy was like that of an Egyptian Pharaoh. Further associations made it clear that the figure was the impersonation of a ruling principle which was characterized as 'imperator-like principle', of which Julius Caesar is the most outstanding representative. This dream took place just about the time when the new German Government was formed. The imperator-like principle is the principle of leadership where the capable man, in [a] time of disorientation and disintegration, is able to see the immediate necessities from a new angle, and to take things into his own hands. Of course, the dream was also relevant to the dreamer himself. But it certainly is, at the same time, an expression of a political situation which becomes more and more apparent in Europe and, at the time of the dream, was even obvious in the United States.

(Wolff, 1934, pp. 13–14)

As we see, Wolff has tied the dream to the time of the early days of the German government under Adolph Hitler. In the same month as she dates the dream, the Weimar Constitution was amended to give the German cabinet, and thus in effect the new Chancellor, Hitler, the power to enact laws without the participation of the Reichstag.

In support of her view, which I share, that the nightmare of the awakened mummy contained the dreamer's reflection on the emerging political situation being felt transnationally, Wolff cites a more recent dream of the same man that she notes came at the time of great civil unrest in France and Austria.[2]

Wolff also notes that at the same time that "we had some upstirring political events in Switzerland"[3] (p. 14).

In his dream from this more recent, politically charged time, Wolff's "most cultured man of about 60" dreamed that he

> [...] went to the Zurich playhouse, where Shakespeare's *Julius Caesar* was given in modern setting and clothes. He remembered having seen several scenes; but when it came to the great scene at the Forum he thought he could not bear to see Caesar in a modern suit, and he left the theatre.
>
> (p. 14)

To demonstrate how she applied tenets of the analytical psychology she practiced in responding to this dream, Wolff let her audience in London hear her conversation with the dreamer:

> I asked him what political principle Caesar and Brutus would represent, not in Shakespeare's tragedy, but in real history; he said that Brutus was the conservative element who conspired against Caesar because he thought he was violating democratic and constitutional ideas. But this was a quite unjust accusation, as Caesar was the one blameless figure in history who never defiled himself by breaking the law or by seeking merely personal ends. He was the leader and dictator first because the epoch was in need of this, and then also by his genius
>
> (Wolff, 1934, p. 14)

Let's pause here to note that in working with both dreams Wolff dismisses the affective reaction of the dream ego, treating it as an error in judgment, rather than as a valuable message from the psyche. This is not a stance in dream interpretation that I would endorse. It is especially dangerous when dealing with dreams that have political content, because the analyst's political leanings may too easily lead him or her astray.

What is the impact of such interpretations on the dreamer? By now, it may have occurred to you that I suspect C. G. Jung of being "the most cultured man," living in Switzerland, whose dreams Wolff is speaking of. The evidence I have is circumstantial, but I find it compelling. Jung was Swiss, he was a most "cultured man," he was about to turn 60 the following year, and his hobby was certainly history. And, more important, Julius Caesar was one of his heroes. We know this from a photograph Sonu Shamdasani includes in his book, *C. G. Jung: A Biography in Books* (2012, p. 9), which takes us into Jung's library. There is a picture of the library in 1909, which shows portrait busts of Voltaire, Nietzsche, and Julius Caesar. Jung (1912/1947, pp. 317–319) quotes Shakespeare's Julius Caesar at length in the second part of *Wandlungen und Symbole der Libido*. And in the second of his *Two Essays on Analytical Psychology*, which was published in 1935, Jung (1935/1966, p. 217, para. 352) he mentions, to show the way some people concretize their self-idealized inner figures, a man who by day is a shoemaker and yet sits every night among his circle of Freemasons as a grandee, "a reincarnation of Julius Caesar, fallible as a man, but in his official capacity infallible." And of course, Wolff was a close confidant of Jung's in a position to comment interpretatively on his inner life (Healy, 2017).

The revisionary Jungian analyst James Hillman (1978, p. 152) once quoted an Icelandic proverb: "Every dream comes true in the way it is interpreted." Wolff's comments on these dreams, if, as I believe, they were shared by her with Jung himself, certainly had an effect. Jung's notorious June 26, 1933 Interview on Radio Berlin occurred three months after the time of the first dream that Wolff reported in London. We can hear Jung declaring even through the watered-down translation we have in English (see von der Tann, 1989) that Hitler has responded in an appropriate way to the needs of the time. Jung said:

> The need of the whole always calls forth a leader, regardless of the form a state may take. Only in times of aimless acquiescence does the aimless conversation of parliamentary deliberations drone on, which always demonstrates the absence of a stirring in the depths or of a definite emergency.... It is perfectly natural that a leader should stand at the head of an élite, which in earlier centuries was formed by the nobility. The nobility believe... [in] the law of the nature in the blood and exclusiveness of the race. Western Europe doesn't understand the special psychic emergency of the young German nation because it does not find itself in the same situation either historically or psychologically.
>
> (McGuire & Hull, 1977, pp. 65–66)

By the time he gave this interview, Jung apparently had decided that Hitler, like the "blameless" Julius Caesar had assumed dictatorial powers because only he was capable of enacting and embodying the organic principle of leadership. It was on this basis that Hitler deserved to be called the Führer now. The precedent of history convinced Jung that it would be unfair to criticize Hitler for having done what was needed. If Jung was the dreamer who did not want to see Julius Caesar in modern dress, it is amazing that he does not even consider that in the wake of Caesar's deciding he was the man of the hour came the historical tragedy recorded so memorably by Shakespeare, which caused parliamentary democracy to disappear from Europe for 1,700 years. Nor did it seem important to Wolff that the first dream she mentioned hearing from the dreamer I have suggested was Jung, unmistakably conveys how frightened he was to see the awakening of a dynastic Pharaoh. This image hardly felt natural or organic in the dream, rather, it was monstrous.

Whoever had this dream, it came exactly when Hitler assumed dictatorial powers and reveals a dreaming self plainly horrified that this sort of absolute dictatorial leadership had been propelled by a perverse historical process back into life.

I assign to the citizen in this man's psyche the anxiety that the revival of the autocratic principle evoked. His psychological citizenship was communicating itself to the dreamer through the *affect* that overwhelmed him in the dream itself.

The dream interpretation that Wolff facilitated leads away from the dream's horror that such a long-buried avatar of undemocratic leadership has managed to unwrap itself. Arrived at on the basis of conscious associations tinged with cultural complexes, this interpretation argues that the delirious phantom that has been awakened from its long historical sleep to intrude into modern history is actually a blameless human personage whose return one is wrong to fear. The dreamer is assured that the "imperator-like" presence that can still be recognized in the vivified mummy points to a restorative archetypal "principle of leadership where the capable man, in [a] time of disorientation and disintegration, is able to see the immediate necessities from a new angle, and to take things into his own hands."

And when, a year later, this dreamer had a follow-up dream that I think tries to correct that optimistic interpretation, by showing him in no uncertain terms that his dream ego really "cannot bear to see Caesar in modern dress" and wants to leave this dream theater altogether, Wolff quelled the dreamer's doubts once again by calling him back to his associated idealization of Julius Caesar, noting: "He was the leader and dictator first because the epoch was in need of this, and then also by his genius."

If the dreamer was in fact Jung, and his dreams the expression of instinctive alarm at the contemporary emergence, under Hitler, of a new archaic autocracy, being asked to associate to the good dictator image he had found in the historical figure of Julius Caesar, whom he had always idealized, probably helped Jung to deny the degree of his immediate anxiety about Hitler. Wolff's strategy of asking for historical associations carried with it its own danger, an appeal to pre-established values that could effectively silence the concerns of the citizen in Jung's psyche. I hear that citizen clearly expressing uneasiness about contemporary historical developments in these dreams. If I am right, we have in Wolff's account a document that shows that Jung's psyche did harbor, early on, doubts about Hitler's way of coming to absolute power, as well as how through a misapplication of Jung's own historical method those doubts were put down.

The rest is history, to which we cannot, as Wolff says, return. The certainty that Jung displays all through the Berlin Radio interview is exactly the confidence in capacity that in his *Red Book* Jung had assigned to "the spirit of this time, who changes with the generations" (Jung, 2009, p. 229). He is convinced that Hitler is acting in accord with his identity as the man of the hour, and if I am right how he arrived at that conviction is no longer such a mystery.

But let's say I am wrong. Let's say the dreamer is not Jung, despite the coincidences I have offered. If anything, I feel even worse about this possibility. It is even sadder to think that it was the citizen in the psyche of some anonymous dreamer that Wolff's analytical psychology managed to silence. The approach to dream interpretation that Wolff practiced allowed the numinous uncanniness of a dream archetype to dominate the interpretation, crowding out the expressed affect of the dreamer toward the archetype. Isn't such silencing of the worry of the citizen in the psyche the analyst's form of political repression? And shouldn't we recognize that, when we see it, as the outrage it is?

Acknowledgments

I'm grateful to Vicky Jo Varner for making me aware of Toni Wolff's lecture and to the C. G. Jung Club of London for permitting me to quote from it.

Notes

1 "In March 1933, Goebbels had proclaimed, in his first speech as Minister of Propaganda and Public Information," "The best place for the woman to serve her people is in her marriage, in the family, in motherhood." In 1934, Hitler proclaimed, "[Woman's] world is her husband, her family, her children, her house."... Women's highest calling was to be motherhood. Laws that had protected women's rights were repealed and new laws were introduced to restrict women to the home and in their roles as wives and mothers. Women were barred from government and university positions. https://en.wikipedia.org/wiki/Feminism_in_Germany consulted November 29, 2017. Cf. Goebbels speech in Munich, March 1933: "The first best and most suitable place for the women is in the family" (http://www.spartacus-educational.com/GERwomen.htm, consulted December 3, 2017).

2 In early February 1934, riots by right wing French fascists and veterans succeeded in toppling France's center left government. In Austria, a brief civil war, the "February uprising," broke out between socialist and conservative-fascist forces.

3 She may be referring to the referendum held on March 11, 1934 on whether to approve a federal law on maintaining public order, a proposal that was rejected by Swiss voters.

References

Healy, N. S. (2017). *Toni Wolff & C.G. Jung: A Collaboration*. Los Angeles: Tiberius Press.

Hillman, J. (1978). Further Notes on Images. *Spring*, 152–182.

Jung, C. G. (1912/1947). *The Psychology of the Unconscious* (B. Hinkle, Trans.) New York: Dodd Mead.

Jung, C. G. (1935/1966). *Two Essays in Analytical Psychology*, 2nd ed. (R.F.C. Hull, Trans.) *Collected Works*, Vol. 7. Princeton. Princeton University Press.

Jung, C. G. (2009). *The Red Book=Liber Novus* (S. Shamdasani, Ed.; M. Kiburz, J. Peck & S. Shamdasani, Trans.) New York: W.W. Norton.

McGuire, W. & Hull, R. F. C. (Eds.) (1977). *C. G. Jung Speaking: Interviews and Encounters*. Princeton: Princeton University Press.

Samuels, A. (2007). *Politics on the Couch: Citizenship and the Internal Life*. London: Karnac Books.

Shamdasani, S. (2012). *C. G. Jung: A Biography in Books*. New York: W.W. Norton.

Singer, T. (2019). The Analyst as a Citizen in the World. *Journal of Analytical Psychology*, 64/2, 206–224.

Von der Tann, M. (1989). A Jungian Perspective on the Berlin Institute for Psychotherapy: A Basis for Mourning. *The San Francisco Jung Institute Library Journal*, 8/4, 43–47.

Wolff, T. (1934). Some Principles of Dream Interpretation. Lecture given to Analytical Psychology Club of London.

Chapter 14

Learned helplessness and Roma, the most marginalized of all ethnic groups in Europe

Heather Formaini

In this short chapter I address the relationship between psychoanalysis and human rights, documenting in part a legal case with which I have been professionally involved. I hope to show the way in which poverty is reproduced through existing social and cultural structures in Romania and Italy.

The case concerns the rights, or lack thereof, of a family from an ethnic minority in Romania, the legal aspect of which began in Italy in January 2015 and continues still. At the time of writing, this case has been in the Supreme Court in Rome for around nine months, following three and a half years in the Juvenile Court and Appeal Court in Florence. A judicial response is expected very soon and this will indicate whether two Romanian Roma parents can visit their children, presently held 'in care' by the State. The two elder children are in institutional care while the younger children have been placed for adoption, without the parents' permission. If the judges in the Supreme Court in Rome deny such a visit, a final appeal will then be lodged in the European Court of Human Rights in Strasbourg. Given the backlog of cases in Strasbourg, such a process could take several more years and thus mean that the parents will have had to wait for almost a decade to know their children's future as well as their own. As things stand, the parents fervently hope for and believe in the children's return to them forthwith, while those of us working on the case know that this is now an impossibility and that their best hope is to gain some kind of visiting rights to their children. While there are some countries that allow biological parents visiting rights to their children even when they have been legally adopted, Italy does not yet provide for this. It is important to note here that at the time the children were taken, the parents owned a house in Romania where the maternal grandparents also lived.

The two young Romanian Roma parents concerned in this case are, in a sense, typical of many impoverished Roma families which are forced to leave their home country in order to search for work. If they can find work in another part of the European Union, they are then able to send money home to provide for their extended families, most of whom live in abject poverty. This couple, called here Diamanta and Fiorello, came to Florence with their four very young children at the invitation of a German woman they met in a library. After appearing to befriend them, she then invited them to leave their home in Romania to come and work in the countryside outside Florence, and they believed this offer to be genuine. However, when they arrived, they found that there was no work for them and neither was there a place to live as had been promised. They had been betrayed by the person who had made this offer and who had, moreover, taken their documents from them for 'safekeeping'. They were placed in an old car in one of the main squares in Florence and were brought cold spaghetti to eat with their fingers, thus making it appear that they were uncivilized as well as poor and homeless. While at first this woman's intentions appeared benevolent, in fact her intention was to take the children from the parents and educate them on her own, thus separating the parents and children. I met this woman on several occasions and she appeared to feel as though she had been wronged for wishing to educate the four children, one of whom was a baby at the time.

Not long after their arrival in Florence, and in the middle of a winter's afternoon, when three of the four children were playing in the street near their father, they were seized by police and immediately placed into institutional 'care'. This took place in one of the most elegant squares of Florence with passers-by paying little or no attention to what was happening in front of them. At this time, the children's mother was at a nearby hospital with the youngest child. On learning of this, the police went to the hospital and seized that child, the baby.

Being Romanian Roma, and now without any documentation, they had no idea how to act, being unfamiliar with Italian bureaucracy. How should they go about finding why their children had been taken and what had happened to them? They believed that it must be possible to find them and then return home to Romania. They were left stranded and entirely desperate.

This family's case was brought to my attention by a nun whom the couple sought out soon after the children were taken. She offered them a refuge and promised to contact a local lawyer and me. I then went to Florence to meet the couple and interview them, before writing a psychological report for the lawyer and the Court. From this moment on we were all engaged for the next 18 months or so in moment-by-moment and day-by-day activities, mostly concerned with the Juvenile Court in Florence and the Social Services, two state authorities deeply mistrustful of each other. On several occasions Social Services refused to follow the Court's instructions to allow the parents to see their children. I too was made such a promise which was never honoured by Social Services. During this time, a number of visits were made by the parents to the Romanian embassy in Bologna to garner more official documents and indeed some help from the Romanian authorities. Also during this period, the Juvenile Court in Florence questioned whether the parents were actually involved in selling their children. To add insult to injury, the father's paternity was queried and he then had to go through agonizing months of waiting for the results of a DNA test.

The question I raise at this point concerns the Italian Constitution in which the sanctity of human rights is embedded as is the application of those human rights at the level of the State. I contend that when the State does not accept its own responsibility, it is the task of a citizen to stand up and follow the Constitution, that citizen then being a representative of that State and hence acting on behalf of the Constitution.

In what is described here, several citizens stand in the place of the State, while at the same time working against that State in order to try to achieve justice for the two parents. This kind of (psychoanalytic) work is in a category of its own and has given me the opportunity to recognize our interdependence with other professional disciplines, specifically anthropology from within Roma culture, and of the law as it applies to human rights and the Italian constitution.

The citizens contesting this action contend that the State has infringed the rights of the children (as well as the parents' rights), enshrined in the UN Convention of the Rights of the Child, to which this State is a signatory. Such citizens contend that the rights of the children are discounted by the State even though the State purports to be acting only in the 'interests of the child', begging the question of whether it can ever be lawful forcefully to separate children from their parents in the absence of violence or abuse. It appears that the children were seized because they are ethnically Roma, and therefore outside the Italian state's apparent mono-culturalism. The citizens also argue that the Italian state has infringed the rights of the parents, given that the constitution explicitly states that everyone must be assisted to live to their maximum potentiality. We therefore believed, and continue to believe, that it was the State's constitutional duty to help the abandoned Roma parents rather than to 'abduct' their children and then allow them to be adopted by Italian families. The citizens in this case include two lawyers, an honorary judge (a child specialist), and a psychoanalyst. As that psychoanalyst, I argue that our work can and does extend way beyond the consulting room, taking us to the streets, to the point of disidentifying from our expertise, to stand alongside those who are entirely helpless and vulnerable.

It is obvious that there exists a contradiction between the State and the State's citizens, and this contradiction could be described as a form of disassociation on the part of the State, the left hand (the Constitution) refusing to acknowledge what the right hand is doing (the Juvenile Court and the Social Services in Florence). I illustrate what happens when an ethnic group is marginalized to the point of being outcast, whether wilfully or out of ignorance.

Speaking from the standpoint of theory, I suggest that our understanding of the structure of the psyche can provide insight into the failure of the function of the ego when a very weak ego makes it almost impossible to speak of a sense of 'self' with a capacity to act intentionally. What I have found indicates that some Romanian Roma do not yet have functioning egos but rather transfer the ego function – the capacity to act on one's own behalf – on to those who are not Roma and who appear to know the way the world functions. This is, I believe, because many, if not most Roma, feel excluded from the world, and because their sense of helplessness is both actual and learned, inherited over many generations. This sense of exclusion, again both actual and learned, stems, in my view, from the consequences of hundreds of years of slavery in Romania, rendering many people helpless and dependent. Helplessness and dependence have therefore become a way of being. While there are some exceptions among Romanian Roma who have had a good education, this is not what happens generally throughout most of Romania, or indeed the rest of Europe. Until very recently most Roma were forbidden the right of education and were turned away at the school-gates.[1] Even when they were allowed through those gates the financial cost was very high, as it still is. The cost of education, even for children in primary school, is beyond the reach of most Roma, so the majority remain illiterate and hence unemployable.

It is my view that, psychologically speaking, we are working in the region of inter-generational transmission of trauma, a consequence of 500 years of slavery in Romania and of the generations since the Nazi Holocaust. It came as a great shock to learn that, according to the work of the Roma historian, Vania de Gila Kochanowski, it is estimated that 75% of all European Roma, some 7–8 million people, were murdered during those years.[2] While most non-Roma (gadjikane) sources say 250,000–500,000 thousand were murdered, the Simon Weisenthal centre acknowledges 2,000,000–2,500,000 million, based on records.[3] Most deaths, however, were not recorded, since most Roma were killed in open country by Einsatzgruppen, not in the camps themselves.

Although focussing on one particular case, I argue that it provides an opportunity to see how a part of our humanity has been lost, buried in what Jungians might call a collective shadow, functioning under the burden of capitalism and neoliberalism, the emphasis placed on that part of capital which works against social and human capital.

On a political level, I propose that the writings of the Italian political theorist, Antonio Gramsci,[4] on cultural hegemony, are those most likely to bring about necessary change in Roma culture which has rarely experienced any kind of unity, though there is now some movement in that direction. In recognizing the hegemony of the dominant class in society, European Roma could become united as a (non-geographical) Roma nation, thereby becoming a political force. Gramsci's theorizing indicates that only when those who are marginalized begin to identify with each other can they have access to political power through their unity. As things stand, Roma clans still tend to keep to themselves, for reasons which are obvious. My experience among this particular clan's extended family indicates that they have not yet found meaning in unity since the main focus of daily life is concerned with survival, living a kind of communal depression. I see a connection between an unactivated ego function and a difficulty in being united in order to have social and political power. I also see a connection between Roma who are prepared to struggle for their people and the development of individual and collective ego functioning. There are now some outstanding examples.

The following narrative will provide an example of what this particular Roma family has been up against over these last years. After two and a half years in the courts in Florence, and a monumental degree of work on the part of two dedicated lawyers, it was finally agreed that the parents could have a one-hour visit to their children at an unknown location on the outskirts of Florence. I was designated to be the person to accompany them to this meeting.

We meet at 7.30 am on a warm September morning. Two young and very excited Roma parents are waiting for me at the railway station of Santa Maria Novella in Florence. We have a mission for which we are all prepared. Not only will the parents be with their children for a time, but the visit will be monitored by an ethnic specialist and a team of psychologists. I personally have great hope in this ethnic specialist, though I have never met him.

First we prepare ourselves for the bus trip with a coffee at a bar downstairs, where the mother, who is almost beside herself with excitement, takes to the piano provided in every major Italian railway station. Although as yet she is no musician, she lays claim to her heritage, being of the Lautari musical clan, and now communicates something to the world: that she is a musician of an ancient culture, however unrecognized it is here. And she is communicating much more than this, though not in words, since her Romani language will not be recognized, nor will she be heard, coming from a despised caste.

This morning, however, Diamanta is dressed as 'gadje' (non-Roma), in order not to upset anyone of influence who may be present at the meeting with the children. Then, quickly, which bus must we take? Do we have the correct address? This part is easy and on arrival we are ushered into a small flat by a very gentle man who tells us not to move a muscle. Five minutes later a bustle of young women appears in the room, imitating – I do not exaggerate – Mussolini's brown shirts. A senior member of their brigade enters and I recognize her as one of the appeal court's psychologists.

What follows next is more violent and brutal than I could ever have imagined. I cannot recognize this as psychological or anything remotely human. This very senior psychologist, a professor indeed, bellows at the young man, the father, as though he is the lowest form of life, of a criminal class. He is dressed, as always, like a young Italian, in regulation black jeans, T-shirt, and jacket. The cause of offence is a small piece of his lower neck appearing beneath the T-shirt. When she leaves the room we adapt the T-shirt by turning it back to front.

A few minutes later there are tiny footsteps in the hall outside. Our door opens and the parents are ushered out. Although I am the only professional who has been engaged on this work since its outset, I am allowed no part in the observations, even though my psychological reports are among the documents in court.

The shouts of joy that follow are heard all over the building: 'Mamma, Papa....'. This is the first time that children and parents have been allowed to meet since the day they were taken.

The band of psychologists, along with the gentle man, stand behind the regulation glass in order to examine everyone's reactions, the psychologists convinced that the children will not recognize their parents. They are, however, much mistaken ... and the next hour is filled with the noise of the games they are set to play.

On our return to Florence the parents talk of nothing else ... they are hugely elated at how much their children have grown, how beautiful they all are, how many languages they now speak.

Fast forward a month, during which time there have been a great deal of upheaval, many tears, a thousand accusations, a notification of a seven-month prison sentence for the young mother,[5] and then, finally, a gentle calming of the waters. This kind of rhythm has by now become very familiar and it is one I hope to address once this work is brought to a conclusion. I now believe that we are confronted with not just one family's trials over these few years but more likely hundreds of years of inherited depression, the consequences of dispossession.

At 3.00 pm on 24 October, I receive an email message from the person with whom the parents now stay, in order that the prison sentence be avoided. (Diamanta has a kind of house imprisonment and may not move beyond the city of Florence.)

She indicates that the person 'adopting' two young children will have a very hard time. This message appears to come from nowhere. I know nothing about any adoption, and have been working for the return of all four 'stolen' children. I feel powerless. Can this be a solution to marginalizaton, slavery, itself originating in racism, leading to poverty, self-hatred, and other psychosocial catastrophes? Funds required for foster care and adoption can be found by the State but no provisions made to help the parents. They have been set-up for failure.

On 2 November I receive more news. Knowing that the young mother has had some blood tests I contact the person with whom she stays and ask about the results. The answer is that she has or has had Hepatitis B. Nothing more is clear at the moment. Attached to this message is a rider to say that 'a psychologist' has not given a good report of the young parents. Someone has communicated this report beyond the court's boundaries. I ask for a copy. There is none, since it has come by word of mouth. I write to the special lawyer in Rome.

Early in the morning of 6 November I hear from the lawyer in Rome. She has received the report by the ethnic expert and now understands that he has changed his view since the September meeting. Will I read this report? There are 350 pages and I choke in horror as I go through it. Every half an hour I pause to take in what is being said about the young mother. Immediately I am put in mind of the old 'stop and search' tactics used in Britain to apprehend and frighten people of colour. Nothing about the young mother's life in Florence passes without being recorded, and I speak of some years. Nothing about her is appreciated.

On countless occasions Diamanta resists arrest, and still the authorities do not, or will not, understand that she comes from a slave caste, once called Dalits (in fact, still) in India. After all of those years of slavery it still appears that it is not possible to understand why Roma are so suspicious of authority.

When I reach the end of the document I realize that the ethnic specialist is no specialist at all, but is just as monoculturally biased as others in this drama. He has seen the love between the parents and children but does not see this as a basis on which to make a decision for the family to stay together.

I use here the present tense to demonstrate the day-by-day ups and downs. Earlier on, in the first year of this work, such events took place several times a day, and were often seen as much more serious, with the young mother being placed in prison for a night, police searching her and taking her possessions, including her phone, on which she is reliant. Only much later did I realize that many of these were based upon a form of projective identification by the person who was supposedly 'saving' the family.

Each problem took an extraordinary amount of time to unravel due to the complexity of Italian bureaucracy and human psychology. The deconstructing of the fields of projective identification took not only time but also great delicacy, moving backwards and forwards between the players. At that point I had had little training or education in understanding the culture of Romanian Roma and did not realize the degree to which Roma 'clans' stay together.

I offer an example: the Lautari clan, musicians, stays very close to each other in one particular square in Florence, and other clans do not come here though, fascinatingly, they come to the very edge of the square. Other clans gather elsewhere. Asking members of the Lautari clan to move away from their square would be tantamount to making them homeless a second time.

The priests and the nuns at the church in the square know some of this clan and often are kind and thoughtful towards them. The clan keeps the common areas around the church spotlessly clean, sweeping and washing them several times a day, as though they are cleaning their own home.

So a kind of life has been created and it is here that the story already described had its origins, when a small Romanian Roma family came to seek medical care for their youngest child, treatment not being available to them in Romania. A woman appears to befriend this family offering them a home and work. While the mother is at a hospital with the youngest child, this woman denounces the parents to the police, who seize three children in broad daylight. The morning after the police go to the hospital and take the baby from his mother.

On hearing of this atrocity, another woman then enters the scene to manage the situation. It was then that I received a request to act for the parents, and although I did not know the person who invited me to do this, I supposed her to be of good character with a genuine wish to help Romanian Roma. She knew that I had worked with Slovakian Roma in the refugee courts in London.

As already indicated, I was soon able to meet the two parents, interviewing them at length. Considering what they were enduring, I found them to be very solid and indeed in possession of a remarkable equanimity. Since then I have come to know them very well and have written psychological reports for the courts which have been taken seriously, save for one section where I discussed ethnic cleansing. Given the situation, it has been neither appropriate nor necessary to work analytically with the parents. Much more important, in my view, is the need to offer ongoing support and understanding, trying to work on sorting out the everyday issues that come up. I therefore keep in touch by telephone, sometimes daily. I go to Florence regularly to have lunch with the mother, the father on occasion having some work during the day.

At other times it has been necessary to keep the peace between some of the difficult and volatile characters who inhabit this landscape, given to outbreaks of anger and accusations. This is perhaps the most difficult of all tasks: how to work with warring factions to reunite them to their common purpose: the return of the children from State custody.

These interactions require some delicate reckoning, negotiating separately with the parties but never together at this point, while engaging the help of one or both of the lawyers. Bowlby and Main's attachment theory plays a central role at this point and demonstrates the way in which the parents and the highly privileged person all suffer insecure attachment, both avoidant and ambivalent. It is likely that all three experience a fragmentation of the ego.

The three of us – the lawyers and I – have our goal set on achieving something which could be considered straightforward in a country which has a most dignified constitution. Article 3 of the Italian constitution, for example, states that 'All citizens have equal social dignity and are equal before the law, without distinction of sex, race, language, religion, political opinion, personal and social conditions. It is the duty of the Republic to remove those obstacles of an economic or social nature which constrain the freedom and equality of citizens, thereby impeding the full development of the human person and the effective participation of all working in the political, economic and social organization of the country'.[6]

When this couple arrived in Italy, four and a half years ago at the time of writing, they owned a house in Romania which was in Diamanta's name. They shared their house with the maternal grandparents, one of whom has since died. Being forced to stay in Italy because of the legal processes, Diamanta had to put the house into her mother's name, believing that she could secure their future. Her mother, however, not understanding fully the consequences of what she was doing, sold the house in order to pay for a medical operation. The family has therefore lost their home in Romania and have been forced to live a precarious existence while still waiting, after four and a half years, for news of their 'stolen' children. They are now more impoverished than they were and even more marginalized, being separated from their community in Romania.

Postscript: At the very moment of going to press I received a message from the lawyer in Rome. She had been in Strasbourg all week and returned home to discover the judgement from the Supreme Court. We have very very good news!

Antonio Gramsci

The following articles are very useful in elaborating Gramsci's theories of cultural hegemony, the subaltern, contradictory consciousness, and revolutionary processes, his understanding of history.

http://www.internationalgramscisociety.org/resources/online_articles/
    articles/Green-Marcus-2002.pdf
https://petejcrawford.wordpress.com/2016/04/26/hegemony-in-antonio-
    gramscis-theory-of-revolution/

Notes

1 http://www.errc.org/video/bettertogether-stop-school-segregation-
   of-roma
2 Parlons tsigane: Histoire, culture et langue du peuple tsigane, Vania De Gi-
   la-Kochanowski, Collection "Parlons", French ed, 1994.
3 Historical Amnesia: The Romani Holocaust, C. R. Sridhar. *Economic and Political Weekly* Vol. 41, No. 3 (August 19–25, 2006), pp. 3569–3571.
4 http://www.internationalgramscisociety.org/resources/online_articles/articles/
   Green-Marcus-2002.pdf
5 Mihaela Dragan is an excellent example of a Romanian Roma woman, highly
   educated, an actor and activist.
6 Constitution of Italy, 22 December 1947.
   On 16 March 1997, German President Roman Herzog declared

   The genocide of the Sinti and Roma was motivated by the same obsession
   with race, carried out with the same resolve and the same intent to achieve
   their methodical and final extermination as the genocide against the Jews.

Throughout the National Socialists' sphere of influence, the Sinti and Roma were murdered systematically, family by family, from the very young to the very old

(ibid)

The whole evolution of German post-Holocaust treatment of Roma and Sinti is a disturbing study. From not acknowledging the Roma/Sinti as genuine victims (they were still classified as 'asocial criminals' in the immediate aftermath of WWII), to the acknowledgement of the Genocide to placing Romani Holocaust victims on a par with Jews in terms of both groups being targeted for the Final Solution. That said, compensation claims for many Holocaust victims in Europe are still pending (ibid). 9. See also https://www.theguardian.com/world/2013/aug/23/king-of-gypsie.

Chapter 15

Nowhere to go

The limits of therapeutic practice

Ali Zarbafi

Introduction

I saw Reza in 2006 in the National Health Service. The following chapter is a summary of the therapeutic work and the challenges and difficulties this presented to my role as a psychotherapist working for an arm of Government, i.e. the health service. I myself am Anglo-Iranian. The therapy was conducted in Farsi (Persian). My mother is English, so English is my mother-tongue even though I lived in Iran until the age of 14. My father is Iranian. I feel very comfortable and *at home* in Farsi and I have visited Iran regularly throughout my life. I am both a child refugee and a migrant so identify with the experience of exile.

In exile

Reza was referred to me by a woman Iranian doctor for depression. He came into the room and greeted me in Farsi by shaking my hand. Reza was 32, slim and around 6 ft with a gentle manner and countenance. The session was conducted in Farsi as his English was poor.

R: I have been here for about six months. I had to leave Iran and life here is not what I expected. I feel quite lonely and not sure what to do with myself. I am safe, that is true, which is good – it is very different – people leave you to yourself. In Iran you cannot get away from family and friends. Here nobody bothers you.

A: You have not met anyone here?

R: Yes, well I have been going to English classes, but it is difficult, and my concentration isn't good. I keep thinking about home and have avoided other Iranians here. My communication with non-Iranians is very limited. I also have nightmares and am not sleeping very well.

A: Nightmares – any one you care to tell me about?

R: Oh nothing, just rubbish really, it does not make any sense....

I wait, looking at him.

R: Well a recurrent dream I have had is that I am untying my shoes next to my bed and as I untie them I start falling and I find myself in a muddy arena and there is a huge pig attacking my right arm and people are watching. I have a little girl with me whom I am trying to protect with my left arm, but the pig is ferocious, and I don't think I can hold it off as it tears at my arm, and then I wake up frightened and cannot sleep.

   I wait a while, taking in the image.

A: That is quite a powerful dream – do you have any thoughts about it.

R: *'No'*, looking at me blankly. *'It's just a dream'*. Nobody has ever asked him this question before.

A: The dream starts with shoes, do shoes mean anything for you?

R: Shoes. Well yes, I was a shoe maker in Tehran. I had a shop in the bazaar with my brother. We made a decent living – not rich but we enjoyed it. We made leather shoes which are very expensive over here. I don't think I could do the same here. I cannot work anyway as I am waiting to get a decision on my refugee status. I have to go to Croydon every week to register with the Home Office.

   I am aware that I do not know anything about this man and the dream is important but maybe a bit early for me to have a sense of its place in the context of his life.

A: So do you want to tell me why you had to leave Iran?

   He sits there quietly for a while.

R: I had to leave because I am a homosexual (this is the closest translation from Farsi which actually translates 'playing with the same sex'). I was visiting a friend of mine I saw regularly. In Iran relations between homosexuals go on very secretly and is not generally noticed too much but some busybody neighbours reported something to the police. They poured into the house, arrested us, whipped us both and told us to pray to God and that if it happened again we would face the death penalty. We were in jail for a few weeks and we were beaten and humiliated.

   When I was released my family spat at me – my brothers told me not to come back home because they might kill me as I had brought shame to the family. My father would not see me. I had been arrested before a couple of times when I met friends in parks, but it was only ever a suspicion and I generally paid off the officers. This time it was much more serious as friends and family now knew as well.

   I could feel how difficult this was for him to tell me as I was an older Iranian man and we were speaking in Farsi about a subject that most Iranians would not speak openly about in any serious way. It was in the shadows and there was a different approach to this than in the West. In Iran sexual identity is not an issue unless you make it so publicly. Identity is located in masculinity, patriarchy and honour. To declare being gay as a sexual identity is also to declare your individuality in a culture which is very group based and it is the latter which brings danger, i.e. putting your individual self before your family (Afary, 2009).

R: I had some money and left and came here via Turkey, Bulgaria, Greece, Italy and France. It took me a year. In France I made 6 attempts to cross and finally got over unseen.

A: You were very determined to get to England – that is quite a journey.

R: I had relations in London but when I got here they had emigrated to Canada, so I was alone. This was a shock and it does not help that I was still receiving texts from my older brother telling me that wherever I go he will find me and kill me. I changed my number as it was getting me down.

Reza told me that the younger brother he shared a shop with helped him financially only. His mother, although horrified, contacted him for a while pleading that he should meet a nice girl and put these things aside, but the rest of the family have shunned him and are in shock. When he got to England he applied for asylum and, although the Home Office accepted that he was gay, they said his story was not convincing. He was waiting for a decision.

A: So you were a shoemaker and your dream starts with untying shoes.

R: I always liked shoes – you need them to protect you from the rough ground. There was something very comforting about making shoes. I put a lot of myself into it. I felt creative when I made shoes for people. It was a craft and I was respected for my work.

Craftsmanship of which there is a huge variety in Iran is highly thought of and there is pride in this work. We both knew this culturally.

A: 'What about the pig' I asked.

R: Well in Islam the pig is haram – dirty and forbidden – you are not supposed to eat it. This pig was more like a boar, so it was male.

A: In the dream you fall through shoes, having untied them or opened them I suppose, and find yourself fighting off something forbidden or dirty and masculine, i.e. a boar in a public arena and you are protecting a young girl.

R: The only important young girl in my life was my little sister. I was very close to her. I always felt protective towards her as she was the youngest. She was always full of life and very bright, but I seemed to be the only one who noticed.

A: So with your right arm you are battling with something dirty, unacceptable and with your left arm you are protecting an alive and bright but unnoticed little girl and nobody it seems is helping you. You are alone in this. What is the crowd doing?

R: They are just watching quietly as though it is a spectacle, like watching an accident on a road when you drive by.

A: This feeling of being unnoticed, is it familiar to you in your life?

R: I had a fairly normal big family life with lots of cousins and family gath-
     erings. My mother was always busy cooking. There were 6 of us in the
     family. My father worked and seemed rather uninterested in the chil-
     dren in general. I seemed to grow up with my many cousins and children
     in the streets with neighbours' families. Lots of games.
        He looks at me.
R: You have lived in Iran.
A: Yes many years ago.
R: So you know what it is like to grow up there.
A: Yes I have a general idea.
        There is a pause.
A: It sounds like you are telling me that you were not close to your father.
R: No, I felt closer to my mother – but she is 'the mother' so to speak, so
     that is natural. I grew up being quite responsible and independent hence
     the shoe business. I worked hard and played in the shadows. I got on
     with people and did not have any trouble. I am not a troublemaker.
A: Why not?
R: Well partly because being homosexual I did not want to draw attention
     to myself and so tried to blend into the background where people did
     not have to think about me.
A: You did not want to be noticed.
R: I suppose so – it was too dangerous.

As he said this I was aware that he had a very easy manner – a seamlessness –
not intrusive and on the surface quite self-contained. I was also aware that
what he was talking about was about the birth of individual identity in Iran
rather than just homosexuality as such and how this is part of the challenge
to his life – there is a political dimension to this.

The dream gave me a sense of how he experienced himself and the world.
The untying or opening up of something creative or interior seemed to be
very important as were the girl, the pig, the mud, the publicness of his struggle and the indifferent crowd. He was alone within himself, but also in his
own culture, where something could not be thought or expressed.

I was aware that this cultural attitude was also something he carried about
himself. His seamlessness was also very social and hid his individual identity. Most Iranians cultivate a socially easy manner and are generally quite
socially skilled and comfortable. Men occupy a homosocial space where
affection and touching are demonstrated, and so homosexuality is invisible.
The same applies to women (Afary, 2009).

A: It seems to me that maybe one of the themes in the dream points to how
     you experience yourself as 'haram'.
        He looked at me.

R: How can something that you are or that God decided for you be unacceptable. What kind of God or religion can deny your very being. I did
not choose to be what I am. I cannot fix it or behave. I did not think at
14 well what is my sexual orientation? I just was what I was but in Iran
you are not supposed to be what you are only what you are supposed
to be.

He then spent a few minutes expressing his anger at this denial of his individual identity and life within a culture that he felt part of. The introduction here of God and Islam made me think of Haram and the muddy arena
and the sexual connotations of this. In Islam anal intercourse is haram and
forbidden, but in Iranian culture it was practised as long as it was part of
being manly and most of the great poets (Hafez, Rumi, etc.,) speak of love
between men and boys. If you were the passive receiver this was seen as a
source of masculine shame, hence the practice was always between older,
generally wealthier men and younger men or boys who were looked after by
the elder. This did not preclude men having wives and families. It was part
of being masculine (Afary, 2009).

Feeling accepted and hopeful

We met weekly, but he was too isolated, so I suggested there were organisations in London who supported the gay community. He was interested in
this and expressed his surprise that such organisations existed openly and
publicly. I referred him to one of the organisations in London which run
workshops and support groups for the gay community. He went along and
attended a few of these workshops where with his very broken English he
met other gay men and women who were from various cultures.

He attended these workshops and groups weekly.

R: I did not understand quite a lot of what people were talking about in
these workshops, but people were very kind and explained things to me
patiently. I felt part of something, accepted and known. I realised that
other gays also experienced these prejudices in different ways but at
least it could be talked about and you were not shunned for being who
you were. You were allowed to have a private life, publicly.

I was aware that this experience had allowed him to be with the 'little girl
in the dream' rather than just protecting her from annihilation, so he was
feeling 'alive' and connected to a precious banished part of himself.

I saw Reza for around 12 sessions and then saw him monthly for another
three sessions. Then I did not see him for 18 months after which he contacted me again through the Doctor quite distressed.

In limbo

In the first session he told me that after he saw me last he started a relationship with another Iranian man and he was feeling much better. Something he had always felt ashamed of or had to hide could now be expressed much more freely. This new lease of life had somehow helped him to put behind him the loss of his family, friends and country.

But his asylum application had failed, and he had appealed. Meanwhile he had been thrown out of where he was living due to the cut in state benefit and was living on various friends' and sometimes under an arch or just on a bench somewhere. He was still in a relationship, but it was a strain. His boyfriend lived in a bed and breakfast and so could not house him regularly without being thrown out himself.

R: I have been outside my country for over two years now and am still waiting to be accepted into this country. I have not been able to do any work. My English has improved, and I have met kind and not so kind people but now feel I am just waiting around. I did not apply to become a tramp. It is like I am at a train station waiting for the train to take me to my destination, but nobody knows when the train will arrive.
      Pause.

R: There is an indifference even though I am being shown all the marvellous destinations on the brochures in the train station. In Iran I knew where I stood because I was hated. Hatred is much easier to face than indifference. I sometimes think I should have disappeared into the mountains in Iran and changed my name and identity but then I would not have discovered being allowed to be openly gay as I have here.
      Pause.

R: What is the use of me feeling accepted, on the one hand, as a gay person and having a relationship and then not being accepted as a refugee – what are they waiting for, what sort of thinking is this? Do they think like Afghanistan that if things settle down I can go back? I am unwanted as a gay Iranian and a Muslim. I am a shameful dirty pig! He then burst into tears.
      I waited and then said – 'the way you speak makes it sound like you sometimes find yourself agreeing with them – that maybe you are a shameful dirty pig'.

R: I am not!!! I used to think that before I came here but being here has enabled me to feel more normal, more balanced – but what is the use if I am not allowed to live, to plan, to hope for my future?

R: I cannot live my life in a waiting room!

Transference: individual and cultural

It was at this point that it occurred to me that maybe there was another dimension to this.

A: I remember introducing you to the organisations which helped you in accepting your gay identity.
R: Yes, you did, and I am very grateful, but I am also feeling angry that you, like the system, like the doctor, are good to me and put out a hand to me when you are doing something unrealistic .
A: You feel we are somehow misleading you.
R: You don't mean it, but you are. You helped me see something which gave me hope and now look at me.
A: So you feel I was somehow irresponsible in showing you something that you feel could never truly have.
R: No, I feel you understood, but I feel I have been set up, not just by you but this whole damn situation but knowingly or not you are part of it.

We sat there silently together. He was in tears and taking tissues and I was waiting to see if it was possible to think and say something useful. I was aware now that I was feeling powerless and was being challenged as a therapist. What was my role here? What was the point of 'my role' in a system which brutally panders to the latest opinion polls and stranger phobia? I was working for the Health Service but the Home Office which was responsible for immigration was working to a different agenda.

After a while I said to him. 'It seems to me that you have felt quite alive in the last few months. You are now expressing what is important to you, you are very angry, maybe have been for years – you feel the importance of your life. You have tasted feeling known and understood which is important to all of us. You are right, it is difficult to wait – the system here can be quite indifferent'.

R: Yes I have felt alive and more accepted in ways I have not felt before culturally. I have felt free for once in my life, but I don't know how long I can keep going. I have started having nightmares again.
     I wait.
R: In the dream I come out of my flat into the street and start walking to-wards my shop. The street is very crowded, and people are surging from the right, so I keep getting pulled into side roads. I make my way back again and the same happens. I come back and see that this road is very long with thousands of people in the way. I start panicking – I am not going to get through. I struggle and push people aside but get pushed back and then I wake up sweating and shouting.

We sat with this dream and it felt quite overwhelming. I was aware that internally he was being flooded with anxiety to do with psychic survival.

He looked at me.

R: You see the dream is telling me there is no hope. I cannot get to my destination, my shoe shop, where I made a living and had control over my life. I am not a person anymore but am at the mercy of events. Anything could happen to me

A: Well I would say that the dream is also showing how you are feeling inside, rather than what is going to happen to you.

R: How do you know that? Are you God? How can you say things so comfortably?

He gets up and starts walking around the room. He was right, it was a comfortable statement and I was assuming too much, as he was talking about how he could not negotiate his destiny here as it was so impersonal.

R: Look at me I get up and yet I have nowhere to go. I want to believe you but there is too much at stake – what if you don't know. I mean how can you know. People die every day. Things happen which are beyond what you say be it here or Iran.

I was aware that his distress and situation meant that he was taking what I was saying very literally, because it was real, and I was trying to create an internal space as there was no external space left for him, but I was mistaken.

A: You are right. I ultimately do not have any control over the political environment in England or Iran.

R: You have more control than me!

I was increasingly aware of the transference in this work where I had slowly become the indifferent parent/culture who showed him life but was indifferent to his individual identity – the feminine in the dream. He was not only feeling the shape of his own former life up until he lost it and came to England, he was now re-experiencing it here in a more alienated way through the Home Office. In his eyes I was a naive trickster which culturally for him would have resonated as sweet-talking male politicians and elders who do not do what they say.

Now he was having to believe that this rejection of his individual identity was not going to happen to him here again bureaucratically. In Iran he had some power and control represented by the shoe shop and his ability to read his culture and life.

Therapeutically we had a good alliance as he fundamentally trusted me, hence his ability to express very difficult things. However, the difficulty was that he was in a situation of limbo where the therapy was being overshadowed by a seemingly hopeless situation. He was not only bringing me his situation as a refugee and his feelings of exclusion and being a stranger in his own country but, more importantly, how he felt unwanted in Britain. Everything was a trick of some sort with indifference below the surface.

The end

I saw Reza for a few more months and wrote a report for his appeal as did the GP. His appeal was rejected on the grounds that his life was not in danger in Iran as he had been released from jail, despite the beatings. He was not given a deportation date. Again, he was in limbo – now it was official that he was not wanted and was waiting for a deportation date. This was very difficult for him.

R: So I will get back to my shop it seems but not quite the way I expected.
A: Have you any thoughts about returning?
R: You mean how do I feel about my impending funeral?
A: Is it going to be your funeral?
R: I have no idea but most likely – it may just as well be – I cannot go back to the way I was before, now that I have tasted feeling free and alive here! My boyfriend has even suggested he comes with me, but it is out of the question.
A: You would like him to come with you?
R: Yes, of course I would, but it would be madness. Who knows what will happen at the airport when we arrive? They have those computers. I will be arrested immediately and so will he and then we may not see each other anyway so I think it would be better for me if I knew he was alive.
   I thought of him protecting the self and meaning again through knowing that his boyfriend was safe. He thought of all sorts of options like just disappearing here or maybe hiding in a church for sanctuary like others had done.
R: It is my fate maybe I should just face it with honour rather than live illegally over here. I don't know which is worse – living with the possibility of death in my own country where at least I know their ways or just existing as an outsider over here as a criminal! These are my options!
   Pause
R: I remember a story once of a Jewish mother who had two children and the Nazi officer gave her an impossible option. 'Which of your two children do you want to die first'? he said. I find myself in a situation which feels the same except it is about me which is easier than if I had children.
   I was thinking of the girl in the pig dream as he said this and how to protect her. I was very moved but also was aware that he was being a bit fatalistic which in Iran is very common. Religion and folklore in Iran are full of tales of destiny and fate. Nature or God in the end somehow

determines your life. This is part of a history which has intermittently been invaded or influenced by foreign powers.

This felt beyond us both in reality now, but I decided to say something.

A: The choice you pose is between a part of you that does not care about yourself – the indifferent part like the crowd, and a part of you that needs to take a chance for the future for the little girl in your dream and your relationship. The one who risked his life when he left Iran and somehow got to England. If you return you may give up on yourself, if you disappear you buy yourself time and there is still hope. The choice is yours. You either allow the pig to devour you or you keep going in the crowd despite all odds.

He thought about this for a while.

R: I think staying here is giving up as I have no real control but maybe going back is better for my soul than being a coward and disappearing.

I realised the proud Iranian man was now speaking. His cultural identity was now very present which had a heroic quality even though it also felt rather reckless at the same time which may have been more to do with my pragmatic Western psychological and cultural thinking.

As he left he shook my hand. He always shook my hand when he left. An Iranian custom. It was the firmest handshake he had given me.

R: I hope to see you next month.

A month later he did not appear at a session time we had arranged. His mobile was not working or had been switched off. I wondered whether the Home Office had arrived at his address one evening and deported him or whether he had disappeared.

I never heard from him again. I assumed he had been deported but I did not know this for sure.

Concluding thoughts

Reza's decision to go back to Iran was important for his sense of self, identity and meaning rather than disappearing and living a life in the shadows as an illegal immigrant in this country. The hope that the West provided in the Iranian imagination was clearly hollow, in that there was a promise but ultimately very little concern for Reza over here as an individual in contrast to the community life he had in Iran. Reza had come to me partly to receive some sense of normality, i.e. seeing a man from his own culture and language who he could share his thoughts with. The Iranian GP recognised this as well. I sent him to the gay community in London in order for him to feel part of something shared among many in London, so he did not feel alone and alienated. Alienation on a social level can be thought of as 'estrangement from the emotional connections and values of one's family and society' (Akhtar, 2009, p. 10). Just as his gay identity had led to his loss of home in Iran – a huge price to pay, it was not enough in this country to save him. He was not given refugee status. Both the GP and I were imagining what Reza needed based on our lives and history in Britain or the West.

Reza's challenge to me can be thought of in the following way. In Iran the older man may look after the young gay man and help him in his life but ultimately the older man has the power and represents a patriarchal system which insists on the dominance of men over woman, girls and younger men and boys. I was the older man in this therapeutic contract and I was very helpful and encouraging of his gay identity. This for Reza is both benign and malign. I, however, also stand for the West, which through media and education and historical interference, has influenced young Iranians and encouraged or inspired them to develop their gay identities and communities at great risk to themselves in Iran and this is not about being gay but about being openly gay and insisting on their individual identity (Afary, 2009). So, the human rights dimension of Western influence also gets embedded in me. I am not only a seemingly kind patriarch but also an enlightened Westerner, but these are both hollow as ultimately, I am not being truthful on both counts. As a Westerner I lure him into exploring his gay identity but am happy to send him back hence not really taking gay identity seriously enough as a human right. As an Iranian patriarch I need to look after him for my own purposes as well as maintaining the social order in which I have power.

My psychotherapeutic interventions in the work, though seemingly helpful in the beginning, become more bizarre to Reza as though I am some mystic not really connected to his actual material life. I say things 'too easily' and maybe from a very comfortable place as his life and meaning are ultimately in danger. Initially my words were full for him but became emptied out as his situation became more desperate. Here Reza may be talking about the seduction of the language of power where one can say seemingly profound and deep things but not 'walk the talk'. Religion in Iran also has this quality of profundity without empathy. It also applies to Western ideas/ promises which seem to be in the service of power politics and dominance and not necessarily relevant to the context in which they are being applied (Said, 1978). I can say profound things about what is going on in his dream world, but he feels that it is just more seduction like the idea of Western individualism taken out of context. I am aware that the dreams seem to point to being overwhelmed internally but I am less prepared to actually realise the looming hopelessness externally and how I am part of the very state apparatus which is sending him back.

I, as a psychotherapist, have the luxury of being able to travel between Iran and England, both psychologically and literally, but my patient Reza had no such luxury. This makes our encounter culturally at odds with each other due to life experience, and my projections of hope onto him and assumption of possibility is at odds with the culture and country I am in. I became aware that the main threat to Reza was not his own country where the 'trauma' was located but the country he was in now in not taking him seriously.

This case illustrates how the patient teaches the therapist something that he cannot see very clearly. He, the therapist in the transference both psychically and culturally, becomes the unrealistic colluder who is thoughtful but whose cultural shadow gets represented by the Home Office or the Iranian State which does not take gay identity seriously enough as a human right thereby undermining the very project of individual consciousness which the therapist is offering to the patient. The therapeutic project is challenged to be more conscious of its cultural limits, interests and assumptions and how this may be experienced negatively by other cultures.

References

Afary, J. (2009). *Sexual politics in modern Iran*. Cambridge, UK: Cambridge University Press.

Akhtar, S. (2009). *Comprehensive dictionary of psychoanalysis*. London, UK: Karnac.

Said, E. W. (1978). *Orientalism*. London, UK: Henley, Routledge Keegan & Paul.

Chapter 16

Catalyzing influences of immigrants for developing a multicultural perspective in psychotherapy training institutes

Lynn Alicia Franco

In the publication from the second "Analysis and Activism Conference" held in Rome 2015, Stefano Carta reminded us that, "One is always contained in a society and at the same time contains a society" (*The Analyst in the Polis,* Vol. I, p. 20). His statement challenged me to ask what culture contains an immigrant's multicultural subjectivity? I focused my inquiry on how I and other immigrant-trainees had been contained by the cultures of two psychotherapy-training "societies": "The Psychotherapy Institute" in Berkeley, California ("TPI") and the "C.G. Jung Institute of San Francisco" (CGJISF). I hypothesized that the process of immigration and pro-culturation activated immigrant-trainees' political energies toward creating resettlement in a multicultural community. By contributing their vitality and desire for inclusion, I speculated that immigrants would nudge their training Institutes toward greater social responsibility of embracing greater cultural diversity in candidates' curriculum and, demographically, in who was admitted to train. I reasoned that such changes would depend upon origin mythologies and the receptivity of present-day members for altering established cultural traditions. This study was guided by both personal experiences as an immigrant-trainee in both Institutes and based on responses of 25 members I surveyed, some of whom were also immigrants. I offer my findings with the hope that they may be relevant and helpful to the concerns of psychotherapists from all traditions regarding who gets to receive therapy and who is entitled to offer it (Note 16.1).

Inspired by the analytic concept of Tom Singer and Sam Kimbles regarding the theory of cultural complexes (*The Emerging Theory of Cultural Complexes,* 2004a) in their expansion of Jung's theory of the collective unconscious and Joseph Henderson's concept of a cultural unconscious, and by Andrew Samuels' notion of the political energy in the social channel of our psyches (A. Samuels, *The Political Psyche*, pp. 58–59), I envisioned a cultural complex particular to the psyche of immigrants: that of a multicultural complex. As archetypal yearnings for belonging and identity are

NOTE 16.1 SURVEY QUESTIONS AND SUMMARY OF RESPONSES

Survey questions

(Survey was either emailed or used in face-to-face interviews of 25 members of either and both, The Psychotherapy Institute and the C.G. Jung Institute of San Francisco, California).

- Describe your role in the organization:
- Describe evidence, if any, of multicultural (racial and ethnic) inclusivity in your organization.
- What multicultural programs and/or projects have been established?
- If you note greater multicultural inclusivity now than when you first became a member, how has this occurred?
- Have multicultural projects/programs been initiated that did not succeed as original purposed? Why do you think they did not? Did they seed future projects?
- Have immigrant and 1st generation immigrant-trainees been catalyzing influences of multicultural changes in your organization? Can you describe examples of their presence and their influence?
- Have immigrant-trainees, either during training or after completing the program, left the organization without contributing to a multicultural conversation? Please describe how you understand the circumstances.
- Has a multicultural perspective in your training program been accepted? If so, how do you sense it has transformed the organization's culture?

Summary of responses

- Social/cultural concepts require further psychological elaboration and integration, especially examining systemic racialization in the organizations' structures and values and how race maybe embedded in psychological theories. This work requires personal and organizational commitment, dedication and persistent leadership.
- Supervisors and teachers need to invite ethnic and racial conversations with individual specificity which includes an exploration of one's relationship to group affiliation and identity. Key to counterbalancing inherent asymmetrical power dynamics in training programs is to hold the privilege of one's role with an attitude of mutual respect and humility.

- For an organization to develop an ethos which supports a multicultural perspective, facilitated group conversations and processes are crucial for deepening dialogues about cultural identities and cultural complexes. Planned inter-group dialogues and activities are needed, such as between diversity committees and other educational and governing committees.

disrupted during the transit from one's home of origin to the proculturation process in a new culture, where relational, cultural and socioeconomic attachments are severed, often traumatically, immigrants in search of community and identity weave a narrative of change and continuity that must include multiple losses and cultures. Included in their narratives one often finds depressive and anxious symptoms that also contain dissociated anguishes and "phantom narratives" of immigrant parents, grandparents and associated cultural traumas (Kimbles, *Phantom Narratives*, p. 17). While such acute and prolonged suffering results in psychic vulnerability, these circumstances also invite resiliency, flexibility and ingenuity. I suggest that this psychological confluence in immigrants, that I called a multicultural complex, catalyzes their political energy toward creating new settlement in a multicultural society (Note 16.2).

NOTE 16.2 DEFINITIONS OF TERMS

a. "Cultural Complexes" (CC) is based on Samuel Kimbles, *Phantom Narratives*, (2014), Chapter 1, pp. 2–14, Rowman & Littlefield and from Tom Singer ed., (2012) in *Listen to Latin America*, pp 5–6, Spring Journal. Basic issues of invisibility and namelessness, marginalization, powerlessness and rootlessness are existential issues facing us all. When these issues are melded with class, racism, gender and ethnicity, the psychology of differences comes into play as group survival seems to be at stake. Cultural structures function to provide a context for our need to belong, have identity and be recognized. When these needs are not implicitly functioning, fear, hate and alienation dynamically organize our psyche's way of narrating it relationship to the group—its definition of itself, its destiny, and its sense of its uniqueness form cultural complexes.
    - CC express themselves in powerful moods, emotions and repetitive behaviors in both individuals and groups, unless one's individual cultural identity is ego syntonic with the culture of group's identity.

- CC is a dynamic system of relationships that serve the need for belonging and identity and are linked through ethnicity, race, religion, class and gender processes. They also serve to alienate and differentiate group from group and/or an individual within a group.
- CC are highly resistant to consciousness. They have an archetypal core rooted primordial ideas about what is meaningful. They function involuntarily, autonomously and tend to affirm simplistic, often self-righteous attitudes. They impose constraints on the perception of differences and/or accentuate them.
- CC accumulates experiences that validate its point of view and creates self-affirming ancestral memories experienced in the group's expectations, in its definition of itself, in its sense of uniqueness, and through its attitudes and fears of other groups. They often, but not invariably, originate in traumatic events of past generations.
- "Phantom phenomenon" are untranslatable and unbearable experiences that haunt the psychological ambiance of culture. They are represented with less certainty than are CC's per se, haunting us in an ambiguous manner of subject with object and individual with group, held together in an affective field.

b. An "immigrant's multicultural complex" originates in the journey of immigration and proculturation, an inner-subjective process of adaptation after one's sense of belonging and identity have been dislodged and must be rediscovered. For the immigrant relational, cultural, socioeconomic and geographic attachments have been severed, often traumatically, and one must navigate the tensions of multiple cultural complexes and identifications while searching for identity, community and safety/security. Depression and anxiety are frequent symptoms and may include the dissociated anguish of cultural traumas and phantom narratives of immigrant parents and grandparents. Stressors of transculturation are both acute and prolonged and if disruptions were sudden and violent, the immigrant's capacity to cope may temporarily overwhelm adequate mourning these multiple and complicated losses. In the process of acculturating to new cultural structures, a multicultural identity is forged, which includes not only the vulnerabilities described, but also wounds to self-worth when social mirroring in the host culture includes racial prejudices and ethnic biases. Self-esteem declines when a new language reduces communication competence and when norms and social expectations are unfamiliar. As an immigrant navigates the constant tension and play of complexes and identifications in search for identity and community, a psychological resilience, flexibility and ingenuity are promoted. Individuation dynamically circumambulates not as a centered achievement, but as nonlinear, loosely continuous states of consciousness within a multicultural narrative of continuity and change. When sufficiently received by the host society, an intersectional coherence develops, which may also creatively impact the existing culture. ("AN IMMIGRANTS' TRANSIT: FROM A MULTICULTURAL COMPLEX TO A MULTICULTURAL MIND" to be published by Routledge in *The American Cultural Complexes*, edited by Tom Singer.)

c. Intersectionality: Feminists in the 1970s introduced the idea of "intersectionality," as the confluence of multiple identities in each individual, which includes one's social location along with the elevation and subjugation associated with these identities. (See Dee-Watt Jones, "Location of Self," *Family Process* p. 409.)

d. Political Psyche as defined by Andrew Samuels is a way of being that recognizes that individual and collective psychic energies are inseparable and though primarily envisioned as a collective response to social political events, political energies manifest in each individual as a social channel, much like spiritual and moral channels referred to by Jung. (Andrew Samuels. (2015) *A New Therapy for Politics,* p. 6, Karnac, London.)

e. Proculturation: "Reflects real-life human experiences and the role of intersubjectivity in the process of adaptation in emigration or elsewhere in any unfamiliar environment...Most importantly proculturation implies triadic semiotic relations and the possibility of the creation of novel fusions of meanings, by mixing various ingredients in the process of mediation between familiar and unfamiliar ideas and experiences." Vladimer Lado Gamsakhurdia, "Proculturation: Self-reconstruction by making 'fusion cocktails' of alien and familiar meaning," (2019) *Culture & Psychology,* Sage Publication.

Consciousness of my own multicultural complex

This began in 1987 when as a candidate I encountered with the Eurocentric cultural bias of the "C.G. Jung Institute of San Francisco." Although I had completed four years of clinical and supervisory training at another training institute, "The Psychotherapy Institute," a society similar in psychological orientation, I entered analytic training unsuspecting that the "intersectionality" of my own cultural identities, that of being a white, Latinx, Jewish/Catholic, upper-class Colombian and poor North American immigrant, would not contain nor be contained by the relatively homogeneous culture of the Jung Institute. Furthermore, although we studied theory of the collective unconscious, scant attention was paid to how cultural dynamics lived in us and in the group. As such, the alienation and vulnerability I had earlier experienced was available to me for new insight and integration. After certification as an analyst, when the concept of "cultural complexes" emerged, my psycho/cultural struggles began to clarify. I felt renewed energy, this time politically toward developing greater sociocultural awareness and integration in the work with my patients and in each of these societies as a member, organizationally and through supervising and teaching.

Founding legacies shaped each society's receptivity to diversity

The egalitarian spirit of the 1960s oriented the theoretically eclectic psychodynamic therapists who founded TPI not to advantage professional titles, gender nor seniority. Roles are voluntary and assigned by choice and differentiated by task. After a rigorous and competitive application process, if accepted to train, one becomes a member with voting and governing privileges and responsibilities from the beginning. For the first 35 years, its governance operated as a "coordinating" council of members, some of whom were also trainees. Fifty years since its birth, TPI's membership has increased four-fold to 400 therapists now under the guidance of a Board that reviews missions and structural operations.

The Jung Institute, inspired by two heterosexual, white, male psychiatrists (both analyzed by Jung) founded a small medical society to study analytic ideas, which officially became the C.G. Jung Institute of S.F. also in the 1960s. They structured the organization hierarchically, with only analysts authorized to vote and govern. Candidates advance toward certification predicated on continued personal Jungian analysis, supervision, course completion and a comprehensive clinical paper, usually taking 7–10 years. Once certified as an analyst, one becomes a voting member. Full participation on training committees, however, requires another five years post certification. Today the Jung Institute has 130 members and 28 candidates.

What demographic and sociocultural shifts have occurred since these beginnings?

In both societies, females and non-medical degrees now comprise the majority of members, along with significant membership increase in LGBTQ (lesbian, gay, bi-sexual, transgender and queer) representation. Although middle-class values hold sway in both organizations, a wealthier and older representation is evident at the Jung Institute. The racial/ethnic composition with therapists of color or minority social location at TPI has increased about 15–20%, many of whom are immigrants. At the Jung Institute the increase in number of therapists of color and minority social location is much less, with an increase of about 2–3%, and of these most are immigrants. In spite of these changes and of great import, is the fact that the racial/ethnic composition of the leadership in both Institutes continues to be conspicuously, white.

How responsive has each society been to multicultural representation?

Changes were initiated in 2004 at TPI in response to members' concerns regarding the meaning and consequence of the discrepancy of white, middle-class therapist treating people of color in the training program's low fee clinic. The Institute invited an organizational assessment to be made by an outside consulting firm and found that the organization had what the assessment termed as a "conflict-avoidant" culture. Based on these findings, members and especially the trainees, pressed for sociocultural theories to be included in their program's psychodynamic orientation. As noted by a supervisor, "trainees work with people of color and have 'a must-change' attitude." TPI's leadership met these challenges by asking every sector to analyze how the lack of diversity psychologically limited the organization. Thereafter, deliberate strategies were constructed and initiated for developing awareness, educating and processing where implicit racial, gendered and class biases was present and how we could become psychologically more inclusive of differences.

At the Jung Institute, notwithstanding occasional public seminars offered and support for the training of an international student in the candidate program, intentional focus on its internal psychosocial culture only began in 2014, after several years of a reduced applicant pool. Two initiatives were approved: a public service scholarship fund for clinicians working in community agencies and the appointment of a diversity committee. (The committee members changed the name to Diversity and Inclusivity Committee the following year.) The Committee approached its task with the assumption that as a community, we were mostly unconscious of our own sociocultural locations and the historical factors contributing to these attitudes and values. Consciousness and attitudinal change, we speculated, might come if members became more familiar with one another's cultural backgrounds. We began by offered forums for in-depth exploration regarding race, ethnicity and cultural identity. Thus far we have provided multiple in-house opportunities during members' monthly dinner meetings and through intramural seminars, which are for both members and candidates, which focus on racial and ethnic cultural complexes and perspectives where self-reflective interchanges regarding cultural values and identities occur. We have encouraged the faculty to address cultural biases and projections in how we inherited analytic concepts and in those that emanate from our own cultural biases. We have also asked training committees to hold such awareness consciously in their assessment of candidates. The committee has prepared a statement for the CGJISF website acknowledging and apologizing for past racialized cultural bias and specifies intent to be actively inclusive of training a diverse community of psychological practitioners. For our committee work we included the full participation of two candidate representatives. We will present our work thus far at the IAAP International Congress in Vienna 2019 (Note 16.3).

NOTE 16.3 SPECIFIC STRATEGIES AND PROGRAMS IN EACH INSTITUTE

The Psychotherapy Institute

- Retreats planned for various committees where the subject of social/cultural diversity is taken up. One such retreat, planned in 2017 for members of the Diversity Committee, facilitated the advanced training group with a title, "Mosaics."
- Establishing a social/cultural group for trainees in the advanced training to deal with clinical issues.
- Mentorship program began in 2017 to bring in therapists of color to be mentors for trainees of color in the advanced training program.
- The diversity in the Supervisors Group is considering how to alter criteria to be more inclusive—to invite supervisors in who may have specific skills in various areas though they have not had the sufficient experience of doing long-term psychodynamic supervision.

C.G. Jung Institute of San Francisco

Programs sponsored by the Diversity and Inclusivity Committee:

- **Member Analysts Monthly Dinner Meetings**: varying topics of 30 minutes presentations and small groups discussions for 60 minutes: Examples of these were conversations regarding individuals' cultural identities; an Iranian-German immigrant analyst's use of his cultural perspectives in analytic work with two Muslim patients; two immigrant Asian analysts discussed their differing notions of familial piety; "Euro-centrism, Then and Now" offer an examination of Jung's racial biases, specifically with regards to Africans and African Americans; Consideration of "White" identity by two analysts; and "Spector of Other" a report on The International Association for Jungian Studies (IAJS) conference and "the American White Shadow."

- **Intramural seminars** for both candidates and analysts; co-sponsored by the Diversity and Inclusivity and Curriculum committees:

  - *Phantom Narratives* presentation by Sam Kimbles and experiential small groups to consider phantom narratives in-vivo and large group discussion (Spring 2015).

  - Fanny Brewster on *Archetypal Grief of the African – American Mother*, co-sponsored with the Extended Education Committee

  - Alan Vaughn, (Spring 2016), *Cultural transmission of the African Diaspora through art, music.*

  - Alan Vaughn (Spring 2017), *African Diaspora: a clinical example of working with the archetypal layer of a Caribbean-African immigrant.*

  - The China Intensive-reflections and conversations regarding cross-cultural teaching, supervision and analysis (November 11, 2017).

  - Examining our cultural complexes with Tom Singer.

Written by the Diversity and Inclusivity Committee at CGJISF for faculty:

Analytical psychology is founded on the richness of the primordial, archetypal forces that have formed the world's cultures; it is important to include other than European origins in use of fairy tales, myths, etc. Factors such as privilege, economic power dynamics, historical and institutional forms of oppression, are also often relevant in discussions of psychological processes and treatment. But how to include such topics in a course is not always so obvious.

When framing your subject matter, consider providing the historical, cultural context in which the ideas were formulated. (i.e. What was the social milieu? What are the cultural identifiers associated with theorists? How are those reflected in their ideas? How might these theories and this subject matter be adapted when working in a contemporary milieu and with a diverse population of clients?)

Some instructors have found that briefly discussing their personal socio-cultural location, vis-à-vis, race, class, etc., can foster an openness in which students feel invited to freely self-reflect on their own subjectivity, and how their cultural identifications influence their thinking and clinical practice. You may also want to directly invite them to express these observations.

As you are no doubt aware, when case material is presented without providing culturally significant data, there is a tendency to assume the individual is of the dominant culture: European-American descent, heterosexual orientation, and so on. To avoid these assumptions, you could include such identifying information in your case material—to the extent possible, without compromising confidentiality. And, if appropriate, you may want to ponder with candidates the potential clinical impacts of these cultural identifications.

Encourage candidates' thoughts and discussion about how issues about the impacts of socio-cultural issues in society, and on individuals might be relevant to your topic.

While most members surveyed described both Institutes as being more able to address the connection between the individual psyche and the sociocultural context, it appears that founding legacies and traditions implicitly structured each organization's political will and receptivity for cultural change. TPI's theoretical eclecticism and egalitarian governing structure moved earlier and more intentionally to develop a psychodynamic multicultural membership and training program. Since the Jung Institute has a hierarchal structure, naming and changing this organization's lack of diversity required the leadership of the president to appoint a task force, that is the ad hoc Diversity Committee. However, once authorized, Jungian members' socio and political energies have eagerly engaged in developing consciousness and supporting concrete actions for cultural changes. One of the most significant being the decision to move our location from "Laurel Heights," an economically exclusive neighborhood in San Francisco to the "Mission," which is a multicultural neighborhood predominantly populated by Latinx and Asian first-generation-born Americans and newly entering millennials. In our new home (projected to open in the fall of 2020) we intend not only to offer greater access to more diverse populations but to be enriched by educational and clinical exchanges and services with the community.

Do immigrant-trainees serve as catalyzing influences?

With an increase in immigrant-trainees, TPI has racially and ethnically become more diverse. After completing training many have become leaders and brought to bear their multicultural mindsets. Similarly, at the Jung Institute, immigrants' multicultural perspective and political energy has been significant in changes being sought—for example, six of eleven members of the Diversity and Inclusivity Committee are immigrants. From personal experience as a participant and graduate of both training programs, now a member, supervisor and teacher in each, I have concluded that when immigrant-trainees' views are expressed and valued by those in authority, they contribute responsibly and creatively in nudging the group's cultural awareness. "Training-wounds" while common for most trainees, for immigrants being misrecognized or prejudicially diminished, while offensive and hurtful, has also stimulated creative and political impulses for developing a more sensitive and inclusive culture. As one respondent at TPI noted, "immigrants have been leaders in noting blind spots and micro-aggressions. Through their courage and by raising their voices they have been instruments of raising consciousness…" A member of the Jung Institute wrote, "without their thinking, not much would move—too much inertia in the large white community—not out of malice, but out of more complicated cultural limitations, blindness, and ignorance and because of a general lack of personal urgency."

While it seemed that trainees and members who were immigrants and second-generation American-born immigrants contributed toward sociocultural changes in their societies by their presence and differing cultural perspectives and in their clinical sensitivity to psychological needs not previously considered, the impetus for change, however, also required leadership and receptivity of members holding authority roles (Note 16.4).

NOTE 16.4 CONTRIBUTIONS OF IMMIGRANTS TO THEIR TRAINING PROGRAMS

- Development of and participation as consultant to a two-year supervision-training program (SSP).
- Teaching "diversity" didactics in various sectors of both organizations.
- Presentations for public education courses on the psychology of immigration and the cultural biases in psychological theories.
- Co-chairing the Diversity and Inclusivity Committee at the Jung Institute which entails in-house programs for membership and candidates, a Diversity Reading file for the library, interfacing

with the IAAP (survey and compilation of thoughts from our members regarding Institute diversity statement and participation in presentation for conferences).
- Chairing study groups on "The Psychology of Cultural Identities" and "Dialogues on Difference"—TPI.
- Re-writing Intake-sheet to reflect social/cultural concerns and preferences, TPI.
- Developing a program of Mentors for Therapist of Color—TPI.
- Holding a Clinical Director Role with a commitment to integrating social issues into theory and practice.
- Becoming supervisors and contributing to classes and symposiums in both Institutes.
- Participating in governing roles.
- Publishing papers in journals.

From responses of those surveyed four recommendations coalesced:

1 Historical and social/cultural research requires more thorough psychological elaboration and clinical integration, with emphasis on the psychodynamics of implicit racialized and oppressive cultural attitudes and values.
2 Key to counterbalancing inherent asymmetrical power dynamics in training programs is for those in privileged roles to recognize the power of the position and that it be held with an attitude of mutual respect and cultural humility. Supervisors and teachers have the responsibility for inviting ethnic and racial conversations with individual specificity that includes one's relationship to group affiliation and identity.
3 Intentional and facilitated group conversations are essential for deepening understanding. Attention to group dynamics is essential and crucial when the minority voice is small in number, as individuals are particularly vulnerable in a group to becoming scapegoated or invisible. Planned inter-group diversity dialogs and activities between committees are crucial for building awareness of a "group-as-a-whole" perspective that includes cultural multiplicities.
4 Conscientious cultural change requires a team of persistent and dedicated leaders who are supported by the organization's commitment to diversify membership and attitudes.

San Francisco's confluence of multiple, overlapping cultures and identities is comprised of over a third foreign born, with Asians and Latinx being the largest percentage, who are economically interspersed geographically throughout the city. Given this environment, most surveyed respondents from both Institutes voiced a need and desire for a more inclusive and diverse training institute, albeit with the cautious reflection, as articulated by one analyst who wrote, "while being productive, this work has also been painful…"

I have concluded that though immigrants' contributions have been significant and meaningful, the legacy of values and governing structures created by founding leaders was also most important in how quickly the lack of cultural diversity needed to be addressed. The generational divide in both institutes has been felt to be a significant factor for integrating a social-cultural context in psychological theory and practice. Concerns were expressed that such a focus would diminish the core mission of training programs. Resistances were subtly expressed with statement such as, "diversity is important but it's not my interest and though I participate, I do not follow up" or by a lack of participation in educational opportunities offered. Some surveyed expressed pessimism that "as long as leadership remains almost exclusively white, middle-aged, middle-class, neither society seems like a place that someone from a different background is likely to feel at home." Fear and helplessness were expressed as, "something terrible is present, but I cannot find language to put it into words—I feel great despair" and though "outreach might be helpful, we are psychologists, not community organizer."

Although neither organization had consciously foreseen the inevitable experiences of cultural de-integration when multicultural integration pressed for inclusion and cultural transformation, the movement toward such change, nonetheless, persists. It appears necessary not only for the survival of the training programs, but also as being ethically and morally important. Cultural integration of greater diversity and representation seem to have come more successfully where members are empowered to share leadership across generations sharing responsibility for ideas unfolding in practice. Balancing the pain, fear, and confusion felt with an acknowledgement of these difficult but natural emotional states, along with attitudes of mutual respect and cultural humility, supports learning from destabilizing experiences. Leaders are also learning that they need to persist with faith and patience, operationalizing the value of continuous community dialogs and group self-reflectiveness. To paraphrase Professor of Consciousness, Donna Haraway, we must **"stay with trouble"** as we experience anew what belonging means. (Haraway, Donna J. (2016) *Staying with the Trouble,* Duke University Press, Durham & London pp. 58–98.)

As post script to the process of cultural change which I have documented up to December 2017, in May 2019, at the CGJISF after months of collaboration between the Diversity and Inclusivity, Development, and Outreach Committees a statement that articulates **"our commitment to identify and**

Figure 16.1 "O Snail/Climb Mount Fuji/But slowly, slowly!", by Kobyashi Issa (1763–1828).

challenge racial and cultural biases in ourselves in our teaching and practice, and in our Institute" was unanimously approved by the Executive Committee and was posted on the Institute's website.

Figures 16.1 and 16.2 reveal a subtle change in the cultural attitude at the C.G. Jung Institute of San Francisco over the past 40 years.

This snail image in figure 16.1 was adopted as the official Logo in the 1980s. The design was created by Dick Lumaghi with the basic idea that individuation spirals upwards and occurs slowly involving all four functions of consciousness. The idea was taken from a famous haiku by Kobyashi Issa (1763–1828), which translates as, "O Snail/Climb Mount Fuji/But slowly, slowly!" The cultural attitude reveals a contained, introverted manner which also unconsciously discloses a protective approach for maintaining cultural cohesion.

The flower on the cover of *At the Institute* 2017–2018, the annual public brochure, was created by artist FANNY BOWDITCH KATZ (1874–1967), a patient of C.G. Jung from 1913 to 1918 (Figure 16.2). Her portfolio was donated to CGJISF in 1997 by her grandnephew, Peter Childs. Written on the back cover are the words, "The chalky delicacy of her pastels and her translucent watercolors hint at a sense of fragility. But the bold imagery Katz chose as her subject matter also suggests an inner strength and determination. **It is with that same paradoxical footing that the Institute looks forward to its own exciting future.**" (Bold font is mine)

Figure 16.2 The Flower by Fanny Bowditch Katz (1874–1967), patient of Jung.

References

Berry, J.W. (1998) Psychology of Acculturation, in *The Culture and Psychological Reader*, ed. Nancy Goldberg and Judy B. Veroff, New York University Press.

Boulanger, Ghislaine. (2007) Wounded by Reality, Mahwah, NJ: Psychological Press.

Boulanger, Ghislaine. (2003) "Lot's wife, Cary Grant, and the American dream, *Contemporary Psychoanalysis,* 40(3).

Carta, Stefano. (2015) Introduction, p. 20, in *The Analyst in the Polis*, Vol. 1, ed. Carta, Stefano, Adorisio, A. Mercurio, R. Rome, Streetlib.

Cavalli, Alessandra. (2012) Transgenerational transmission of indigestible facts: From trauma, deadly ghosts and mental voids to meaning making interpretations, *Journal of Analytic Psychology*, 57, 597–614.

Csillag, Veronica. (2017) Emmy grant: Immigration as repetition of trauma and as potential space, *Psychoanalytic Dialogues*, 27(4).

Gamsakhurdia, Vladimer Lado. (2019) Proculturation: Self-reconstruction by making 'fusion cocktails' of alien and familiar meaning, *Culture & Psychology*, Sage Publication.

Gamsakhurdia, Vladimer Lado. (2018a) Adaptation in a dialogical perspective — From acculturation to proculturation, *Culture and Psychology*, 24, 545–559.

Gonzales, Francisco. (2016) Only What is Human can Truly be Foreign: The Trope of Immigration as a Creative Force in Psychoanalysis, pp. 15–38, in *Immigration in Psychoanalysis*, ed. Julia Beltsiou, Routledge, London and New York.

Gonzales, Francisco. (2017). Iteration and homologies of difference: A discussion of Veronica Csillag's Emmy grant: Immigrations as repetition of trauma and as potential space, *Psychoanalytic Dialogues*, 27(4).

Henderson, Joseph L. (1997) Reflections on the History and Practice of Jungian Analysis, pp. 3–28, in *Jungian Analysis*, 2nd edition, ed. By Murray Stein, Open Court, Chicago and La Salle Illinois.

Henderson, Joseph L.

Haraway, Donna J. (2016) *Staying with the Trouble*, Duke University Press, Durham and London.

Jung, Carl. The Transformation of Libido, p. 142, in *Symbols of Transformation*, Vol. 5, Bolligen Series, Princeton University Press.

Jung, Carl. The Undiscovered Self, p. 245, in *Civilization in Transition*, Vol. 10.

Jung, Carl. The Psychological View of Conscience, p. 437, in *Civilization in Transition*, Vol. 10.

Kimbles, Samuel. (2014) *Phantom Narratives,* Rowman & Littlefield, London.

Kimbles, Samuel. (2006) Cultural trauma and the transmission of group traumas. *Psychological Perspectives,* 49(1), 96–110.

Kimbles, Samuel. (2010) Chaos and fragmentation in training institutes and societies. Presented at IAAP, Montreal Canada.

Layton, Lynn. (2013) *Enacting Distinctions: Normative unconscious processes in the Clinic, Keynote address at Turning a blind eye: working with 'race,' culture and ethnicity in Practice,* Tavistock Center, London. November 8.

McRae, Mary B. and Ellen L. Short. (2010) *Racial and Cultural Dynamics in Group and Organizational Life,* Sage Publications, Los Angeles.

Morales, Ed. (2018) *Latinx The New force in American Politics and Culture,* Verso, London and New York.

Navridis, Kilmis. (2017) Conflicts and Social Transferences in Groups, pp. 196–118, in *A Bridge Over Troubled Water*, ed. Gila Ofer, Karnac, London.

Oguz, Timur F. (2012) Concrete expressions of an "unformulated" discontinuity, *Contemporary Psychoanalysis*, 48(1), 54–71.

Olivier Dubose, Fabrice. (2015) Lampedusa Constellation. The great Immigrant Exodus and Other signs of the Times, p. 245, in *The Analyst in the Polis*, vol 1. 1, ed. Carta, Adorisio, Mercurio, StreetLib.

Popadopolos, Rene. (2003) Refugees, Home and Trauma, in *Therapeutic care for Refugees,* ed. R. Papadopolos, Karnac Books.

Rozmarin, Eyal. (2017) Immigration, belonging and the tension between center and margin in psychoanalysis, *Psychoanalytic Dialogues,* 27(4).

Samuels, Andrew. (1993) *The Political Psyche,* Routledge, London.

Samuels, A. (2015) *A New Therapy for Politics,* p. 6, Karnac, London.

Singer, Thomas and Sam Kimbles. (2004a) *The Cultural Complex: Contemporary Jungian Perspectives on Psyche and Society,* Routledge, New York.

Singer, Thomas. (2006) The cultural complex: A statement of the theory and its application, *Psychotherapy and Politics International,* 4(3).

Suarez-Orozco, Carola and Marcelo m. Suarez-Orozco. (2001) *Children of Immigration,* Harvard University Press.

Tummala-Narra, Pratyusha. (2013). Psychoanalytic applications in a diverse society, *Psychoanalytic Psychology,* 30, 471–487.

Tummala-Narra, Pratyusha. (2014) Cultural identity in the context of trauma and immigration from a psychoanalytic perspective, *Psychoanalytic Psychology,* 31, 396–409.

Tummala-Narra, Pratyusha. (2016) Discussion of 'Emmy grant: Immigration as repetition of trauma and as potential space, *Commentary on paper by Veronica Csillag,* 27(4).

Yadlin-Gadot, Shlomit. (2017) Psychoanalytic approaches to conflict resolution: The limits of intersubjective engagement, pp. 205–212, in *A Bridge Over Troubled Water,* ed. Gila Ofer, Karnac, London.

Index

Note: *Italic* page numbers refer to figures and page numbers followed by "n" denote endnotes.

Printed in Great Britain
by Amazon